NOT ON MY WATCH

Not On My Watch

Copyright 2022 © Bob and Joan Hatrak

ISBN HARDCOVER: 978-1-940178-67-7
ISBN SOFTCOVER: 978-1-940178-68-4
Library of Congress Control Number: 2022914446

Publisher: Villa Magna Publishing
Cover design and interior design: Noel Hagman-Kiziltan

For information, contact:
Villa Magna Publishing, LLC
4705 Columbus Street
Suite 300
Virginia Beach, VA 23462
www.villamagnapublishing.com

Not On My Watch

Bob Hatrak & Joan Hatrak

FOREWORD

You are about to begin a unique and memorable reading experience. You don't have to be famous to write a memoir or autobiography that is compelling and worth reading, as you are about to see in *Not on My Watch*.

How many wardens or administrators of maximum-security prisons have shared their experiences and stories? How many people who run prisons and jails make national news for positive reasons? How many wardens can boast about championship boxing matches, network television documentaries, and an Academy Award, all behind bars? Only one I can think of: Robert Hatrak, the co-author of this book.

If Bob had devoted this entire book to just his time running prisons, he would not have run out of material. The best of his time "behind bars" is included in this book. But there is so much more to his life – before and after those years – as well.

To call Bob courageous, innovative, and an effective leader is accurate, but just part of his story. Yet, it is the part I know best, from personal experience. I am writing this foreword because Bob Hatrak changed my life, and I changed his.

No, I am not a convict or ex-con. Even though I have spent time inside at least three dozen prisons and jails across America, I have never been arrested, convicted, or served time. I am a filmmaker of documentaries and other non-fiction network television programs.

You might have seen or heard about an Academy Award- and Emmy Award-winning television documentary called *Scared Straight!*. I was its producer, director, and writer. It was filmed inside Rahway State Prison (now East Jersey State Prison) in 1978, when Bob was the superintendent (warden). I needed his permission to make a film about of group of inmates known as "The Lifers," who ran a powerful, unique program to dissuade at-risk teens from become future inmates. This program would not have existed without first, the permission and encouragement of Superintendent Hatrak; and second, the Rahway Lifers group. The Lifers risked their future by exposing their crimes on national television when they agreed to participate in the filming of the Juvenile Awareness Program sessions.

After interviewing me at length, Mr. Hatrak allowed me to film The Lifer's Program, which – with the later success of the film on national television – became known as the "Scared Straight! Program," the title I had created for my documentary. I had no idea the film would receive the national recognition it did, inspiring numerous other prisons and jails to develop their own effective programs for at-risk juveniles.

Had Robert Hatrak not been the forward-thinking visionary he was, there would have been no Lifer's Program and no *Scared Straight! Film*, which changed my life and Bob's. I will never forget the entire *Scared Straight!* Phenomenon that I executive produced (two sequel films, a CBS TV movie, and a five-year series on A&E called *Beyond Scared Straight*), all begun with Superintendent Hatrak's approval, support, trust, and influence as I prepared to produce the original *Scared Straight!*.

I have received countless letters over the years from adults who said watching the film on television or in school as teenagers, without actually being inside the prison, changed their lives, and in some cases, saved their lives. For a film to be such a profound influence on young people's lives is beyond gratifying...not only for me, but for The Lifers, and for Bob Hatrak.

I will never forget the picture of Bob and his family, beaming with pride, being photographed at home, holding my Academy Award for *Scared Straight!*
Even though the Academy Award brought national attention to The Lifers and Superintendent Hatrak, it was just one of the events in his career showing him to be innovative, original, and impressive.

I am so happy Robert Hatrak is alive and well so he can know how special and important he is to those of us who know him, and to so many young people over the decades who don't know him, but are living their lives not as inmates but as productive citizens. I am honored to introduce you to a memorable man and the remarkable life he has led.

Arnold Shapiro
Academy Award and sixteen-time Emmy Award-winning executive producer, producer, and Writer
April 2023

FOREWORD

It's clichéd but factual to say there are a lot of great tales in boxing.

Often, the most powerful stories are of redemption, but not everyone is willing to give someone the opportunity to redeem themselves.

Bob Hatrak earned respect by doing that. He is a man of second chances, of giving the benefit of the doubt, and he is a man of principle.

In particular, what he did at Rahway through the 1970s will and should never be forgotten. His place in boxing lore is certainly secure because Hatrak created a boxing program that has gone into the history books. He used the sport for all of its positive qualities: getting inmates involved in the noble art to improve their discipline, self-respect, self-esteem, and work ethic and helping them learn to respect others.

We might not have heard about that period of the New Jersey justice system in the boxing world had it not been for the program's figurehead, James Scott.

Scott, an amateur boxer in New Jersey who was always in trouble with the law, and in and out of correctional facilities, became an up-and-coming contender in Miami, but he'd spent most of his life on the wrong side of the tracks. He wound up back in New Jersey, and he had a lot of time to serve.

Hatrak had known Scott from the time they'd spent together years earlier, with Scott as an inmate and Hatrak as a prison official, but when they reconnected in Rahway, they created something quite magical.

What happened might have been wrong in a lot of people's eyes, but it will never be replicated. With Scott leading the program, encouraging inmates to box and become trainers, cutmen, referees, and judges, remarkably James rose through the light-heavyweight world rankings.

Hatrak, in his own words, would turn Rahway State Penitentiary into Madison Square Garden for James Scott's fights against the world's best contenders and leading 175-pounders.

A ring was set up either in the sports hall or outside on the prison's recreation field. Members of the public would pay to attend, prisoners would box on the undercard, and journalists would go through security protocols to sit ringside and cover the extraordinary story of James Scott and his miraculous rise through the light-heavyweight division.

Hatrak and Scott formed an implausible alliance but a winning combination. In all, Scott would have eleven professional bouts behind the prison walls, broadcast around America on national television. His reputation was, of course, fierce.

They knew him as Superman, for his incredible engine, punch output, and punishing training regime.

It's hard enough going into enemy territory to take on a "home" fighter when you go to their hometown, let alone when you have to challenge an inmate in prison. Clearly and understandably, some opponents were psyched out by the whole experience.

Others felt a ring was a ring, no matter where it was placed, and they were happy to do battle.

Ironically, one such man was Dwight Braxton, familiar to both Scott and Hatrak as a former inmate and member of the boxing program. That's a story in itself.

Perhaps – today, in a different time – we should not romanticize the legend of what happened in Rahway between 1975 and 1981, but you cannot deny its existence, nor should you.

What Hatrak and Scott implemented achieved outstanding results. Several members of the program went on to have careers in boxing afterward, on both sides of the ropes.

Scott didn't get out for decades, long after Bob had been moved on, but after the boxing was gone, James studiously learned politics, history, religion, and literature, gaining dozens of college credits, and when he was finally released, he helped coach young amateurs at a gym in Trenton before he became too unwell to do so. The old gym owner would say of Scott, "He's great with the kids."

It will always be a shame that Hatrak and Scott never reunited after James became a free man. They could have toured the country, talking about their unusual coalition, the big fights, the boxing and political wheeling and dealing they encountered and life in Rahway. They could have inspired and educated students, prisoners, and prison staff and helped others from all walks of life; how the middle-class white man and the black kid who'd had it so rough forged a tight bond that had Scott a whisker from a shot at the world title, either in prison or on license at a venue in New Jersey.

What then? What if they'd pulled it off from Rahway? What if Scott had captured the world title? Chances are, you would have already heard about this incredible, unlikely story, the one that could not and would not take place today and will never happen again.

Maybe one day you'll be able to find it on Netflix, with actors, informing future generations about what happened when Bob and James took one another almost to the top of the sporting world from a prison cell on the East Coast.

Tris Dixon
Author, journalist, TV commentator, and former editor of *Boxing News*
Boxing Life Stories – podcast

FOREWORD

I met Robert "Bob" Hatrak in a most unconventional scenario. In September 1973, I was an eighteen-year-old sophomore at William Paterson College in New Jersey. I received a letter from my former amateur boxing instructor, Eddie "Mad Dog" Johnson, who was incarcerated at Rahway State Prison, inviting me to meet with the Inmate Council on a Saturday afternoon. Eddie's letter gave little detail as to what was the purpose of this meeting, but with Eddie being a longtime friend of my family, my brother Bob and I agree to attend. This was two years after the infamous deadly uprising at Attica State Prison in New York State and almost two years after the Thanksgiving weekend riot at Rahway.

The huge green dome of the prison was an imposing structure visible from miles away as our car approached the institution. About fifteen minutes after our arrival, we were escorted by a corrections officer into the interior of the prison, passing hundreds of inmates silently staring at us. We were dropped off in what I later learned was the school wing of the prison and entered a classroom. Eddie Johnson was seated with about twenty-five other inmates at desks. My brother and I were politely motioned to sit at a long table in front of the classroom.

The president of the Inmate Council introduced himself as Samuel J. Williams. Sam was a tall, African-American about forty-five years of age. He was extremely articulate and conveyed his thoughts as if he were a college professor. Among the central goals of the Inmate Council was to increase education and counseling services within the prison to help reduce recidivism.

After about an hour into our meeting I asked Sam a question: "How would you feel about students at my college circulating a petition asking the warden to support your objectives, which seem quite reasonable?"

The response from Sam was that there was no need for such a petition because Warden Robert Hatrak already supported and advocated increasing education and counseling. "Hatrak is a former teacher, a decent man who we can work with. Our focus is not on him but for the New Jersey legislature to understand our needs and allocate resources. The fact that Hatrak allows us to interact in-person with college students, such as yourselves, professors, and members of community organizations proves to us that he is serious about reversing recidivism and bringing humanity into this penal system."

Those words from Sam Williams remain in my memory to this day. Over the next several years, the inmate singing group the Escorts cut an album in the prison and performed in Newark (accompanied by corrections officers). There was the creation of the Lifers Group's Juvenile Awareness Project (aka "Scared Straight"). A boxing program began in Rahway that attracted national publicity and there was expansion of a college program within the prison, which I later learned was started in Trenton State Prison by Bob. These developed a sense of pride and hope among the inmates, as well as their families. He walked the inner-most areas of the prison, speaking with inmates, listening to their concerns, and taking notes, and he treated them with respect. The interactions I experienced with inmates, administrators, and corrections officers increased my social capital and insights of societal problems beyond my college courses. I credit Bob for that opportunity.

Unfortunately, Bob's work was abruptly interrupted without any real explanation. His transfer left staff, inmates, families, and social workers with agencies involved with the Lifers Group Juvenile Awareness Project shocked and disheartened. Bob never sought publicity, letting inmates speak with the media. He blended accountability with compassion, aware that his endeavors impacted people within and outside of prison walls. If I were in his position, I would have felt a bit better if the person replacing me shared my vision of preparing inmates for their return to society. Bob left a foundation of accomplishments that could have significantly reduced intergenerational incarceration if they were allowed to develop and expand to other prisons. Instead, subsequent administrators dismantled Bob's initiatives. Hope and optimism were replaced by an increase of despair and violence within Rahway Prison.

I believe that Commissioner William Fauver never took into consideration the negative consequences of transferring Bob out of Rahway State Prison and reassigning him from the front lines of reform. His actions went beyond Robert Hatrak as an individual. At that time, there were competing philosophies of how to deal with America's social problems: locking up and warehousing as many people as possible or holding people responsible for their actions while treating them humanely and providing opportunities for them to change their lives. Fauver's arbitrary actions sent a political signal to reactionary elements of society that punishment and mass incarceration was a logical strategy for addressing societal problems. Bob was not allowed the opportunity and time to fully develop his vision of progressive corrections in New Jersey, which had the very real potential of changing our nation's correctional system as well as becoming a model on a global level.

While teaching sociology courses to my college students, I relate my experiences at Rahway during the "Hatrak era." Young people often have stereotyped ideas of what a warden should be, based on popular culture films such as Shawshank Redemption. I enjoy the students' reactions as I relate Robert's accomplishments.

In light of the problems our society is confronting today, Robert Hatrak's story needs to be told.

Sanford "Sandy" Shevack, Doctor of Education
Adjunct Professor of Sociology, Montclair State University and Ramapo College
2020 New Jersey Governor's Jefferson Award for Community Service

DEDICATION

To our three amazing children,
now wonderful adults,
whom we are very proud of:
Sharon Marie Hatrak,
Robert S. Hatrak II,
Cadence Paige Champ

And to our four terrific grandchildren:
Benjamin, Levy, Colton + Robby

Love to you all ♡

AUTHORS' NOTE

We began writing this story a couple of years prior to our sixtieth wedding anniversary, which took place on June 30, 2022. The goal was to present to our kids a written chronicle of the years and events of our lives.

We spent many long afternoons documenting our adventures and had a blast reminiscing about the wonderful people we met along the way. However, it wasn't long before we realized that our story had a message we wanted to share. One that could provide guidance and hope. It was about second chances, overcoming adversity, and offering opportunities and courage to those facing a challenge. It was really, mostly, about Bob; the events that changed the trajectory of his life and his career as a prison warden.

In 1973, two years following the infamous 1971 riot, Bob was appointed superintendent of Rahway State Prison. In his early thirties, he became the youngest maximum-security warden in America at that time. Bob definitely wondered about what he was getting himself into. He had researched the 1824, 1952, 1969, and 1971 riots at the prison. Each disturbance played a significant role in the prison's violent past. On the day he was appointed he promised himself that this reign of terror would not continue, not on his watch!

He is often referred to as a "great reformer." What he accomplished at Rahway, and the hundreds of thousands of lives he touched through his countless endeavors, is certainly a testament to that. However, as Bob sees it, he's always been for the underdog. "Those inmates were underdogs. Nobody wanted to do anything for or with them. It was my job, I thought, to care."

Bob and Joan Hatrak
March 12, 2023

INTRODUCTION

The thread that weaves through a person's life, the culmination of experience that leads to a vocation or passion, is not always clear to the outside world. We have been asked through the years how our dad became a warden. The "warden's son or daughter" is an odd distinction for a little boy and two girls growing up in New Jersey.

We lived as a part of a multigenerational East coast family who immigrated to America from Eastern Europe and struggled to create a safe and secure existence. We grew up as witnesses to our dad's career as seen through the lens of our childhood experiences, hearing stories of past generations and Dad's early life. We learned firsthand how abrupt and devastating changes in direction led to the development of ideals and values that guided his life's journey.

Being impressionable, we learned about second chances, that if lucky, become apparent in the face of difficult transitions through loss and grief; how it takes the support of others who offer hope, structure, support, and opportunity to succeed. It's the devastating effects of violence, lack of education and opportunity on the vulnerable, and the belief that everyone deserves a real chance to find an alternate path.

This is a book about the transformational power of respect, of having a voice, and of having agency in creation and participation in something bigger than self. This book illustrates how, throughout a lifetime of invention, our dad became who he is and how that provided the foundation for an innovative career in corrections. His achievements are still studied and praised for successfully creating safer and more life-affirming practices in a setting where historically there was little safety and few second chances.

Sharon Marie Hatrak
Robert S. Hatrak II
Cadence Paige Champ
February 7, 2023

TABLE OF CONTENTS

Forewords
Dedication
Authors' Note
Introduction

Am I seeing things? — 1
Lessons Learned — 2
It's A Trenton Thing — 3
Great Expectations — 4
Adversity & Perseverence — 5
Welcome Back Hatch — 6
School Daze Behind "The Wall" — 7
Techy Times — 7½
Out Of The Flames & Into The Fire — 8
Under The Dome — 9
Forging A Path Never Taken — 10

11 — Correction Officer Control Time
12 — Violence Control
13 — Threats & Promises
14 — Unexpected Inheritence
15 — The Lifers' Group
16 — Scared Straight
17 — Boxing Association
18 — Boxing Vocational Training
19 — Live From Rahway
20 — Footsteps

BOOK ONE

The Early Years

CHAPTER 1

Am I Seeing Things?

Wednesday, November 23, 1971 – Thanksgiving Eve
Front elevation view of Rahway State Prison
The night of the 1971 riot

"...a riot is the language of the unheard..."

– Martin Luther King

On the Eve of Thanksgiving in 1971, it was cold and wet. I was a rain-soaked and tired passenger aboard an Amtrak train that left from a bustling Grand Central Station in New York City and was headed for Trenton Train Depot in New Jersey. From there, it was just a short drive to my home in Morrisville, Pennsylvania.

At that time, I was the director of Education at the Trenton State Prison, while also taking classes at New York University, where I'd just completed the coursework for my doctorate in public administration and could finally move on to the dissertation phase. That week – only half over – had felt endless, and I was so looking forward to spending the holiday weekend relaxing and eating turkey at my Mom's house with my wife Joan, our little girl Sharon, and my extended family.

Sometime around 9 p.m., while enjoying a cold beer in the dingy club car, I peered out through the rain-streaked windows and what I saw made the hair on the back of my neck stand up straight. The diorama passing before me, as we sped along, was suddenly as bright as day. I leaned in closer against the cold glass window for a better look. Illuminating floodlights arcing across the black night sky suddenly exposed Trenton Prison's sister institution, Rahway State Prison.

Although the activity looked inviting, like Yankee Stadium on game night, I knew better and understood something was very wrong within the prison compound. *Could it be a riot?* Riots were on my mind because two months earlier, Attica State Prison in New York State suffered a significant bloody uprising. Its ruthlessness attracted national media attention.

Now, looking out from the train and seeing the glaring emergency lights on full blast here, I felt my stomach clench in dread and apprehension. *Was this the "son of the Attica riot" in the making right here before my very eyes? Or was I seeing things?*

I didn't know it then, but the scene unfolding before me, incredulously and by chance, would significantly affect my life and career.

About thirty minutes later I winced as the train's screeching iron brakes announced our arrival at Trenton Station. Stepping onto the wooden arrival platform and joining the impatient crowd, I headed for the nearby escalator. Hustling to reach my car and turn on the radio, I hoped to catch the New Jersey evening news. Toggling the dial from station to station, it frustrated me to find that Rahway Prison wasn't even mentioned. Still, my gut instinct knew there was something serious happening there right now.

The drive home was a fifteen-minute trip. The quick peek at the disturbance at Rahway triggered vivid flashbacks of violence at the Trenton Prison. It reminded me that I worked in the middle of what Joan, my wife, called a "war zone." Trenton was ripe and ready to join in on an angry blowup at Rahway – if that's what I saw.

*

During the past two years while working at the Trenton State Prison, I sensed there would eventually be a major disturbance there. If asked to predict the future, I would have guessed that someday Trenton Prison would host a full-blown riot, just like Attica's and just like the one I suspected was going on right now at Rahway.

I had seen my share of violence at Trenton. But nothing can duplicate the intensity of a real riot – happening in real time.

The most violent eruptions nearly always involved prison gangs and inmate threat groups. The dominant factions operating inside our prison were the Nation of Islam, the New World of Islam, smaller Black Power blocs, a strong mafia presence, and motorcycle clubs. These informal communities included inmates with similar motivations, interests, objectives, and ideologies. They devoted most of their time to raping inmates, shanking, drug trafficking, retaliatory violence, and extortion. In addition, we routinely dealt with escape attempts, organized disruptions, intimidation, strong-arming, and other occurrences that demanded our full attention.

One of the most significant and easily carried-out acts of violence was an inmate tossing a container of flammable liquid into another inmate's cell, followed by a lit book of matches. This was a murderous event, with severe consequences. Some inmates suffered life-threatening burns, and others didn't recover because they weren't rescued in time. I wondered if Rahway, too, was experiencing the senseless violence I witnessed every day working at Trenton.

Attacks by inmates on inmates, inmates on officers, and officers on inmates were not just continuing but were disturbingly escalating. The scariest part was that retaliatory assaults always followed these attacks. Cohorts of those assaulted found ways and places to deliver "get-even" responses, depending on who got clobbered first.

An example of a retaliatory beating I saw occurred as an aftermath of an inmate assaulted by an officer on the "goon squad" (a non-sanctioned secret group of officers whose self-appointed mission is to even the score). I watched several officers leaving a segregation unit cell in four-wing escorting a badly beaten inmate. He was being ushered to the infirmary to be tended to by a nurse. It took little imagination to figure out that the inmate wouldn't dare identify his attackers when they all reached the infirmary.

One mid-afternoon, a couple of days later, I saw the inmate retaliation for this beating; it occurred while I was standing in "Center" waiting for a mass movement to finish before heading for my office. Under escort from the prison's recreation yard, an angry group of inmates surrounded their accompanying officer and beat him to within an inch of his life. The attackers ran posthaste from the beating scene. They stomped into Center, which controlled all communications and movement in the institution, and which also housed the armory. There I stood, frozen as a witness, certain they saw me. I remember wondering what the odds were that they might decide *I'm just not worth killing.*

In a flash, the large group of menacing inmates surrounded me. They were yelling and screaming profanities. I couldn't tell you what they were saying, but it was apparent that they realized I saw the assault. Thankfully, quick thinking by the Center keeper, Captain Richard Curran, prevented me from becoming their next victim.

Curran steadily pointed the business end of a tommy gun through a gunport in the bulletproof but see-through glass wall of the Control Center. In a loud voice, he ordered the crowd to disperse, yelling "Get the f**k out of here and return to your housing units!"

In a suspended moment that seemed to last forever, all eyes were fixated on the weapon staring them unwaveringly in the face. Finally, the pissed-off group of inmates disbanded and reluctantly headed toward their wings. It all happened too fast for me to get scared, but when it was over, it was all I could do to keep my knees from knocking. I'm certain Captain Curran saved my life that day. I also knew, instinctively, that the departing men were thinking to themselves, *There's always next time.*

*

My intuition had been correct about a potential riot. However, I was off at my expected location. I worried about Trenton's volatility and hadn't focused on Rahway. Only thirty minutes away, its proximity to Trenton could mean trouble for us. It was possible Trenton's inmates would act out in sympathy for Rahway rioters.

It looked like I would spend Thanksgiving Day working. How quickly things can change. I thought about how anxious I had been to begin the holiday weekend with my family. I knew it wouldn't make Joan happy – she and my mom had been cooking and baking for days to make this a special gathering for everyone.

As I turned into our driveway, I breathed a sigh of relief. I was just happy to be home. The minute I walked inside, I told

Joan what I had seen on the train. As soon as I caught my breath, I called my boss, Warden Howard Yeager, at his Trenton Prison residence to tell him what I had witnessed from the train on the way home. He confirmed what I had seen. It was no surprise to me that he already knew Rahway inmates were rioting, but it was a surprise to him to hear that I had seen it.

Mr. Yeager asked me to report to the prison tomorrow at 4:30 a.m. sharp! He told me that he had called a white hat (security officer supervisors) meeting to decide tomorrow morning's routine, considering Rahway's situation. Foremost would be to determine what security and levels of operation to implement. *Do we open the prison in the morning according to our regular schedule or do we lock everything down?*

The warden voiced what we all knew: "A lockdown will invite an ugly reaction from the residents and will mean that the men will eat in their cells." I knew it also meant that the inmates would not be allowed to see visitors. They would not be able to attend their classes, do work duty, or exercise. Furloughs would be canceled. Non-correctional employees (educators, volunteers, supplementary staff) would not be allowed in the facility. Only the warden, officers, medical staff, and prisoners would be permitted on site. Lockdowns are a measure meant to protect both the inmates and the staff. Even so, I couldn't help my thoughts from reminding me what I also knew: It could also result in more unrest and incite violence. Lockdown is not intended to be punitive, but the inmates find it to be so. "Opening up" after an unwarranted lockdown could mean cutting loose a beehive of angry men.

Before ending our telephone conversation, the warden told me one last thing. "To make the right call, we need information, and fast. I'm asking the chief deputy tonight to choose several supervisors who have a good rapport with a cross-section of the population to walk through all housing units and tiers. They will spend as many hours as necessary walking throughout the entire institution, talking to the residents and gathering information on the grounds."

Our conversation ended with me saying, "Sure, boss, I'll be there," and then I hung up the phone to share this update with Joan.

It seems that with this evolving event and escalating crisis, my role as director of Education was further changing. I recognized that Mr. Yeager was drawing me into the upper echelons of management and prison security. Although I didn't exactly know why, I did know that the opportunity to work with him and absorb the wisdom of his long years of experience was something that suited me just fine. I was also worried that a riot at Rahway (or even the real possibility of one) would cause the warden a great deal of stress – and could cause a serious impact on his health given the recent heart attack he was still recovering from.

Not too long ago, he had asked me to join his emergency evaluation and control workgroup. At the time, I just thought he wanted me on the team to assist him with the copious amount of paperwork and "after-incident" reports flooding his office, which was something I was more than happy to do. Now, I was not exactly sure of how he intended to use me.

*

Joan and I spent the rest of Wednesday evening glued to the television watching the news, which eventually confirmed what Warden Yeager had already told me. "Rahway's riot began in the prison's auditorium. Warden Samuel Vukcevich and five of his 'blue hats' (correction officers) were hostages."

My thoughts kept returning to Trenton Prison. How would our inmates react once they learned what was happening at Rahway? The inmate communications system had an active grapevine, and news traveled fast. I'd bet they already knew. Inmates received daily newspapers, and they had access to a radio system in their cells using headphones. They could also make and receive monitored telephone calls with immediate family members, which was also a prudent conduit for information.

Before breakfast, the institution would be buzzing. We needed to evaluate the feedback from the white hats and then develop a plan of action…fast. I couldn't turn off my thoughts. Sleep wouldn't come to me, so at 3 a.m., I gave up trying. I got out of bed, showered, dressed, drank a cup of coffee, and left for the prison while Joan and our little Sharon slept upstairs.

I ARRIVED AT the institution at 4:15 a.m. Walking to the front door, through a nasty pre-dawn November drizzle, I recalled my very first peek at this historic old building. The street was once again dark, cold, and raining just as it had been on that long-ago night twenty-six years before, when my family and I drove wide-eyed past the looming prison on our arrival in South Trenton from modest little Jessup, Pennsylvania.

I had grown up in this same neighborhood. Once more I wondered why, ever since that dreary night so long ago, I had always felt a strange connection to this "spooky old place," long-standing in this same spot since 1836.

Shivering, I rang the polished, old brass doorbell at the front entrance to the intimidating stone fortress. When I was granted access through the massive black iron door by Harry Ibbs, the friendly front door officer, the echo of the heavy metal door slamming shut behind me added its grumble to the hushed pre-dawn "hubbub" in the front house. I walked quickly through and headed straight for the boardroom.

Administrators had been reserving this boardroom for special meetings, monthly warden's meetings, parole board hearings, classification committee meetings, and strategy planning situations such as this one for almost two hundred years!

As I expected, I was not the first to arrive. The warden and several sleepy white hats sat talking at the long, ancient, gleaming table and chairs, the only furniture in the enormous room's center. Conversations were subdued and the tone in the room was somber. I took a seat at my usual place, to the warden's left. My back faced a barred window, revealing a tiny recreation yard beyond. It ran parallel to five-wing, which housed minimum custody inmates.

In the future, when renovated, this wing housed inmates sentenced to death, and the warden renamed it the "death house."

Warden Yeager had stopped smoking after his heart attack, so the room was strangely absent of the heavy cigarette, cigar, and Captain Driber's pipe smoke that it was usually filled with. "No smoking" signs had never appeared, and the warden hadn't issued an inter-departmental memo directing us not to smoke, but the big, brown, glass ashtrays had been strategically removed from the old mahogany table. There was an unspoken awareness that this subtle change was the handiwork of the warden's tiny, cheerful, and determined executive secretary, Evie Grover. The message was clear and hung poised in the air instead of the missing smoke.

As the early morning inmate kitchen detail was already up and rolling to prepare breakfast and operate our regular morning feeding schedule, the most urgent issue to decide on was whether or not to initiate a lockdown. If the boss locked down the institution, the men would get in-cell meals of either hot/cold cereal with milk or a peanut butter and jelly sandwich on a metal tray. This would cause many angry inmates, seeing as none of them had created any trouble. They would ask every white hat they encountered, "Why am I being punished on Thanksgiving Day? What's going on?"

A lockdown might cause some inmates, even those who were "with us" most of the time, to turn against us. Especially since today was Thanksgiving Day, and the men expected a visit from family members, a good hot meal, and special activities in the recreation yard. Food and visits were the only incentives for inmates to look forward to and the only thing that kept some men from causing us trouble. I hoped our population would display sound judgment and not do something stupid. A dramatic display of support for their fellow Rahway inmates was not beyond the realm of possibility. We were all aware violence was always lurking around the corner, and some men needed little to no reason for acting out.

The white hats returned from their mission and filed into the boardroom with the information they had gathered. Their impressions were all positive. They explained to the warden that "it should be safe to open for business as usual and everything is under control."

After more discussion, the warden had made his decision, "Okay then, we agree. We'll provide the morning meal in the dining room." We were all relieved. Mr. Yeager turned to Chief Deputy Edmonds and said, "Art, see to it that we have enough additional staff on duty to help should something unexpected jump off."

Breakfast was without incident, and we followed our usual routine for the rest of the day. I figured that most inmates saw nothing in it for them if they caused trouble. With the prison locked down, inmates knew what to expect. We would cancel family visits and indoor and outdoor activities, and the mess hall would remain closed which meant cold bologna sandwiches would replace the traditional Thanksgiving Day meal of turkey, dressing, and pumpkin pie. In prison life, these simplicities are truly what can maintain daily sanity and are held at supreme value.

Gratefully, that day at Trenton was a quiet one. Thanksgiving festivities took place as scheduled, upholding rare moments that are equally cherished by both the inmates and their loved ones on the outside. Most importantly, inmates and staff alike were spared from unnecessary adversity.

*

Meanwhile, at Rahway, the rebellion took on a life of its own as angry inmates continued to riot, raucously roaming through the four tiers in four-wing, plundering and out of control, breaking and destroying everything within grasp. Wearing wet masks made from torn sheets in anticipation of tear gas, they burned sheets, blankets, and mattresses, broke windows, smashed furniture, and damaged locking systems.

The bedlam went on all day on that Thursday. Rahway was officially in a state of chaos. The inmates had turned savagely on Warden Vukcevich. He received two stab wounds in the back, two punctures in front, a razor slash in the abdomen, and four broken bones at the back of his neck. Determined, the rioters relentlessly held the seriously injured warden and five officer's hostage. Inmates who wanted no part in the rebellion closed themselves off within their cells and simply didn't take part. Overall, hell persisted at Rahway, flames, tragedy, and all.

At one point, correction officers and the New Jersey State Police planned to storm the institution in a joint operation. Had that happened, mayhem would have occurred just as it had at Attica. Prisoner Alfred Ravenel, the riot ringleader, ordered Vukcevich killed if the state police stormed the facility. Knowing him well, I'm sure it would have happened. To the press covering the riot, Ravenel had declared himself the "would-be executioner." We later learned that our governor, William Cahill, had established a disciplined command post at the neighboring and peaceful Woodbridge State School early in the day. From there, he led stress-free negotiations and ended the riot. Trenton's staff, assisting at Rahway returned safely to Trenton. Surrendering inmates submitted a list of demands to Carl Zeitz, a news reporter. By this time, twenty-four hours had elapsed.

Late Thursday night, once we knew the uprising had ended, Warden Yeager instructed Chief Deputy Edmonds to go to Rahway Prison early Monday morning. He took with him a captain and two other supervisors. They were instructed to help, however needed, and to interview both the staff and the inmates. In addition, Chief Edmonds agreed to prepare a verbal presentation for a white hat meeting.

Friday remained uneventful at both facilities. Our staff at Trenton remained on alert for potential signs of trouble. Other than that, we operated on a regular schedule. Under the landmark dome, at Rahway, the inmates remained on lockdown and the staff began the monumental job of cleaning up the wreckage created by the rioters. An official investigation to determine the riot's ringleaders began and continued through the weekend.

On Monday morning, Chief Edmonds and his team arrived at Rahway. They began their tour in the auditorium where the conflict began. From there, they proceeded to four-wing – the area that had suffered the most destruction. It took all day for them to complete their inspection and interviews of the still shell-shocked staff and residents. Late that evening, before leaving for home, they went to Rahway General Hospital to visit Warden Vukcevich and the officers.

Warden Yeager's Tuesday afternoon white hat meeting began at 1 p.m. in the boardroom. Chief Edmonds started his presentation:

"On Wednesday evening, at about 8:45 p.m., from the Rahway Control Center, Lieutenant Carstens alerted Warden Vukcevich that a loud commotion was going on in the auditorium. Several inmates might be high, drunk, or both. Almost immediately, Warden Vukcevich determined that the situation was serious enough for him to get involved, so he left his home which is located on prison grounds and walked across the street to the prison. He stopped in the Control Center to leave his watch and wallet there, and proceeded, unescorted, to the auditorium. Once there, he climbed up on the stage and approached an inebriated inmate – Clay Thomas, a 'Black Power instigator' [as described by the *New York Times*] – who had arrived at the prison's auditorium just as the holiday movie ended and was as high as a kite." (The most probable intoxicant was "Hooch," the popular name for prison-made moonshine.)

The room grew quiet. Staff members standing nearby who were present at the incident reported that they saw a brief conversation occur between the two men. (Later, although I was never able to verify this information, I learned from several Rahway correction officers on-duty when the riot started that

Sam Vukcevich had leaned forward and whispered to Thomas, "You guys are acting like a bunch of losers.")

The chief went on, "In response to the brief interaction that took place, the apparently stoned Thomas punched Vukcevich in the face, knocking him down. Next, he shoved the stunned warden off the stage, where he landed with a sickening thud, falling onto the wooden floor in front of the stage. Thomas then jumped down to the floor, grabbed a wooden chair, and slammed it across the warden's back, shattering the chair into several flying pieces. Seeing the warden dazed and disabled encouraged other inmates to join in and stab him in the back with shives." (Shives are homemade, metal stabbing and cutting weapons manufactured by inmates from commonplace metal scraps stolen from the prison's shops. Many of these handmade weapons are long, thin, and pointed, leaving no trace behind when pulled out of a wound. So instead, they seal, and the victim bleeds internally.)

He continued, "We learned that in the surging pandemonium, inmates dragged the warden to the ancient four-wing. [Generally referred to as 'the ghetto.'] The aim was to further humiliate and punish him by making him experience the same awful conditions they endured daily in the eighteenth-century cell block. As they rampaged along with the semi-conscious warden in tow, the group grew larger and more out of control. The celebratory hoots and howls of the men rioting intensified and were both deafening and alarming."

[The crumbling four-wing dated back to 1833, and at the time of the riot, the cells in this wing were terrible. They were about nine feet long and seven feet high. Most prisoners could hold out their arms and touch each side of the cell wall. There was a metal toilet, a metal washbasin, a bunk, a table, a footlocker, and a naked lightbulb dangling from the ceiling that glared in the darkness. New Jersey weather was both simmering hot and humid in the summer and intensely cold and drafty in the winter. The wing was filthy (although the inmates had to assume some responsibility for cleaning their own cells) and was definitely in need of structural renovation. Apparently, the condition of this wing helped contribute to the discontent leading to the riot.

Furthermore, "In the midst of it all, a fistfight at the opposite end of the tier distracted Sam's captors, and they roughly dumped him in a corner. Seizing the moment, three inmates exchanged signals and made a quick decision to grab Sam and pulled him into an empty cell. Sam was not a small man. Somehow, his rescuers slid the semi-conscious warden under the small cot in the cell and concealed him with blankets. They closed the barred cell door and waited with anticipation to see what would happen first – an incredulous opportunity to sneak him out or be discovered with potentially fatal consequences.

"One inmate, in particular, risked his life and remained with Sam in the same cell. The other rescuers rejoined the melee and pretended to take part in the ongoing uproar. Twenty-six-year-old inmate Garrett had been a hospital orderly at the prison before the Thanksgiving Day of rebellion. He had taken blood pressures and pulses but had done nothing more sophisticated. Yet somehow, he found the ability to stitch the bleeding wounds of Warden U. Samuel Vukcevich. Garrett first treated some cuts and bruises for other prisoners and officers. Then, turning his attention to Vukcevich, he applied cold compresses and bandages to deep slashes and cuts on the warden's neck and back. Some of the other inmates brought Garrett the needed materials and let him leave the cell light on, so he could begin sewing butterfly stitches in an effort to close the warden's gaping cuts. After the wounds were tended to, Garrett and the warden talked and puffed his cigarettes, the warden's first, after eight years of swearing off smoking.

"Several other brave inmates also stepped up, involving themselves in a life-risking operation to save and help the warden escape. During an interval in the riot, when no one was watching and the time seemed right, they wrapped Sam up in a blanket, like a burrito. Together, they lifted, carried, and dragged the injured and helpless warden to the end of the shadowy tier. They painstakingly labored to navigate their dead-weight, bundled-up, injured, but still breathing package down the stairs to 'the flats,' four flights of darkened iron stairways below. Officers standing down in the rotunda spotted them struggling at the top of the stairs and demanded they identify themselves. Were these more rioters up to no good?

"Initially suspicious, and with good reason, the gathered staff looked on in disbelief when the blankets came off to reveal a badly beaten and bloody Sam Vukcevich. Without hesitation, someone threw open a barred rotunda door allowing the heroes and Sam to pass into the safety of the secured area. Someone said the scene was all 'Butts and Elbows' as the joyful officers in the rotunda rushed to summon one of the many ambulances standing by in the parking lot. Once safe, the warden left by ambulance for Rahway General Hospital."

WHEN THE PRISONERS finally agreed to end the revolt, the hostages were released and transported to the hospital. The division director ordered Garrett's transfer to another prison, where he lived in a special section with jailed organized crime leaders until his parole.

Garrett did such a terrific job that doctors at the Rahway General Hospital didn't remove the stitches put in Warden Vukcevich's back, stating that "the inmate did an excellent job." Later, in response to his quick medical prowess – using crude makeshift instruments, limited supplies, and a surplus of courage – he stated, "It just came to me, I don't know how. He had confidence in me, and he was giving me confidence in myself."

Crediting Garrett for saving the warden's life in the uprising, the *St. Louis Post-Dispatch* reported about the inmates' daring care of the injured warden in their February 13, 1972, edition. Garrett told reporters he thought of his fellow inmates. "What I did wasn't for the warden so much, but for all the men," he said. "What they don't realize is that if he died, they were dead too."

Governor William T. Cahill reduced the inmate's sentence for a service station robbery by half. It made him eligible for immediate parole, and Governor Cahill promised him his old job as a state youth counselor, saying the man had endangered himself by helping the warden. When the 150 convicts seized control of the two wings of the prison and captured five correction officers and the warden, Garrett recalled, "I was the only thing close to a doctor in the whole joint."

Concluding his presentation, Chief Edmonds reported the list of typical demands that the inmates presented to reporters as the riot neared its end. The list included:

1. <u>Medical Care – Aspirin is the "wonder drug" for everything.</u>
2. Commissary – Prices and the profits are too high.
3. Parole Board – First offenders rarely become eligible for parole hearings after serving one-third of their sentences, the current minimum requirement.
4. Educational/Vocational Program – Education is inadequate, and there is no vocational training at all. Prisoners should learn a skill to help them get employment after release.
5. Disciplinary Action – Guards work out their frustrations on prisoners in a kangaroo court-type atmosphere.
6. Cultural Identity – Blacks and Puerto Ricans are not able to practice their own cultural identity.
7. Religious Freedom – Only certain religions are allowed to conduct religious services.
8. Mail Packages – Mail delivery leaves a lot to be desired and is often rifled.
9. Job Allotment – Inmates may not quit jobs they don't like, and wages are low.
10. Work Release – The program caters to only a few inmates.
11. Rehabilitation – Rehabilitation does not exist.

*

By that next Sunday, both prisons were operating as usual, and the warden gave me a day off. On Monday morning, I returned to my office to get some work done. Just as I had sat down at my desk, the phone rang. It was Warden Yeager calling to say, "Bob, I have an idea I believe you will find interesting. See me sometime on Thursday so we can talk about it."

I couldn't help but think, *"Oh boy, what next?"*

CHAPTER 2

Lessons Learned

Jánko Hatrak And Elizabeth Dobos

"It seems, in fact, as though the second half of a man's life is made up of nothing but the habits he has accumulated during the first half."

– *Fyodor Dostoevsky*

Once people learn I was a prison warden working in one of America's most notoriously violent prisons, I'm often asked, "What prepared you to deal with the situations, staff, and inmates you encountered during your career?" My answer to these inquiries always begins the same way.

"We're all a combination of the total sum of our life's experiences. Hopefully, everyone gathers the wisdom required to deal with life's trials and tribulations."

My outlook on life was shaped as I watched my parents struggle to raise a family during the Depression era in the 1920s. The small anthracite coal mining town of Jessup, in Northwest Pennsylvania, was not an ideal place to raise a family. However, my parents – Jánko (John) and Elizabeth – faced and met the challenges head-on. I genuinely believe any insight I developed while in Jessup came from the exposure to economic hardship and the courage my parents exhibited to keep on trying. These examples naturally became the foundation of my future perspective.

*

My parents' roots trace back to Trebishov, Czechoslovakia, which is where my story ultimately begins. Orphaned at age seven, Jánko was just in the second grade when his only living relative, an uncle, died suddenly. Having no family members left to take care of him, Jánko needed to become a quick genius at survival. He wandered alone from one Trebishov farm to another, and along his quest tried to keep body and soul together. He got lucky when he finally found a safe, dry, and warm barn to camp in. The barn was on the property of farmer and village landowner Mike Dobos. He hid there for several days and gratefully ate the food Mike's friendly farmhands shared with him.

Mike's wife, Anna, discovered Jánko in the barn hiding behind a cow, and she asked him in Slovak, "Go tu robíš?" ("What are you doing here?") He answered through tears saying, "I need a warm place to sleep and eat. Can I sleep in the barn and work with the farmhands?" He must have been a pathetic sight to behold, because once the young mother heard his story, she immediately agreed to help him.

That night, Anna informed Mike that she had discovered a small homeless boy hiding in their barn. She asked him if the child could sleep there, work in the fields, and eat with the other farmhands. Mike usually agreed to her requests, and once more, he said "Áno" ("Yes").

Jánko was an engaging little boy. It wasn't long before he became part of Mike and Anna's extensive family of seven. He was of course thrilled when Anna invited him to live in the main house with them. There, he met Mike's youngest daughter, Elizabeth, who many years later would become his bride – and my mother!

AS THE YEARS passed, Anna busied herself playing matchmaker between Jánko and Elizabeth. Mike voiced staunch objections to Jánko marrying his youngest daughter, calling him a "homeless wanderer." Most often, the still persistent Anna had things her way, and she was determined the outcome of this romance would not be an exception. After all, little Jánko had touched her heart, and she had embraced him into her family. By then, he had become an even more charming young man. Despite Mike's opposition and protests, eventually, Jánko and Elizabeth became a couple and agreed to be married.

Mike, being stubborn, avoided any involvement in the wedding planning and had actually announced that he intended to boycott the wedding ceremony altogether. In small villages such as this one, holidays and weddings were always significant events where people traveled with their families from far and wide – on foot and in wagons – to join in on the festivities that usually lasted for days. Everyone enthusiastically took part in the wedding celebrations; except the father of the bride whose conspicuous absence caused much whispering among the guests.

Now that Jánko and Elizabeth were married, Anna continued planning their future. As the weeks passed, she began squirreling away the money she made from selling eggs from their hens and vegetables from her garden, to finance a trip to America (through Canada) for Jánko. She had decided what his priorities should be – first, find a place to live, and then find a job. Once this major step was accomplished, Jánko's instructions were to send for Elizabeth to join him. From there, the young couple would move to the United States. Jánko, happy with the prospect of eventually getting to America, kissed Elizabeth goodbye, left Czechoslovakia, and journeyed by ship to Canada. Following Anna's plan, he found a place to live and a good job and then accordingly sent for Elizabeth.

After months of planning and packing, Elizabeth left Europe and sailed off to join Jánko. Not long after she arrived, they migrated to Jessup, Pennsylvania. They were eager to be reunited with two families, the Bodnars and the Bobiks, who also immigrated from Trebišov, where they had all grown up together.

*

To say living in Jessup in the 1920s was a challenge is an understatement. Once there, they rented a small, old house on Front Street, found for them by the Bobiks. Front Street was a scattered row of old, faded dwellings that aligned themselves with meandering railroad tracks that led to and from the coal mines. Each house looked much like its equally neglected neighbor.

Smoke and dust showered the houses and yards. Shabby sheds and privies cluttered the small backyards. Any laundry hanging outside collected an unwelcomed gift of soot, courtesy of the Pennsylvania Railroad and the busy coal mines that populated nearby hills. Huge slag piles perpetually dominated neighborhoods as they continued to smolder year after year, filling the air with nameless odors.

Our two-story house sat in the center of a middle-sized yard, which later developed into Mom's very productive vegetable garden. The most intriguing feature of our "estate" was the haunted and abandoned coal mine, which made Mom (who was naturally superstitious) uneasy. The house had no electricity, so Mom would collect candles, taking them first to be blessed in church, to light our home. There was no indoor plumbing, and the water supply came from a well, conveniently stationed outside the back door. A small outdoor hand pump helped her draw water to the surface, which she then spilled into a big bucket. The old and rickety outhouse served as our bathroom. Mom insisted that we each take a weekly bath in a large, galvanized tub, squatting on the floor in what was to us the living room. A coal-fired stove in the kitchen provided heat, but it only warmed the first floor. As a result, the second floor was freezing cold during the long winter months.

Not long after they arrived in Jessup, Jánko took a job as a coal miner. Work began at sunrise and ended at sunset, six days a week. There was no such thing as overtime pay. Jánko knew that mining was a risky business and that it was not unusual for miners to be injured or die during rockslides or gas explosions. He didn't let that deter him because he knew that the job he was about to begin would provide the money needed to support himself and Elizabeth in their new life in America. A powerfully built young man, Jánko was just under six feet tall, bull-necked, with massive biceps, wavy sandy hair, laughing blue eyes, a ruddy complexion, and an ever-ready grin. He was quick to anger and always quicker to have a laugh.

My older brother, Elmer (John), and my big sister, Yolanka (Joan), were born in Jessup before I had arrived on the scene. I'm glad that by the time I was born, my parents had become Americanized enough to simply name me "Bobby." I was born at home on Christmas Day, December 25, 1937.

Pop was worried that a war was coming to America. So, he convinced the midwife who delivered me at home to enter the date on my birth certificate as January 3, 1938, instead of

December 25, 1937, because he hoped that change would delay my being drafted into the military for one extra year. So, my legal birthday is 1/3/38 instead of 12/25/37.

Pop told me I arrived in Jessup with Santa, and without hesitation, I believed him. Mom's girlhood friend from Trebišov, Elizabeth Bobik, helped with my home delivery. Everyone was excited when I made my debut appearance wearing something over my face, which they called a "veil or caul." According to Elizabeth's Eastern European superstitions, a veil's unusual presence at birth predicts the newborn would enjoy good luck and do something special with their life. But, as a kid, after hearing this prediction again and again, I wondered how I would ever meet Mom's expectations. "What exactly was I supposed to do to measure up to her hopes and dreams?"

EVEN THOUGH POP worked incredibly hard at his job in mining, he also contributed to our food supply. He slaughtered a giant hog each fall to supply us with much-needed meat for the winter. Since there was no refrigeration, we hung the pork in the smokehouse that he built behind the house. The cured pork lasted us all winter. I always loved eating the delicious garlicky smoked kielbasa he prepared for us.

Elizabeth was tall, slender, dark-haired, and blue-eyed and wore a somber expression. Yet, she was innovative and very competent. Her energy and perseverance in hard times were an impressive and reliable asset to Jánko. Elizabeth always had too many opinions, while Jánko, being quick and decisive, found it difficult to have patience with her indecisive nature. She rarely, if ever, stuck to her decisions. Elizabeth always meant well, but she could be a very abrasive lady. In these early months she and Jánko were very often at odds.

When it came to food, Mom cooked and baked better than anyone. Always happy to share what little we had with whoever showed up, she made sure no one ever left our home hungry or empty-handed. An overflowing basket of vegetables, flowers, or freshly baked goodies always accompanied departing guests.

What helped her to do so was the small but highly productive garden she diligently tended in our backyard. She always over-planted, so that she had extra to sell or generously give away.

Thanks to her resourcefulness, including the aggressive family of geese she raised and the chickens that populated our backyard, we never went cold or hungry. Without question, it was a luxury to have goose-down quilts and pillows, handmade by Mom to keep us warm during frigid winter nights. The geese also provided seemingly never-ending meals of goose soup with dumplings, goose potpies, goose paprikash, roasted goose, and goose meat sandwiches. Yikes, that was a lot of geese.

Being the smallest member of our family, the geese always picked me to chase screaming around the backyard while honking and snapping at my bottom. So, I wasn't at all that unhappy when the *honking menaces* magically became "dinner and quilts!"

IN THE SPRING of 1942, when I was four years old, Pop suffered a disabling back injury while working in the coal mine. Because of his injuries, he couldn't find other work in Jessup. With Pop unemployed, the family desperately needed money, so Mom took a job working as a laborer on a neighboring farm picking beans seven days a week in order to support us. My brother and sister, Elmer and Yolanka, were less than thrilled to join her during the harvest season.

That summer was miserable, with Mom, along with my brother and sister working and living at the nearby farm. I sadly remember Pop and me visiting them there. We all slept in a tiny, hot, airless room. Mom and Pop slept in the only bed, and we kids slept on the floor. I can remember crying during the night when I felt a bug on my leg. Mom and Pop took me into the narrow bed with them, and I felt safe and sheltered, snuggled there between them…and the family all together.

After visiting Mom and collecting her pay envelope, Pop and I drove home. I missed them, and I often asked Pop, "Kedi idu domov?" ("When are they coming home?")

*

By the winter, everyone was back together at home. Elmer, Yolanka, and I spent many windy days trudging along the snow-covered railroad tracks that passed in front of our house. We collected the coal that bounced to the ground from the passing trains. I always trailed behind with my nearly empty coal bucket, trying to keep up.

We needed the coal to fuel the coal-burning kitchen stove. We depended on the stove to cook our meals and to heat the first floor of our four-room house. The upstairs floor did not have heat. Thank God, we each had our own comforting and sumptuous goose down prikrývka (goose down quilts in Slovak). It was always a shivery race to change out of our clothes and dive under the mountain of goose-down, falling asleep in the blessed warmth.

Life, however, was not without fun. One day, Mom was bathing our fluffy white dog, CheeChee, outside, in the same large, galvanized tub our family used for Saturday night baths in the living room. The dog was impatient while tolerating being scrubbed down to her skin. Finally, she decided she had enough of the rubba-dub-dubbing. Bolting from the tub and soaking Mom, she took off like a streak across the backyard. Later that day, we looked for CheeChee to feed her, but she was nowhere to be found. She remained missing for the rest of the day and was unaccounted for that night when we extinguished the candle lights in the house and went to bed.

Pop was not as superstitious as Mom, and he had little patience with her dramatics. Later that evening, after everyone settled down for the night, Mom kept insisting in a loud stage whisper that she heard eerie *Oooh-Oooh* sounds outside. She was sure the noise she was hearing was a mátoha (ghost in Slovak). The howling, she said, was coming from the abandoned coal mine in the backyard. By now, all three of us kids were crying, and Pop, in exasperation, gave up trying to sleep. Mom continued to pester him to go outside to look for the ghost. When Pop had enough of her fantasies for the night, he got out of bed, dressed, and went slamming out of the kitchen door shouting, "Ježiš, Maria, a Josef!" ("Jesus, Mary, and Joseph!")

This was his usual last resort when dealing with Mom's antics. I wondered if Pop thought his "ghost-busters" search would reassure us, or if he just needed to escape the confusion. I asked my sister Yolanka, "Will Pop find a ghost in the backyard? And if he does, what will he do with it?" I had already decided that I would run. All I know is that it was a long night!

The next day, following his normal morning routine, a sleepy Pop headed for our only bathroom…the outhouse. He found no creature comforts there. Toilet tissue was a luxury, and so we didn't have any. Somewhere, Pop had found some Sears catalogs, which had served as our faux toilet paper for a long time. Pop told us not to use a page with color and to crunch up each sheet before using it. That would make the sheet softer to use. I didn't miss toilet paper because, frankly, I didn't know what it was.

As Pop reached the privy, he realized that the mournful howls Mom had heard the previous night indeed were coming from somewhere close by from a still whimpering CheeChee. Peering down into the darkness through the hole in the wooden seat, Pop saw the shivering and miserable "ghost" … our dog CheeChee. She was no longer white and fluffy, but she was happy to see Pop and thumped her tail into the mess she was sitting in. Pop rescued her by dropping a long rope with a slipknot on one end down into the darkened abyss. Poor CheeChee! Acting as if she was once taught what to do under such circumstances, or maybe by accident, she stepped into the loop, and Pop, being extremely strong, pulled her up to safety.

By this time, the entire family had gathered outside. Everyone was waiting with bated breath to see if the missing dog would emerge dead or alive. It already smelled like she was dead. As soon as Pop removed the rope from her body, she charged like lightning through the outhouse door. Panting, she began running in erratic circles around the entire yard. She paused, joyfully greeting each of us, and shook off the "decorations" she had collected during her adventure. She smelled awful, but holding our noses, we cheered her on, and the louder we cheered, the faster she ran. Since we didn't own a hose, Pop pumped buckets of water from the well to toss at CheeChee as she ran past them. Some water he threw missed its target and hit Mom square on! She squealed so loud I laughed all over myself. Pop insisted to Yolanka that he was truly aiming for the dog. His mischievous grin made us all wonder. Mom remained gloomy for the rest of the day. That night, CheeChee didn't get to sleep in my bed.

*

Pop's back injury had improved only slightly, and it was clear he could never return to working in the mines. Since there were no employment opportunities in Jessup for Pop, he needed to find some other work. He decided that we should move and again follow their friends, the Bobik and Bodnar families, to Trenton, New Jersey, where they had recently relocated. They assured him there was work waiting for him in Trenton's steel mills (the American Steel and Wire Company and the John A. Roebling and Sons Steel Mill).

Pop planned the route that would take us from Jessup to South Trenton. He made one visit by himself to scope things out and find a job and a place to live before moving us there. He had never left our home before, and when he drove off in our new, old black Pontiac, I cried until I had the hiccups. While there, he rented a small row house in a place called "The Burg."

OUR JOURNEY TO Trenton began late on a cold and rainy Friday afternoon. Part of the expedition included driving through the beautiful Pocono Mountains. Once in the mountains, we found heavy snow, hail, and wind, making roadways treacherous. As a result, Pop drove cautiously and slowly. It was no surprise Mom found it necessary to continuously, or so it seemed, warn Pop, by shouting, "Jánko, ísť spomali" ("John, go slow"). It was easy to predict that Pop's response, eventually, would be, "Ježiš, Maria, a Josef!"

Today, traveling the 133 miles from Jessup to Trenton, would take two and a half hours. There was no Pennsylvania or New Jersey turnpikes and no interstate highways back then. So, at that time our journey was a seemingly endless one. The car's heater wasn't working, and we were freezing. Elmer was sitting in the front seat next to Pop. I sat in the back seat between Yolanka and Mom. I snuggled with Mom, covered in blankets, with my head in her lap. The roads were slippery, full of potholes that needed repair. The snowy ride seemed to go on and on forever.

WE FINALLY ARRIVED in the South Trenton section of Chambersburg (The Burg). It enjoyed its reputation as the city's restaurant capital because many of Trenton's best Italian restaurants and most popular eateries were located there. Later, we would discover favorites such as the Hudson Beer Gardens, Peoples Bakery, De Lorenzo's Tomato Pies, Creco's, and Diamonds.

We drove slowly in the drizzle through the silent and dark city streets, searching for Tremont Street. Our friends, the Banyacki family, had invited us to stay with them until Monday and were reliably waiting for us. On the way, we approached a massive stone structure that filled an entire city block. It was bigger than anything I had ever seen! Everyone was agape as we went past. Then, in the car's silence, I asked in my high-pitched, four-year-old voice, "Otče, je to náš nový kostol?" ("Father, is that our new church?") Everyone laughed, and Pop answered me, "I don't think so, Bobby."

It would never have occurred to any of us on that wet and dreary night in 1942 that some twenty years later, the dark, brooding fortress before us would play a pivotal role in my future. Or why, from that night on, it was so often on my mind. In retrospect, the lessons I learned in Jessup included the values my parents exhibited in the face of adversity. The way they lived and handled hard times taught me to never give up. Instead, I learned "to just keep going, even when you really just feel like quitting."

The bullying geese taught me when to retreat, and Pop moving his family to Trenton showed me that sometimes…you just need to cut your losses and move on. These experiences became the lynchpins of my future viewpoint for many things in my life. They also played a big part in who I became as a warden.

I could never understand the connection I felt to the New Jersey State Prison.

CHAPTER 3

It's A Trenton Thing!

"...like pork roll, tomato pie, and Italian hot dogs...
you just wouldn't understand."

"Growing Old is Mandatory – Growing up is Optional."

– Chili Davis

Even though I am proud to be born in Pennsylvania, I'm proud to say both Jessup and Trenton are my hometowns. My heart is still there in New Jersey.

The city of Trenton has a rich history. General George Washington crossed the Delaware River on December 26, 1776, to fight and defeat the Hessians camped in Trenton. In November and December 1784, briefly, Trenton was the nation's capital. Trenton later claimed fame again when John A. Roebling and Sons Steel Mill, founded in 1849, built the Brooklyn Bridge. It was the world's first suspension bridge.

The future would soon bring many industrial successes to the growing city. Nearly every one of them is still going strong today in their exact original locations. They are still integral parts of the base of this mixed hive of active industries established in the nineteenth century. Although not a business enterprise, the Trenton State Prison is still a significant employer of many South Trenton residents. The local community of hard-working immigrants lived in Chambersburg (The Burg) within a ten-square block area of their place of employment.

To celebrate the city's reputation as a manufacturing and industrial area, the city fathers memorialized their town with the motto "Trenton Makes The World Takes." They installed a massive sign with those words prominently displayed in lights on the Lower Trenton Bridge in 1935. It still hangs there today, making it a significant and permanent landmark in the proud city of Trenton.

*

The blended neighborhood we were moving into included immigrants from a handful of European countries. They moved to Trenton to preserve their cultural identities, establish roots, and make a new beginning. Trenton's ethnic neighborhoods provided a familiar setting for those new to America. They offered support in language, particularly if newcomers preferred to speak their native language or were still learning English.

They also provided networking for jobs, housing, religious organizations, and schools, creating a community essential for assimilation ease. The families settling in these neighborhoods found a welcoming environment for their children to be secure.

Our new home, a rental row house nestled in this busy and productive scene, sat waiting for us to arrive at the intersection of Beatty and Tremont Streets. Walking down the street on warm days, with the neighbors' doors and windows open, I could smell wonderful whiffs drifting out to me and filling the entire neighborhood with tantalizing aromas. To a little kid from sleepy Jessup, all this activity was beyond excitement. I wish Pop had not consistently told me, "Don't move off the porch."

Early, that first Saturday morning, I remember how exciting it was to tour our new house. We were pleased and relieved to learn that the house had indoor plumbing and electricity (finally no outhouse and no more candles!). A large black coal stove sat possessively in one warm, cozy kitchen corner. A big white Hoosier cupboard occupied the entire opposite wall. Here would be all of Mom's baking supplies and equipment. Each item in its special place. I would often give in to the temptation to crank the little handle on the flour bin to see the cloud of sifted flour drift out. This action would always prompt Mom to ask the same question: "Bobby, why do you keep doing that?"

I knew if I grinned at her, she wouldn't be mad at me. It was a game we always played, and I think Mom enjoyed it as much as I did.

On the second floor, thank God, was an indoor bathroom with a gleaming white tub – no more public baths in the galvanized tub for me! After all, I was four years old now. We discovered a small plot of ground on the side yard. It was perfect for a garden and my new dog, Blackie! She was a beautiful black cocker spaniel who always curled up and slept with me. She was now my constant companion and only friend so far.

*

Arriving in the Burg from Jessup, that first sighting of the huge Trenton Prison fascinated me. Even though I thought it was our new church, the high, shadowy walls were very scary and intimidating. I recall asking Pop, "Why would anyone want to work on top of a wall, and why are they walking back and forth carrying those long guns?" I just knew there was a secret in there, and Pop's explanations clearly never satisfied me. My eager curiosity must have tried his patience.

Whenever Pop and I went somewhere in the car, if we passed by the Trenton Prison, I asked him to drive me around the four square blocks the institution occupied, so I could take another "good look" at it. He accommodated me most of the time, but he always said, "Yoy, yoy, yoy, again? We've done this so many times. Bobby, why are you so curious about an old prison?" I didn't know why, so I never had an answer for him. Despite that, the fascination never faded away.

*

For many months after we arrived in Trenton, I watched the neighborhood boys play games together and have fun in the street. I sat at the living room window and wished I could join in, but I dared not to venture outside. *How could I?* The boys all spoke English, and I spoke Slovak. No one could understand what I was saying, and how would I know what they were saying? So, I remained indoors, lonely, constantly peering out of our living room window. Learning the lesson of isolation because I couldn't speak English was difficult for me, considering I was naturally a chatterbox.

Slovak was the primary language spoken in our home. But we also spoke three other languages: Polish, Hungarian, and Russian, depending on who was visiting my family that day. It never occurred to me that I was fortunate because I understood and spoke four different languages at just the age of five. I wish I could still do that today. I always sat with our guests, and they encouraged me to join the conversation. It took me almost a year after I arrived in Trenton for my English to progress enough for me to feel comfortable joining the kids playing in the street. I learned they called themselves the Beatty Street Gang. Their ages ranged from five to ten and there were less than a dozen members. The gang was a version of the Little Rascals, except their focus was on athletics and no girls were allowed. I was excited when member Pat Magee, age seven, *knocked on our front door* and asked me to join the group, and happily, I agreed.

*

Many neighborhood residents worked two full-time jobs, including my mom. It was clear, that work and family, also meant work *for* the family. Because so many households had two working members, the neighborhood grandmas, whom I called our Staré Pani (old ladies), kept their watchful eyes on the neighborhood's children playing in the street throughout the day. I remember how the grandmas and the non-working moms sat or stood on their porches, visiting with each other, and observing the children at play. They were the equivalent of today's neighborhood watch.

All the kids knew the surrounding adults and all the grownups knew which child belonged to whom. "No way on God's green earth" could anyone come into the neighborhood to abduct or abuse the children. The women made sure none of the kids got into trouble. Of course, they themselves wouldn't think twice about coming out into the street to slap one of us upside the head. Funny, this never seemed strange to any of us.

That said, intriguing characters visited our Beatty Street neighborhood regularly, and after all these years, I can still hear the ragman. He scared me to death. Long before he appeared, I could hear his gravelly, raspy, monotone voice repeatedly announce his arrival: "Rags, Rags!" I could hardly wait for him to come into view. His old, rickety, horse-drawn, wooden wagon looked like it might not last through the day. I had never seen such a scruffy old guy. His horse's gait never changed as he slowly lumbered past yelling loudly, "Rags! Rags!" Mom was always eager to negotiate with the ragman. She stopped him to sell the rags she had accumulated since his last visit. Some people sold him bones he would resell to others, who used them to make glue and fertilizer.

As a young girl in Europe, Mom learned how to drive a bargain, as she watched her mom skillfully haggle with gypsy hucksters. This poor rag/bone man was the victim of her negotiating talents. Afterward, she always bragged "Dostai som lepsiu dohodu" ("I got the better deal"). Mom enjoyed the contest as she bartered with him until his eyes crossed. He always seemed relieved to get away.

My friends and I gathered and waited at the curb to watch him pass. I think that might have been the first time I had ever seen a horse. We often talked about asking him for a ride. But we never dared to ask, and he never offered.

Another man riding a horse-drawn cart sold ice. He lugged enormous blocks of ice using large metal tongs. Mom met him at our door, saying, "Wipe your feet, wipe your feet." He tromped through our narrow house to the kitchen and placed the ice in the icebox. My job was to empty the wobbly drip tray under the icebox. It took practice getting it to the sink to dump the water without making a mess on the kitchen floor. I wasn't always successful, and Mom would clean up behind me. The vegetable huckster, the mailman, our neighborhood cop who regularly walked the beat, the milk deliverer, and the coalman all made routine rounds and were welcome familiar figures.

*

One didn't need to look too far to find a place to bet on nearly any sporting event imaginable, especially horse races. People even bet on a three-digit number, which was much like today's six-digit jackpot lotteries.

In today's world, no one would permit a little kid to cross the street unaccompanied, let alone go to a store to place a bet. But there in the Burg, in 1942, if anyone thought it unusual, they didn't mention that anything was wrong while seeing me do it! Most mornings around 7 a.m. Mom had already gone to work. I left the house before everyone else was up. Crossing Beatty Street, I headed for the first store open to place Mom's bet. In my pocket was a quarter she had left for me the night before on the corner of the stove, entrusting me to place her daily three-digit wagers. She left the numbers written on a small piece of paper for me to give to the bookie. How did Mom pick the numbers she bet on? One of her methods was to use something she called her dream book. The book offered a simple description of a variety of dreams someone might have, and a brief analysis of each. At the bottom of each page was a series of three-digit numbers. Mom would choose one or some combination of those numbers, and if she didn't have a dream to analyze, she would just randomly select three numbers. She never won, not even once, and from this I learned that gambling was not a smart thing to do.

*

My kindergarten year at Saint Mary's of the Assumption Elementary School was stressful. I was almost one full year younger than everyone else. To start, I had to learn the English language, and then somehow, I had to figure out how to become a student. Following along with the teacher when I didn't know what she was saying was nearly impossible and incredibly frustrating. I soon learned some boys in my class were unfriendly. I didn't know what they were saying since they spoke English, but they laughed at me when I attempted to talk to them. Their loud and snarly voices told me they were hostile, and that I was not welcome because I was different.

My first experience with bullying began the day when the boys pushed and shoved me. I had no other alternative but to defend myself during recess. After that, we fought nearly every day, morning, and afternoon. Being isolated, lonely, and sad took its toll, and eventually, I didn't want to go to school anymore. I had waited so long to be with other boys, but I didn't expect it would be like this. The nuns didn't understand the boys were bullying me. Bullying was also not something people talked about like they do nowadays. The nuns neither stood up for me nor disciplined them.

I felt abandoned. The nuns must have assumed because the other boys stood united that I was the problem. Since no one seemed able TO UNDERSTAND what was going on, I was on my own and left feeling completely overwhelmed. Even the principal didn't figure it out and instead of dealing with the bullies, she turned her attention to me!

AFTER MORNING RECESS one day, the principal finally got involved in one of our commotions. She was short and stout, but boy, could she swing her paddle! My attempt, in Slovak, to convince her it was the bullies and not me that needed paddling made no difference. She kept asking me (in Slovak), "Prosim, prestante bojovat's ostatnymi chlapcami." ("Please stop fighting with the other boys.") I responded with, "Prosim sestra, nie je to moja chyba." ("Please, Sister, it's not my fault.") To which, she replied, "Bend over!" The next thing I knew, she was administering ten solid whacks to my butt with her paddle. Defiantly, I didn't cry. Which prompted her to ask, "Preco neplaces?" ("Why aren't you crying?")

I didn't answer. I was too angry and there was no way I would let her see me cry. I knew I dared not tell Mom or Pop. If I did, I would get walloped again. Mom and Pop believed the sisters were never wrong. Also, it didn't help that each of my report cards proclaimed, "Needs to be more attentive." It was challenging to be attentive when I didn't understand what was happening.

I spent my entire kindergarten year and most of the first grade learning enough English just so my schoolmates no longer laughed when I spoke. Finally, the fighting ended mostly because I learned the only way to deal with a bully was to stand up for myself. This became a lesson I always passed along to my students, the athletes I coached, inmates I was responsible for, and, later, our children.

In kindergarten, I learned about injustice and that things were not always what they appeared to be. From the sisters of Saint Basil, I learned to respect authority, and while fearful of the big paddles, I understood that physicality was not the way to solve problems. Reason and logic were more effective tools in the long run. I found out what it feels like to get bullied, and that it's never acceptable. Somewhere along the line, I figured out that having all the facts before making crucial decisions was, in effect, a game-changer in life.

*

My parents always encouraged me to be productive and do minor jobs that would earn a small kid like me some money. I created a job for myself shining shoes when I was nine years old. Mom saw to it that I banked everything I earned. I thought this was really unfair as there were so many tempting shops in the Burg, like Josephine's Newspaper and Candy store, where I could buy candy, soda, bubblegum, and other goodies.

Once I was in sixth grade, I was a familiar figure at the dim, noisy, and smoke-filled Veteran's Tavern just a block away from my home. Every Friday and Saturday evening, I went there to shine patrons' shoes for a dime. I diligently polished and buffed while customers enjoyed visiting with friends and often argued about the day's sporting events listed on the bar's scorecard delivered every day. I built a small rickety box to store my supplies and on which a customer would place his foot while I was working on his shoe. It took some admonishment from my customers and a little practice to keep from getting shoe polish on a customer's socks – because if I did that, I didn't get paid – so no time was wasted in cleaning up my performance. I was proud of myself and couldn't wait to show my earnings to Mom.

Pop gave me one dollar every Saturday morning to give to Mr. Martin Mayer, the man he found to provide me with trumpet lessons. But he never suspected that when I left the house for a lesson with my trumpet in hand, I stopped off at Josephine's store to visit my friends. Before I knew it, I spent the whole dollar on candy and soda. I hung out for an hour and then went home, never taking a lesson. After "blowing off "my first trumpet lesson, it turned into a habit, and each week I spent that hour a truant yet a reliable customer of Josephine's.

IT WAS EXCITING when my shoe-shining career quickly expanded to include a newspaper route. Josephine's, in the middle of the block, employed me and my friend Pat Magee to deliver morning newspapers to neighborhood customers. We reported for work at 5 a.m. to fold the papers, which we then loaded into our delivery bags. The bags hanging over our bikes' handlebars were heavy at the beginning of the route, but got lighter as we continued, swerving and straining to peddle while zigzagging down the street...determined to deliver the newspapers.

New Jersey sometimes had severe snowstorms during the winter months, making deliveries impossible using my bike. One weekday morning, I think I was ten years old, I awoke to discover a serious, sleeting ice storm had created a treacherous but beautiful winter wonderland, which blanketed the streets and sidewalks with sheets of ice. There was no way to serve my papers, not even on foot. I had never missed one day of deliveries, but now the ice was about to spoil my perfect record.

Suddenly, a solution to my dilemma popped into my head! By substituting my new "clip-on" ice skates I received for Christmas, for my now useless bicycle, I could slide along the ice-covered sidewalks and serve the papers on time...and once I got organized and started, it was fun. As I worked my way from house to house, several neighbors were waiting on their porches and cheered me on my way down the street. I not only had a great time skating, but for the first time, I was aware the morning paper was important to those folks waiting for it. I loved seeing their excitement as they realized their papers would arrive after all. I was proud to have resolved the problem and make the entire neighborhood happy with me. That very well may have been the beginning of my "I can fix that" attitude.

*

Somehow, my eighth-grade teacher, Sister Mary Josaphat, knew about a place called Radices. So, one day in class, she told the boys, "If any of you ever go to a store named Radices, you will go straight to hell!" I sat bolt upright in my seat, wondering what and where this place was. *Why didn't I know about it? It had to be close to the school, but where?* I couldn't wait to learn more about this forbidden destination.

Since my classmate Gregory Feher, the smartest boy in our class, lived a few short blocks from the school, I sought him out and asked, "Hey, Greg! What and where is Radices?"

He said, "It's a small store directly across the street from the RKO Broad Theatre." He further added, "At Radices, they steam-clean men's fancy hats and shine shoes, but also sell penny candy, newspapers, magazines, and paperback books, and they even have a nickel pinball machine!"

I wondered what a pinball machine was, because anything with a ball in it sounded good to me. Gregory was full of information. For example, I learned that the owner, Jimmy Radice, sold loosies or two cigarettes for a nickel. I thought, *Wow, I need to go there to see this all for myself.* So, one day after school, I did just that.

Being a short two-and-a-half-block walk from Saint Mary's of the Assumption Elementary School, it wasn't hard to find, and my first visit began a long-term relationship with the little Burg store. The big attraction there for me was, of course, the flashing and dinging pinball machine. I had seen nothing so glorious. If one became a skilled player, they could win free games. I was as enthusiastic about it as kids are today about video games and things they play on their iPad.

A Burg landmark, Radices quickly became my go-to hangout spot after school until the end of the eighth grade that June. That summer people could book numbers there, as I had done for Mom years before, but they could also place bets on horseraces at major racetracks and sporting events, and play poker or Catch Five (a card game unique to Trenton) in the store's backroom.

EVERY SUNDAY MORNING, I walked to Mass with my parents at Saint Mary's. In grade school I served as an altar boy for the eight o'clock Mass, and sometimes Father Simko chose me to ring the big bell up in the steeple, instead of one of the big boys. The first time he selected me to ring the bell, I climbed with my heart pounding up two flights of stairs to the landing above and was surprised to find my full weight was needed to pull down the bell rope. It was both terrifying and thrilling to feel myself lifted off my feet high into the air by the weight of the swinging bell.

There were times, however, that I told Mom and Pop I would be in the sacristy with the other altar boys but skipped out once Mass began to go play the pinball machine at Radices. Knowing that if I scored enough points I could win free games, this feat became an obsessive goal of mine. I always rushed back to church before Mass ended, so I could innocently walk home with Mom and Pop.

I was, secretly, a daily visitor at the store, playing the pinball machine until the end of eighth grade in June. One day during the summer, I asked Mr. Radice if I could watch the neighborhood men in the backroom playing cards. He answered, "Yeah, you're here all the time. I trust you; go ahead. But remember to close and lock the door behind you."

Jimmy Radice, the store's owner, always kept the backroom locked, and you had to identify yourself before being given access to this "secret place." Standing silently behind "Tool" Radice, the owner's son, I learned from "the best" to play Catch Five. He warned me that I could stand there and watch, "So long as you keep your mouth shut." I never spoke a word. I particularly never repeated the vocabulary words I had learned from them that the sisters had obviously never taught us.

Over time, I was not only a welcomed customer but also had the privilege of being the only kid permitted in the backroom (imagine from age thirteen on) to watch card games in progress. It didn't take long before I was granted more of an "in," when Tool asked me to become a food runner for the group when I was in the ninth grade.

My job was to take the food and soft drink orders for the card players. Once I had everyone's order, I went to the Hole in the Wall, a small fast-food shop several doors down, to place the orders that I had carefully written down. Tool's advice to me was simple: "Never screw up an order, kid." Most of the card players shared their takeout food with me, and some even told me to order something for myself.

Today, as I think back to those days, though she was well-intentioned, Sister Josaphat was wrong – I was not, as she suggested, "on a glide path, headed straight for hell!' The men in Radices taught me a lot. I always enjoyed their acceptance and companionship, especially since usually there was no one at home because everyone worked. Now, I suspect the men knew this and gave me a safe place to hang, out of the goodness of their hearts.

I'm grateful that Pop never found out where I spent so much time. He would have killed me.

From my days at Radices, I learned a particularly valuable lesson – it's the judgments we make as youngsters that shape our future.

*

Beatty Street scooter races, using handmade scooters, were a favorite weekend and holiday activity. The collection of the parts and assembly of our scooters was as much fun as the race itself. To make a scooter, we first walked together to the farmer's market near the Delaware River to collect discarded fruit crates. Next, we had to find sturdy boards about four feet long, onto which we attached one-half of an old metal roller skate, the second half was attached on the back end.

Don't ask where we got the boards because I don't remember, but being an ingenious group of boys, we somehow figured it out. On race day, after dinner, we gathered at Home Avenue and Beatty Street to begin our scooter race. Modest row houses stood judgmentally lining both sides of Beatty Street. At race time, neighbors, parents, and the Staré Pani came outside to cheer us on from the sidewalk. Scooter racing was a new and exciting activity for me, and I didn't mind that I never won a race on my rickety scooter.

Summers in the neighborhood seemed blissfully endless. Everyone consumed lots of ice popsicles and large chunks of watermelon, courtesy of police Sergeant Mike Kane, who lived nearby on Tremont Street. Another fun time I remember was sitting outside on our stoop with the other kids until Mom came home at midnight after finishing the second shift cooking in the kitchen at General Motors. She also worked the day shift at the Horseman Dolls factory. This seemed normal because she had always worked two jobs. Now, I still can't believe how hard she worked for us.

Most of our neighbors sat on their porches until the early morning hours, hoping to catch a cool breeze. Unfortunately, New Jersey's mosquitos were unrelenting and about the size of a baseball. When a city truck fogged the entire neighborhood every evening with DDT to combat the mosquitos, we ran inside momentarily until the air cleared enough for us to stop coughing and return to our porch perches. It's a wonder we survived until autumn after inhaling a summer's worth of bug-killing mist.

DURING THE SUMMER months, we played every day of the week, including Sunday after church, from early morning until the streetlights came on at dusk. My neighborhood friends and I were always together playing games on Orange Street. On summer nights, when everyone was sitting out on their front porches trying to catch the breeze, Mom let me stay outside to play hide and seek in the dark and chase lightning bugs with the other kids. We also played inner-city street games like two-hand touch football, stickball, stoopball, and basketball under the streetlights in the middle of the block.

There wasn't any season, or day, from dawn to dusk, when Orange Street didn't reverberate with shouts, running feet, and balls bouncing off walls. These were the everyday sights and sounds our Beatty Street Gang contributed to the pulse of the environment in our special little neck of the woods.

Stickball was an affordable game because we didn't need to buy bats, gloves, or balls. Our bats were broomstick handles broken off someone's mother's broom. Once, when I contributed a broom handle, Mom yelled at Pop for days, asking, "What happened to my broom?" It seemed prudent for me to remain quiet (that's one thing I specifically retained from what the nuns taught us: "silence is a virtue.") In response, Pop shrugged his shoulders, rolled his eyes, and asked, "What next?" If Mom had asked me, I considered saying what Pop often said, "Ježiš, María Joséf," and then run outside! However, I decided that might not work as well for me as it did for Pop. Good thing Mom never asked me about her broom, and good thing the sisters taught us about virtue.

When our supply of handballs was running low, we held a Beatty Street Gang meeting to discuss how to replenish our dwindling inventory. Pat Magee told us he had often seen small pink balls gliding over the prison's wall onto Third Street and suggested how easy it could be to just grab some of those balls and then run away! After lengthy discussions we settled on that daring plan, retrieving the balls once they sailed over the prison's wall and then making a strategic getaway by running away as fast as our feet could carry us. We understood this was stealing. We rationalized we could either do that or give up playing games requiring a ball. Following a vote, snatching the ball won unanimously.

Our plan's most crucial decision centered on how we would pick who in the gang would go on this mission. We all agreed that a team of three needed to make the trip. We called the group the Street Patrol and Ball Retrieval team. To select the first team of three, we used a game we played often – odds and evens. We took the game very seriously, with all of us wanting to win, because it was the three losers who would make the first journey to the Trenton Prison.

I told the guys that when Pop and I drove past the prison there were always loads of cars parked along the Third Street wall, which would provide excellent hiding places if we waited behind them until a ball landed on the street. I had the misfortune of being on the first team of three sent on this truly terrifying mission. Billy Klank and Pat Magee made the nine-block trek with me. We walked solemnly along Cass Street, completely preoccupied. We barely talked because we were considering the risk we were taking and the grim consequences we would face if one or all of us got caught by the police. After all, this was a prison, and it was scary.

When we arrived, it was a huge surprise to see that we had competition – kids from other neighborhoods were already there, all planning to snatch the wayward balls! Also in the street was a man wearing khaki pants with a blue stripe down each pant leg and carrying a large potato sack. We were all suspiciously curious about him, and personally, I wondered if he might be a police officer. Although, the look on his face showed that he was as surprised to see us appear as we were to see him, so maybe he was just there to collect balls too?

As discussed, we hid behind parked cars and waited for an errant handball to fly over the wall and onto the street. The plan required that whoever was closest to the ball would grab it and head straight home, as fast as possible, to Orange Street. My very worst nightmare was the man standing on top of the high wall carrying what I called a great big gun. *Was he allowed to shoot us?* Suddenly a ball bounced onto the street right in front of me, and I automatically took off like a shot after it. I don't know how, but I beat the others to it. Maybe they let me, since I was the slowest runner on the team. I snatched the ball out of the gutter and looked furtively around.

Once I had the ball in my trembling hands, the man with the potato sack and I just stood there staring at one another. I realized something warm was running down my leg. I looked down and saw, to my horror, that my pants leg was getting soaked because I was peeing my pants. How humiliating! I hoped beyond hope that neither Billy nor Pat noticed what I had done, but I soon realized the man with the sack saw what I had done. Laughing helplessly, he yelled out, "Hey, kid, you just pissed your pants!" I took off with the ball in my sweaty hands and sprinted toward home. It wasn't much of a footrace because he was laughing too hard to try to catch me. (I didn't know it then, but he couldn't move past his designated area.)

The whole time, panting while running at top speed, I was peeking over my shoulder, listening for sirens, whistles, and gunshots from the guy on top of the wall. Fortunately, none of that happened. It seemed like forever until my heart stopped pounding in my ears when I reached home.

I later learned that every ball belonged to an individual inmate who had purchased it and inscribed his prison ID numbers on it. If the trustee in the khaki pants failed to retrieve a ball, he took a lot of heat from the balls' owner. To this day, I still feel bad about what I did. The only one I ever talked to about my leaky accident was one of my two best friends, Billy Klank. Billy laughed his head off but agreed never to tell anyone my secret, and being the good friend he was, Billy kept his promise. (RIP, Billy.)

*

Basketball was our second obsession. We hung an old bushel fruit basket on the streetlight pole in the middle of the Orange Street block to play whenever we could. We abandoned the streets and upgraded our game time once we learned Holy Cross Church and School had an outdoor blacktopped basketball court, with real rims and nets.

Our team now played against other neighborhood teams at Holy Cross. The competition was a real turning point for us.

We had to improve our skills to compete with other players. Until then, our basketball games had been about fun and participation.

Since we had no uniforms, one team took off our shirts and called ourselves The Skins, and the other team still wearing shirts called themselves The Shirts. If a ball went out of bounds, the kid serving as the referee would call out, "Skins' ball" or "Shirts' ball." Once again, we used our odds and evens game to decide which team kept their shirts on. The Shirts team had an obvious advantage when it rained, snowed, or was freezing outside. This new level of competition was a challenging experience that redirected our focus and heightened our passion for winning.

IN ADDITION TO basketball, many of us shared a love for baseball and joined an official team. Our last game together of the baseball season was in August 1951 when we played for the city's thirteen-year-old championship. With the score tied going into the last half of the final inning, I sat on the bench and did what I could by saying a silent prayer for our team. Teammate "Skippy" Klitus was at bat, and there were two outs. Skippy hit a home run to deep left field and won the game for us. I was convinced my prayer had helped. Again, the sisters had taught me well.

We played our last city baseball championship game against an all-black team. It was the best challenge we ever faced. Until then, I never saw a black person. I wasn't sure what to expect. Finally, someone whispered, "If we win the game, there will be a fight." My heart sank. It would be like kindergarten all over again. However, this time I wouldn't need to fight alone. The other team was also expecting a problem. Everyone was trying too hard to be cool. But, as the game progressed, we found we were all genuinely enjoying the contest. Finding common ground with these kids somehow blurred the margins of what we were all expecting from each other. We were happy to have their competition, and it was good for us to learn that lots of other kids played as well as we did and were made of the same grit as we were!

We won the game and the city championship. It was in that same year that I also won the city foul shooting contest, setting a record for Trenton. I made thirty-eight out of forty foul shots, breaking the old record of thirty-seven. That is the only trophy I ever saved, and even today it sits on a shelf in our bookcase. Somehow, I've always felt it was more important than all the others that followed.

The Beatty Street Gang focused on the sport of the current season. *Were we successful? You bet!* Consistently winning was quite a feat for a little bunch of ragamuffins from Beatty Street. Several guys (and me too) played on high school and college baseball and basketball teams, city American Legion League teams, and Sandlot baseball league teams.

*

I was fortunate to receive personal pitching coaching twice a week from a neighbor, Steve Kalapos. Steve was a local city standout high school infielder who took an interest in teaching me to pitch when I was in the third or fourth grade. He worked with me twice a week through all those years to develop me as a pitcher until freshman tryouts at Trenton Catholic Boys High School, which I would attend in September.

He brought me closer to my dream of becoming a professional baseball player. I would soon begin my freshman year, and Steve would turn me over to Father Noel, baseball coach at the all-powerful Trenton Catholic Boys' High School in the spring.

Baseball tryouts, *here I come!!*

CHAPTER 4

Great Expectations

Trenton Catholic Boys' High School

*"There are only two questions in society.
Who will teach the children and what will
we teach them?"*

— Plato

As a tall thirteen-year-old, I was a left-handed pitcher with an all-consuming passion to be a starting pitcher for one of Trenton's athletic powerhouses – the Trenton Catholic Boys High School. As a freshman, I should never have dreamed of making their formidable varsity team. Trenton Catholic's student body included many athletes who gained their skills on the streets of an inner-city ethnic enclave like the one where I grew up. But like many teenage jocks, I believed I was a badass.

City sports fans, newspapers, and local radio shows like Bus Saidt's sports show on station WBUD paid a lot of attention to the city's high school football, basketball, and baseball teams. As a result, it was easy for a top-rated athlete to make a name for himself in the city of Trenton. Talented high school athletes received glowing coverage on Trenton's newspapers' sports pages – *The Trentonian*, the *Trenton Evening Times*, and the big Sunday edition of the *Trenton Times Advertiser*.

The summer before I began my freshman year at Trenton Catholic, I devoted every minute and all of my focus to practice pitching and running wind sprints on Orange Street. I tried to ignore a little voice in the back of my head that continued to remind me *there have been no freshman pitchers in the past at Trenton Catholic who had ever survived the cut to the varsity baseball team.*

Shortly before the school year began, my dedicated trainer and neighbor, Steve Kalapos, paid me a visit at my house. Over the years, he had not only developed and strengthened my ability to pitch but had instilled self-confidence in me as well. The purpose of Steve's visit was to reinforce what he had been telling me for the past year: "Bob, you're a good enough pitcher right now, as an incoming freshman, to make the varsity team." He helped me to cultivate a positive attitude and maintain the determination I needed for tryouts. There was no way I wanted to wait until next year, so I decided to give it my best shot. *What did I have to lose?*

*

When the Beatty Street gang members became old enough to begin high school, some went to Trenton High, but most of us went to Trenton Catholic. On the first day of school, I should have been thinking about the fantastic opportunity I had been given to attend a private all-boys school run by the Franciscan order of priests, but all I could think about were baseball tryouts in the spring.

I met the guys every morning to walk the eight blocks from our clubhouse on Beatty Street to Trenton Catholic on Chestnut Avenue in all kinds of weather – rain or shine, wind or snow, for the next four years, just as most of us had walked to grammar school together over the previous seven years. Sharing my dream with my friends of making the varsity team as a freshman earned me hoots and howls, and they said, "Hey, Hatch, that's a pipedream. Wait until sophomore year like the rest of us!" But that little voice now told me that my goal wasn't just *nonsense on a stick*. I could feel I had a chance, and I was going to take it no matter what they thought!

*

During the first semester, I joined the school band. Not because I wanted to, but because the band's faculty moderator, Father Mathias (aka "the Bear"), wouldn't take no for an answer when I told him I didn't want to be in the band. I lied to him and told him I no longer had a trumpet. I could tell he didn't believe me. He insisted, "That's the way it's gonna be!" And with that, I officially became a member of the band. He expected me to attend band practice on time, every Friday, and with my trumpet. This was an intrusive development in my plans to prepare for baseball tryouts.

I didn't know it then, but a few Beatty Street Gang members cooked up a practical joke to play on me and selected Mickey Popovich, my grade school classmate, to perpetrate the crime. I'm sure they never expected the prank to take on a life of its own, but it did. Mickey told the Bear that I had played the trumpet in the Saint Mary's orchestra. He also told the Bear about the trumpet lessons Pop had paid for, three years earlier, but which I never took. During that time, I had instead been helplessly consumed with both baseball and the mesmerizing pinball machine. His prank sentenced me to four years of being picked on by the Bear, who, after listening to Mickey's story, had determined I needed to be humbled and that he was the force to humble me.

Now, during freshman year in high school, my secret had come back to haunt me. *Oh, Mickey! What were you thinking?* This was beyond the goofy pranks we had all played on each other before. I couldn't figure out why the Bear enjoyed toying with me. He even issued me an ill-fitting and foolish-looking band uniform. It included a ridiculous cape that flapped in the wind and slapped me in the face.

Today, I understand why the Bear decided to teach me a lesson, and that it never mattered to him that I couldn't blow a single note on the trumpet. He sure brought me down to earth by chipping away at my arrogance and for getting one over on Pop. He enjoyed humbling me, and each time he assigned me one of his demeaning tasks he made the point I wasn't the *hot stuff Hatrak* that I thought I was.

AS FATE WOULD have it, the Bear was also my Spanish teacher. Whenever he felt someone in class required discipline, I was the only one he sent to his office in the basement to retrieve "Omar." Omar was a circular wooden paddle about one foot long with a short handle. The unlucky boy requiring Omar's attention had to come to the front of the room, kneel with his forehead touching the floor, and receive wallops on his defenseless bottom before returning to his seat. Fortunately, I never got paddled, but I was very uncomfortable being set apart from my classmates. I was pissed off because he was always on my case.

I labored on in the band, stubbornly refusing to ask for mercy while he enjoyed testing my perseverance. At some point, I finally figured out that the Bear knew the story and was indeed evening the score for Pop – an ad hoc punishment for all the candy and soda I had clandestinely enjoyed at Josephine's with my music lesson money. From the beginning, even when I didn't know why he tested me, I recognized this was a challenge and I was determined that I would win this cold war. I hoped my cocky smile signaled it was game on.

The first half of freshman year had gone by in a blur. One day early in the spring, my heart skipped a beat when I saw the notice posted by the baseball coach, Father Noel Bailey, on the bulletin board outside the athletic director's office. The note read, "Varsity tryouts for the baseball team begin on Monday, April 16. If you wish to try out for the team as a pitcher or catcher, please report to the school's backyard no later than 3:30 p.m."

Eighteen candidates reported on the first day of tryouts. Four catchers and fourteen pitchers. There were several sophomores, and everyone else was a junior. I was the only freshman. Tryouts lasted three days, and in the end, I knew I had done well. It was difficult waiting until the end of the week to learn who made the team.

Walking to school on Friday morning, I was nervous and somewhat preoccupied. One of my friends, Norm Walton, asked me, "What's wrong with you, Hatch? You're kind of quiet today!"

"Well, today at noon, Father Noel is posting the names of the pitchers and catchers that survived the cut. I'm nervous as hell and hoping my name is among the pitchers he's keeping." Feeling my angst, all Norm could say in response was, "Ohhh, well good luck, Hatch!"

Father Noel posted the cut list before lunch. Four pitchers survived the cut, and I was the only freshman making the squad. My first thought was, *Here I am, a tall and bony thirteen-year-old having the chance to play with the big guys in a school where they were the state champions several years earlier…. Woo-hoo!*

I couldn't wait to thank Steve for all the years he had generously worked with me, and to tell the gang. I thought about the many hours I had pitched to the guys in stickball games on Orange Street, and of all the days I spent throwing a handball against both the red brick wall directly across the street from our house and against the house on the corner of Beatty and Orange Street. The purpose of this exercise was to learn to pitch to exact spots within a chalk-defined strike zone. I had achieved precisely what I had worked for, and I was thrilled.

*

When the baseball season finally began, we won our first several games while I warmed the bench. I never expected to play as a freshman, but I watched the games with wild anticipation. On the Monday before our next game, during lunch, Father Noel came to my lunch table to tell me, "Bob, we play Princeton High School next Tuesday, and I want you to know you'll be our starting pitcher." Gulping, I felt a rush of tingling heat surge from the base of my neck up to the roots of my hair, and I answered, "Thank you, Father Noel. I'll be ready to go. I'll do some extra wind sprints in the outfield at Wetzel Field until then."

I couldn't wait to tell everyone I knew, and I couldn't swallow the rest of my lunch. Before Tuesday's game, I prayed for our team's success at Sunday Mass. The Franciscan priests taught us never to ask God for personal achievements, so I prayed for the team to play their best.

The big day finally arrived, and I pitched against Princeton High School that Tuesday, and we won the game. I lasted four innings in a seven-inning game. The scorekeeper, a Trentonian sports reporter, Joe Logue, ruled me the winning pitcher. So, my record began as one win and no losses. After that game, I was named starting pitcher even when we played against the best teams on our schedule. *Who could have believed it?* Never in my wildest dreams had I ever thought I could accomplish such a feat. Now I understood: *You can't just slide into success. You have to work for it, and you can't do it alone. (Joan Hatrak)* Thank God for Steve and Father Noel.

THE NEXT COUPLE of years flew by, filled with all the ups and downs of school, sports, family, and friends. Junior year was a thrill because I got my driver's license! I drove Pop's old, beat-up black Ford back and forth across the Delaware River to school every day. Even if it was shabby – the guys called it "The Singer Six" because it sounded like a sewing machine with six cylinders – having "wheels" was a big freedom for a boy at that age. Funny enough, since our priests didn't have a car at their disposal, they made a deal with me to keep my gas tank full if I let them all pile in to go to our baseball games. Seemed like a win to me.

During that same year, the Bear announced we were invited to march in New York City's famous Saint Patrick's Day Parade! I told myself we would disgrace ourselves. We were not good enough to march in any parade. *How will I look dressed in a pair of pants so short on me they came halfway up my calf?* My hat was far too big and fell over my eyes. And holy cow, our flapping uniform cape looked silly on us all. *How were we going to march in a parade dressed like that?* Even worse, it was on Fifth Avenue in New York City. Much to my dismay, the Bear accepted the invitation, so, off to New York City we went. I had a feeling that my greatest humiliation was yet to come.

Arriving in New York, I was determined not to admit defeat. The Bear positioned me at the end of a row next to a curb, so I was marching closely past a large crowd of viewers. We both knew that I couldn't play the trumpet and would need to fake it as we marched along. The good Father gave me specific instructions. "Junior (I never knew why he called me Junior), under no circumstances are you to blow a note. Just fill out the row and go through the motions." I followed his instructions, but my pantomime act was unconvincing. As we marched along, spectators pointed at me while nudging each other. I knew it had to be the silly uniform I was wearing and the obvious fact I wasn't blowing a single note. Today I still recall the Bear laughing at me on the bus ride back to Trenton. He repeated the phrase "Good job, Junior! Good Job." We laughed together. We had both proved our tenacity, but we knew our game wasn't over yet and I felt sure my nemesis was having fun.

In my senior year, just before graduation and on a day I was set to pitch against archrival Trenton Central High School *in the big game of the season,* the Bear pulled me aside and said, "Junior, don't miss band practice today." This was appalling to me! "But Father, I'm scheduled to pitch against Trenton High today. I'd hate to miss that game. Father Noel depends on me."

"Makes no difference to me, just be at band practice."

"But, Father…."

"No buts, Junior, just be there."

This was taking our contest to an extreme and it wasn't funny. I knew it was only a matter of time before Father Noel sent someone to find me. Dejectedly, I went to band practice. Then, at the very last minute, the Bear said, "Okay, Junior, there's a car waiting for you out front to take you to Wetzel Field so you can pitch in today's important game." Then, as I stood there open-mouthed, he handed me an ice-cold Coke and patted me on the back. As he passed me, he said, "Good luck, Junior. I'll see you there. And I'll be rooting for you!"

No one was happier than the Bear when we won the game. Late in the game I replaced our starting pitcher, and the scorekeeper named me the winning pitcher. Even though I had labored on in the band for four years, somehow, he and I became friends – good friends. However, our contest never ended.

Our 1955 team defeated archrival Trenton Central High School twice. Playing them was like playing in the World Series. Our Trenton Catholic team had terrific players and so did Trenton High. I have many splendid memories of playing terrific games in a real baseball town.

Following the last game in my senior year, as I was leaving the locker room, Father Noel said, "Bob, I'm going to miss you next year. Good luck to you as you pursue a baseball career. I'll be rooting for you!" I grinned all over myself for the whole way home and again, silently, I thanked Steve Kalapos for giving me such a good head-start.

*

One month following graduation in July 1955, the area's head scout for the Philadelphia Athletics (a major league team) talked to me about joining the Athletics organization as a pitcher. Mr. ("Lefty") Lloyd had watched me pitch in my junior and senior years in high school and during the summer months when I pitched for the North Trenton Post 458 American Legion team. I played, and was the starting pitcher, on the all-star team in each of the last two years I played American Legion ball.

In late July, Mr. Maynard ("Mo") Weber visited my pop, sister, and me at Pop's small eight-acre farm in Lower Bucks County, in Morrisville, Pennsylvania. Many of Trenton's most knowledgeable baseball professionals considered Mo to have the best baseball mind in the city. Mo told us he was there as a representative of Winona State Teachers College in Minnesota and brought with him a letter from the school's president offering me a full scholarship. He told us that playing in a strong Basin League (a collegiate minor league) during the summer months could have helped me mature as a pitcher.

Pop decided I was too young (not yet seventeen) to go to school in Minnesota, let alone remain there on my own during the summer months. So that was the end of that. Pop vetoed any thoughts I had about a baseball career, and told me in no uncertain terms that my priority should be to finish college first. In those days, if Pop told me it was dark outside, I never looked to double-check. Now, I'm glad I listened to his sound advice, as hard as it was at the time.

Mom and Pop's goals for my education trumped mine. So, in September 1955, I was off to Pennington Preparatory School for Boys in New Jersey, about twenty miles from home, with a full scholarship for one year to play baseball. There were three reasons for my decision. First, I was a year younger than the other post-graduate students, and adding a year of prep school gave me a chance to gain weight and body and leg strength. Second, I would have another year of playing baseball and could elevate my pitching skills. And third, it was an opportunity to improve my English composition skills. Had these goals been reversed, I might have had a different result from my prep school experience. Prep school presented an excellent opportunity that I foolishly didn't take full advantage of, as I should have. I was too busy focusing on baseball. And school was only something I had to endure to make Pop happy.

FOLLOWING GRADUATION FROM prep school, a Rider College (today Rider University) professor, and friend of my sister's, had arranged a meeting for me with the school Vice President Dr. Goodner Gill. He followed Trenton Catholic's athletic program and knew who I was. Dr. Gill then arranged a meeting with the baseball coach after which I was offered a full scholarship. In 1956, I enrolled as an accounting major, and I had a terrific fall semester. My first semester's grade-point average was a healthy 3.5 (B+), coming close to making the dean's list.

My grades were now okay, but most important to me, I earned a spot on the school's varsity baseball team. I joined Rider's senior-laden varsity pitching staff while still a freshman, just as I had four years earlier at Trenton Catholic. Several Trenton Catholic graduates, including the legendary pitcher Leo "Chavez" Chester and third baseman Eddie Adams, took me under their wings and helped me in more ways than I could count.

Pitching in four games as a freshman, I defeated Mercer County College twice. Pop saw me pitch the first game we played against Mercer, in one of my best games ever, and it thrilled me that Pop saw it. Not only did I pitch well, but I surprised myself by also batting well, which wasn't always the case. In the last inning we tied the score when I hit a home run over the right field fence – the same fence that Babe Ruth had hit three home runs over years earlier – and that day we won the game. Afterward, I headed over to Pop to see him with a big smile on his face. He was hustling down the bleacher steps to meet me and offer his congratulations. I never have, nor will I ever, forget that eventful day. That was the only game I played in that Pop ever came to see. He worked long hours, but really, he never wanted to encourage me to be a ballplayer.

As a freshman, the last game I pitched in was against a powerful Lafayette University team. Unbelievably, I struck out the first ten batters I faced in that game, which was a first for me in my brief career. The Lafayette game was not only exciting, but I felt I was fulfilling my expectations and goals to pursue a professional baseball career. According to the *Trentonian*, my reputation as a pitcher was "soaring," and it satisfied me that my freshman year at Rider College had ended on a high note and I still had three years ahead of me to develop as a pitcher at Rider. I could barely wait for my sophomore season to begin.

During July and the first half of August, I took part in the Trenton Elite baseball league. Some of the city's best baseball players played in this unlimited summer league. I played in a game on Sunday, August 18, 1957, less than three weeks before the start of my sophomore year at Rider, and had another fantastic day pitching and batting. The score was tied at 2-2 in the seventh and last inning in this game. The game could not go into extra innings because it was getting dark. As the team's last batter, I hit a long line drive over the center fielder's head. It was a home run, and we won the game 3-2.

Going to sleep that night, I thought how great it would be to begin my sophomore year. My plan for the upcoming baseball season included training on my own in October. First, I planned to ask the athletic director for permission to use the gym. A workout would comprise of running for one hour, followed by one-half hour of pitching to Father Noel, who had volunteered to be my catcher until spring, and ended with fifteen minutes of wind sprints.

I didn't know it then, but very soon my baseball career would take an immensely different turn than what I was so joyfully anticipating. Had I foreseen what the future held for me, my mind and every fiber of my being would have rejected the actuality I would soon face as a nineteen-year-old college sophomore.

CHAPTER 5

Adversity and Perseverance

Bob rearing back for a high hard one

*"I have been bent and broken,
but – I hope – into a better shape."*

– *Charles Dickens, Great Expectations*

Monday, August 19, 1957, lives forever in my memory. I'll never forget that fateful day, because I had to summon up all the courage I could muster to meet my challenge. Legendary football coach Lou Holtz once hypothesized, "Show me someone great in what they do, and I'll show you a person who's had to persevere, and who showed they have the mental toughness needed to overcome obstacles and adversities that could cripple weaker men."

Real adversity was something I'd never had to live through. Now, I needed to draw on the nurturing relationships available to me and any personal strength I might possess to get me through the most critical test in my young life. *Could I meet Holtz's test of grit?*

The first thing I thought of when I got out of bed on that Monday was yesterday's game, the second-best game I ever played in my life. Eating a light breakfast hurriedly, I headed off to work. It was my first day in the last week of my summer job at Rein's upholstery shop in the Burg. Just after lunch, I was on my way up the flight of stairs from the cellar to wash my hands. There was a delivery of freshly reupholstered furniture to make, and my hands needed to be clean. Meeting "Paps," an older man, on his way down to the basement, his arms loaded with used cotton, I stopped and asked him if I could help. Saying yes, he passed me the bundle of cotton he was carrying. It needed to be processed through a machine in the basement before the upholsterers could reuse it. Never asking him where I could find the machine or how to run it, I turned around and went back down the flight of steps with youthful confidence, carrying the mass of cotton in my arms.

When I reached the cellar, I looked for my friend Jimmy McKeever. All summer, Jimmy worked at Rein's and knew his way around the basement. I told him that Paps had given me a bundle of cotton to run through some machine and was hoping he could guide me in the right direction.

> "Can you tell me where this machine is and how to run it?"

"Sure, Hatch, happy to help. Go to the far-left-hand corner of the cellar, and you'll see it. The old-timers here call it a cotton picker. Turn it on. The on and off switch is in an awkward place. Look near the floor on your left-hand side of the machine to find it.

"It's a little challenging to use because the switch is recessed in a metal u-shaped switch protector, so you can't even use your foot to turn it on or off.

"At the top of the machine, you'll see a short canvas conveyor belt. At the far end of the belt, there are a pair of hard rubber wringers, much like those on your mom's washing machine. The belt will be running.

"Put a handful of cotton on the end of the belt nearest you. Using your hands, spread the cotton out so it's not in a ball. The rollers will grab the cotton suddenly and move it along the belt at a good clip.

"Next, the wringers will grab the cotton and pull it to a spinning wheel of long, sharp spikes. The spikes will hold the cotton and revitalize it. It's now ready to be reused by the men working upstairs. That's all there is to it."

Finding the cotton picker and following Jimmy's instructions to turn it on, I spread the cotton onto the conveyor belt. Suddenly, I experienced piercing pain and realized the rollers had grabbed my left hand and their powerful grip was pulling it deeper into the grinding machine. My instincts took over and told me I had to turn off the device and fast – even before yelling for help. That was difficult because, as Jimmy warned me, the on/off switch was on the machine's left side, close to the floor, and it was my left hand that the machine had in its clamp.

Maneuvering my body to the left over the machine, while lifting my right leg up and back behind me, I attempted to reach down to the switch. Twisting my hips while stretching my right arm in front of my left leg, I determinedly strained down toward the button. It was still several inches away from my desperately searching fingers. Leaning in as far as I could, my fingertips barely brushed the metal. If only I could stretch just a little more. But I couldn't reach any further. All I could think was, *Oh, God please help me!*

Meanwhile, the unforgiving rollers continued to slowly drag my left hand into the machine. Icy prickles of fear were poking at the back of my neck and sweat was now running down over my eyes. Desperately squirming forward for what seemed like forever, I finally felt the switch under my fingertips and was able to push the button into the off position. Still, to this day, I can't believe I was acrobatic enough to accomplish what appeared to be an impossible feat.

Black waves of nausea rolled over me as the rollers maintained their grasp while mercilessly feeding my fingers into the swiftly spinning wheel with its many sharp, pointy spikes until the momentum finally slowed. Then the machine shook as it stopped, followed by a brief moment of silence, before I screamed at the top of my voice, "Help! Help! Somebody please help me!"

The cellar was now spinning and tiny silver sparkles floated before my eyes. I felt as if I was about to pass out. Someone upstairs reupholstering chairs had heard my screams and several men came thundering down the stairs. The first person to reach me unintentionally turned the machine back on again, assuming he was turning it off.... By then, the spinning spikes had already removed all four fingers up to my third knuckle. Now they were ripping into my palm and the wringers were dragging my wrist forward into the unforgiving spikes. Another bite. Then another. Relentlessly gnawing off flesh and bone, inch by inch.

The pain was unbearable, and thankfully someone finally screamed, "Turn the damned thing off!" A worker reached down and pressed the on/off switch. Unfortunately, as before when the button was off again, it didn't stop right away. We watched, not believing what we were seeing, as the old contraption continued running and hungeringly ate away at what remained of my hand.

When someone, at last, pried open the wringers, freeing me, I forced myself to look. What I saw was horrifying. My knees buckled, and I fell helplessly against the machine. What remained of my left hand were long, horsetail-like wisps of skin dangling down. Gone were four fingers and bones and half of my palm. What remained of my pitching hand was only the thumb. My wrist was also oozing blood, having been trapped and crushed between the pair of compressing rollers of the fast-moving conveyor belt.

Had I lost consciousness before I first turned off the machine, it was entirely possible that my whole arm, up to the shoulder, would also have been devoured by those feasting spikes. If arteries had been severed, which easily could have been the case, I probably would have bled to death. Today, when I think about how close I came to dying, I involuntarily shudder.

My fingers and the first half of my palm didn't get cut off in one piece or even in one slice. Instead, the whirling spikes had ripped them off a small amount at a time. It would have been merciful had that dreadful machine just removed everything in one fell swoop.

Freed now, but bleeding profusely, I was afraid I still might bleed to death before reaching St. Francis Hospital. In a panic, I pulled away from my rescuers, who were trying to hold on to me, and broke free, intending to run to the hospital. Trailing blood, I ran up the stairs, out the front door, and finally down the front porch steps onto the sidewalk. Feeling faint and nauseous, I was unsure of which would happen first… *Would I pass out or throw up?* The sidewalk where I was standing had blood everywhere. My clothes and shoes had blood all over them, as did some of the co-workers who had caught up with me. Several employees then helped me into a car and drove me to the hospital at top speed. On the way there, one man tore off his shirt and applied a tourniquet to my upper left arm, stopping the free flow of blood I was watching spurt out of me. He probably saved my life.

When we arrived at the hospital, someone sat me in a wheelchair and wheeled me to the emergency room. Medical personnel were waiting for me. Someone from Rein's called the hospital to tell them I was on my way. That same caller must have called my Pop because he was already in the emergency room awaiting my arrival. Pop was crying. *Oh God, I had never seen him cry.*

Pop immediately took charge. He told the emergency room staff he wouldn't allow any surgeon to treat me other than Dr. John Kustrup, the hospital's chief of staff. Pop and Dr. Kustrup's parents had immigrated to the United States from the same little Czechoslovakian village, Trebishov, and he had been Pop's doctor for a few years here in Trenton.

A nurse told Pop the doctor was in surgery and unavailable. Pop replied, "That's fine. We'll wait until the doctor becomes available." During the next hour, I was in agony and shock. Not accepting what exactly happened, I did believe I would die from the loss of blood. I was freezing and shivering from head to toe, and I couldn't stop the dry heaves that controlled my body. A nurse replaced the DIY tourniquet I had on my arm, and everyone made their best effort to console and comfort me.

The look of relief on Pop's face was noticeable once he saw Dr. Kustrup arrive. He and the doctor huddled briefly, and then suddenly a nurse mercifully stuck me in the left side of my neck with a needle that delivered relief. In a matter of seconds, my left arm went numb, and I heard Dr. Kustrup gruffly tell the staff, "Get him to the O.R. immediately!" Pop hugged me, and the last thing I remember was zooming off on top of a flying gurney, down a long, brilliantly lit hall.

*

Awaking many hours later in the recovery room, I saw several nurses at my bedside, and I was wondering where I was. Then it all came back to me – the accident, Pop in the waiting room, and going into emergency surgery. My next thought was, *What now? I'm still alive, but I'll never pitch again, so I may as well be dead.*

I asked a nurse to call Father Noel at Trenton Catholic, and to tell him where I was, that they were telephoning for me, and that I'd like to see him. I could see it was already getting dark outside, but I hoped that Father would get my message in time to come and see me that night. Somehow, I knew he would. Father Noel had been my first-year algebra teacher and my baseball coach for four years. He instilled self-confidence and leadership in the team and me, and in doing so, he became my mentor and friend and one of the most influential forces in my life. He always had an infectious positive attitude that we'd all admired, and tonight, I really needed that.

Dozing off, I thought I watched myself walking the eight blocks from my home to Trenton Catholic High School. As I drifted further into my dream, I looked down at my feet and I saw the sidewalk puddled with blood. My new black Converse sneakers were stepping through it and I was confused. *What was happening? What is all this blood?* Fitfully, my eyes opened and I struggled trying to sit up. I was both shaken and happy to see Father Noel sitting in a chair beside my bed in the recovery room.

"Hello, Bob. I was about to wake you up because it looked like you were having a bad dream."

"Hi, Father Noel, thanks for coming. I was sure you'd be here."

In a flash, I again remembered what had happened to me, and couldn't stop the flood of tears now pouring out. Father took my right hand in his and whispered something to me. He sat with me for a while, and we reminisced about beating Trenton High, our archrival, twice in my senior year and how proud everyone had been. He spoke to me about the word *possibilities*, and how my attitude would influence my future. He reminded me of the brotherhood our class had formed and suggested I reach out for help from my former classmates and teammates. I promised I'd do it. Father must have noticed I was falling asleep and told me I needed to rest. In no time, I dozed off.

The sound of someone crying roused me, and it startled me when I realized the sobs I'd heard were my own. Through the protective cast on my left forearm and the gauze protecting Dr. Kustrup's work, I could feel my fingers throbbing. How was that possible? I knew my fingers weren't there. I had already seen what little remained of my left hand. When I told a nurse standing nearby about the feeling I was experiencing, she told me, "Bob, we call those phantom pains. You'll be experiencing that sensation for some time."

AT SOME POINT later in that day, several orderlies arrived to move me to the private room Pop had arranged. When I arrived there, my family was already waiting for me. We all tried to console each other. Mom appeared shattered. Seeing her crying so uncontrollably was difficult. We made awkward small talk for a short time, and then the nurse gave me a shot for the pain and to induce sleep. She suggested my family leave because I needed to rest, and that tomorrow would be a busy day, so reluctantly, they did. Once they were gone, I had never felt so alone nor known such abject despair, but I also felt relieved because I no longer needed to compose myself. Finally, the shot took over, and I slept until morning.

In my slumber, I heard someone from what seemed far away saying, "Good morning, Bob." A pleasant but stern-looking nurse appeared at my bedside. She told me Dr. Kustrup had assigned her to work with me full-time, for as long as it took, to help me become right-handed. Pop and the doctor had developed a strategy to help me return to Rider College for my sophomore year, which would begin in less than three weeks. First, they knew I needed to write right-handed to take lecture notes. Second, I needed help learning to dress, bathe, eat with my right hand, and tie my shoes with just one good hand. I needed to know how to do most everything right-handed now.

The nurse spent the entire first day with me trying to get started. I was incorrigible during that whole day.

For eleven more days, I continued to be uncooperative and nasty. After all, I was an excellent student and a damn talented baseball player with a promising future. *Why should I have to reinvent myself?* (God bless that saintly, patient lady.) She never lost her temper or reacted to my stubbornness. When I felt low and bared my soul to her, she shared her thoughts about adversity and gave me the courage to keep on trying. Despite the hard time I gave her, she hung in there with me and truly did a terrific job that I am forever grateful for.

Years later, my sister Joan shared a conversation with my wife Joan that she had with Dr. Kustrup following the surgery he performed on me. She told him, "They got to him just in time. It could have been much worse." Apparently, he snapped back at her with definitive advice, "Never say that to Bob. Considering his plans as an athlete, this was the worst thing that could have ever happened to him." He was 100 percent correct.

On my second day after my morning session with the nurse, Steve Kalapos, my first pitching mentor and neighbor, visited me. We spent the better part of the afternoon recalling the many hours we had trained in the corner bakery's side yard. As you know, Steve was the first to encourage me to be a pitcher. He believed in my potential when I was just eight years old. I learned to be determined and consistent from him, qualities I certainly needed now. He had worked with me throughout grammar school but stepped back when Father Noel entered the picture my freshman year in high school. Now, it was as if no time had passed, and he was once again encouraging me to think forward and not give up. When I told him how powerless I felt to go on, he countered my admission, and explained to me that I could only lose my power if I believed I didn't have any – *and indeed, I still did.*

THE REST OF my days in the hospital dragged on in slow motion. Grumpily, I devoted my time to working with the nurse and visiting with my friends. The empty nights also crept by listlessly.

Questions swirled through my mind. *What was I going to do with my life? Who and what was I now? Did I even care about being a student?* Being an athlete made me happy. All my close friends excelled in some sport, and I had thrived on our camaraderie. *Would I always feel like a freak? What was waiting for me inside these bandages?* Never had I imagined I wouldn't be an athlete. Feeling lost and hopeless, I asked God, *please help me get through this night somehow.*

*

Once I was back home, I remained in my blue funk and kept to myself, which was fine by me. I hadn't yet seen my hand without the cast.

Stupidly, I acted as if I had learned nothing from all the supportive people in my life – those who helped me grow up, by instilling in me the skills I needed to pursue my dream, and now, the inspirational individuals who were assisting in my rehabilitation. With the way I was going, slowly walking toward nothingness, I would soon become nothing but an angry bum living in some park.

Feeling sorry for myself meant spending my time drinking too many draft beers at Mickey's Bar in the Burg and hanging out at Radices playing Catch Five. The older guys at Radices welcomed me back and they did everything imaginable to help me recover from the shock of the accident.

When it was time to have my cast removed, I insisted on making the long walk from Radices to Dr. Kustrup's office alone, because I didn't want anyone to see my reaction *or* my hand once the doctor took my cast off. By the time I got there, I was shaking, not ready to face the reality of what remained of my hand. As the doctor cut through the plaster and snipped away the bandages, I closed my eyes.

Stepping back, he said, "Bob, look."

When I didn't, he kept insisting.

I asked, "Are you finished?"

When he said yes, I replied, "Thank you very much, sir, for helping me. Excuse me, please," and quickly left his office.

It was a long walk back straight down South Broad Street, and I found myself again back at Radices, still not having looked at my hand. When I entered the room, it became hushed. Probably because I *felt* completely helpless, I must have *looked* bereft of all hope. Numbly, I sat down at the card table in the back room without being invited to sit. Everyone remained still and didn't seem to know what to say or do. There was an awkward silence as I sat there with my hand still jammed into my pocket.

Tool Radice finally said, "Hey, Hatch, let me see your hand." Reluctantly, I removed my hand from my pocket, and everyone saw it simultaneously. There were audible gasps, my own included. At the same time, they all attempted to reassure me, saying, "Don't worry, everything will be all right." Of course, I didn't believe them. Everything would never be all right again.

After sitting there in silence for a long time, I thought about how many years I had spent playing cards and "shooting the bull" with these men. Even though I felt the comfort of their presence, I knew nothing anyone could say would help.

Leaving the safety of that place, I walked back to my sister's house to show her and her husband my hand. My sister Joan made me a sandwich, and I went to bed thinking about how quickly my future had changed. Somehow, it had turned from the promising and shiny place I once was, with an optimistic future, to the despairingly dark place where I now found myself.

*

Three Rider College deans saved my future. The first was Dean Alexander Poyda. Early in the fall semester, he began looking for me on our downtown city campus. He talked with several of my friends and learned I had not registered for the fall semester or appeared on campus. He worried about how I was dealing with my accident. Based on what he heard from my friends, the dean telephoned Pop. Tactfully, he told him he needed to see me and that tomorrow I should get to school a little early. When I got his message, I realized if I didn't see him, he might snitch on me and tell Pop I hadn't enrolled for the fall semester. Reluctantly, I did as instructed.

When I knocked on his office door, he invited me in. The dean was a mountain of a man, and before I knew it, he had me pinned to one of his office walls! Then, with his face inches from mine, he hurled a rhetorical question at me, saying quite assertively, "What do you think you're doing? You're irresponsibly throwing away your future. That's what you're doing!" He let go of my shirt collar and growled, "Now sit your ass down, young man!"

He then shared a story about his youth. During a summer recess from college, he worked in the Pacific Northwest as a lumberjack. Not having heard this story until then, I didn't know he had lived through his own, eerily similar tragedy. He showed me he had lost his right hand in a dynamite accident, and that he had been right-handed. Recognizing he was telling me his story because he uniquely understood how I was currently feeling, I sat still and listened.

Now that he had my attention, he escorted me to the registrar's office and stayed with me until they fully enrolled me as a sophomore. I'm sure he had the registrar break some rules because I was registering very late. There was no choice now but to return to school. If it were up to me, I would have preferred to spend my time at Radices playing Catch Five or drinking draft beer at Mickey's with the guys.

Somehow, my friends from Beatty Street learned about my meeting with Dean Poyda. Not trusting I would go to school the following day, a few of them, also entering their sophomore year, came to my sister's house where I was temporarily staying. They "escorted" me to a waiting car and forcibly put me in the back seat. Frankie Kopp said, "Hatch, like it or not, you're going to school with us." So, there I was, sprawled across the back seat with Kopp sitting on top of me. I was madder than hell at him.

But, thanks to my Beatty Street gang members, they helped me get my life back in order.

As we drove along South Clinton Avenue, rolling past familiar scenes, I remembered the many hours we spent as eight-year-olds playing whatever sport we could on Orange Street. Still, I felt removed from everything and knew the day would be a long one. My only saving grace, thanks to that devoted nurse, was that I would begin this new school year able to write right-handed and I could tie my shoes one-handed. Everything else remained a work in progress.

Another dean, Robert McBain, sent for me once I returned to school. When I went to see him, he handed me a copy of a letter addressed to Pop. In effect, the letter said my athletic grant-in-aid would continue even though I couldn't play ball. However, he said I would need to referee intramural basketball games instead of playing baseball. I appreciated his message, and I realized what the dean was tactfully implying that *I shouldn't expect a free ride in life simply because I lost my fingers, and it was time to rejoin life on campus.*

That letter from the dean was crucial. Had my scholarship not continued, Mom and Pop's dream of me finishing college would have ended without question. My parents were hard-working people who provided for our family, but paying for my continuing education was not something we could afford. That was foremost in my mind because I knew this was a devastating reality for them. Later in life, I wished the fog would have lifted from over my head, and I would have taken it upon myself to find a job and pay my own way.

At the end of that week, a third dean, Dr. Carl Zoerner, stopped me on Clinton Street as I walked on campus from South Hall to the Main Building. Since I took Accounting I from him as a freshman, he knew I was a pitcher on the varsity baseball team, and he too was an athlete. In college, Dr. Zoerner was an All-American soccer player. The dean took the time to convince me to change my major from accounting to education. He explained coaching at the high school level would help me remain involved in athletics. He was a tough, firm, but compassionate man. I admired him, and it was easy for me to take his advice and switch majors. Making this change allowed me to take my first deep breath since the accident. *Maybe there was a future for me after all?*

SINCE I COULDN'T play baseball any longer and couldn't bear to go back to Rein's, I hoped to find an after-school job to earn some pocket money to help get me through my sophomore year. In November, three months after my accident, I applied for and received a job in the mailroom at the Trenton State Prison. During my junior and senior years in high school, I had worked summers in the business office. It felt good to return to the familiar feeling of connection I still experienced within this inner sanctum. I never expected it would remain dominant in my life for many years to come.

The mailroom job included censoring incoming inmate mail, processing food packages left for inmates, and taking the shoes of new inmates to a shoe store every Saturday to fluoroscope (x-ray) them. Some shoe stores used these machines to show customers' feet inside their shoes and check how they fit. We used the machine to examine shoes for contraband possibly hidden in them. In all the time we did this, we never found anything.

When censoring mail, they required me first to read the entire letter and then mark the first page and the front of the envelope with a rubber stamp that identified the clerk processing that piece of mail. My stamp number was four. Arriving at work one day after morning classes, it shocked me when my boss in the mailroom told me I was to report to Warden Howard Yeager's office immediately. When I entered the warden's office, he gruffly said, "Have a seat." I knew this would not be good because he sat at his desk, holding his head in his hands. Once I sat down, he quietly but angrily said, "Bob, please tell me it's not so!" I had no idea what he was talking about. *What could I possibly have done wrong?* The warden handed me an envelope.

On the front I saw my number four stamp. Again, I wondered to myself, *What the heck is going on?* I soon found out.

"Bob, to whom is the envelope addressed?"

"To you, Mr. Yeager."

"Why in the world would you open and then censor a letter addressed to me?"

Feeling like a fool, I said, "I don't know, sir."

"Let me tell you something. First, you should never have read the letter because of the information it contained, and because it was addressed to the warden of this prison! Also, if that weren't bad enough, you sent the letter to inmate Yeager and his first name isn't even Howard! So…now, Bob, please read the letter out loud."

The letter began, "The execution would occur soon…"

What?! Now all I could think was, *Holy crap, I'm a dead man! No pun intended.*

In his letter to the warden, the executioner informed Mr. Yeager of the date, time, and location of his arrival for the upcoming "event." The executioner's identity was a strict secret and so were his travel arrangements. And here I was sending the executioner's letter, addressed to the warden, to an inmate with the same last name, but a different first name.

"Bob, you need to know the inmate who received this letter became very frightened because he thought he was about to be executed! He gave the letter to the first white hat (supervisor) he saw, pleading with him to take the letter to the warden. What do you have to say for yourself?"

"Mr. Yeager, sir, please accept my apology. I was careless."

"Yes, you were, Bob."

"No doubt the inmate must have been frightened," I said remorsefully.

Mr. Yeager said, "Thank God for the way this inmate handled the situation! He could easily have broadcast this confidential information throughout the entire prison population! Some inmates would have been happy to intercept his travel plans, making sure he didn't arrive anywhere – EVER! Instead, he promised me he would not betray our confidence."

"Bob, I should fire you, but I won't. Let this be a valuable lesson on the importance of being careful. *Remember this is prison!* Now, get out of here, and don't you ever get into such a predicament again or anything requiring you to come see me. The next time you do something this stupid, I won't be so lenient."

The warden should have fired me. But, in addition to giving me a royal chewing out, he treated me with understanding and kindness.

BOOK TWO

Bob's Careers

CHAPTER 6

Welcome Back, Hatch!

Trenton Catholic Boys High School, –1960.
Principal Father Robert Yudin is in the first row, third from left.
I'm the tall, slim guy at the far left of the top row.

"Wherever you go and whatever ends you pursue, you must always fulfill the trust reposed, in you by your nation, your parents and your alma mater."

– Samar Mubarakmand

At the start of my senior year at Rider College, I resigned from my mailroom job at Trenton Prison. Since I was an education major at Rider, I had to complete a ten-week student teaching internship. I fulfilled my requirement at Solebury High School in New Hope, Pennsylvania, during the spring semester of 1960. It pleased and relieved me when I realized I loved every minute there and that I had a future without baseball.

In June, I was a proud graduate, with a Bachelor of Science degree in Education, and eager to get going with my newly put together future – teaching and coaching athletes. But before I got the chance to look for a teaching job, in early July, I received a telephone call from Father Robert Yudin. He was the principal at my alma mater, Trenton Catholic, and I was clueless as to why he was calling me.

He said, "H"llo Robert. Your guidance counselor, Father Casimir, tells me you were an education major at Rider College and that you majored in business education."

"Yes, that's right, Father. I graduated last month."

"Terrific! I spoke with Dr. Carl Zoerner, your dean at Rider, about a vacancy I have. We need a business education teacher here beginning next month. I asked the dean if there were any recent graduates he would recommend that I interview and he recommended you highly. So, I think I'd like to offer you a job. The school year begins early next month. Are you interested?"

"What subjects would I teach, Father?"

"Bookkeeping and accounting, business math, economics, and general business."

"Father, I'm honored to be offered a position to teach at my old stomping grounds. Thank you, and yes, I'm definitely interested in the job! However, that's a somewhat heavy course load considering I'll have five separate lesson plans to prepare every night, a lot of papers to correct, and grades to compute. I'll be happy to see the weekends!"

Knowing I could make it work, I was thrilled that, at last, my life seemed to fall into place. I told myself that the rest of my plan, to coach, would happen soon as well. Being patient and doing my best to teach with such a respected group of educators was the priority. Coaching could wait a little while longer.

*

Classes began on Tuesday, September 5, 1960. I'll never forget how warmly the faculty greeted me and welcomed me back. Several of the priests reminded me of the days I spent as a student at the school. Some talked about my pitching prowess. Their acceptance of me as a teacher made me feel as if I had come home. Each Friday, the faculty decompressed by celebrating the end of the week with a drink together in the cafeteria. At my first get-together, Father Mathias, aka the Bear (my freshman-year nemesis), reminded me about the day early in high school when he drafted me to play in the school's band. He laughed and confessed it was clear I didn't know how to play the trumpet, and that someone had told him how I spent the one-dollar Pop gave me every Saturday to pay for lessons I never took. Still laughing, he continued, "Bob, you needed to learn a lesson. I simply couldn't let you believe you had gotten away with fooling everyone. It was all part of teaching humility. I'm happy you're joining us, and I promise, no more lessons." I smiled and said, "Thanks a lot, Bear." He blinked and punched me in the arm. To my knowledge, no one ever called him Bear while in his presence.

After school one day, as I was leaving, Father Robert, our principal, stopped me. "Wait one second, Robert. Listen, I have four tickets to the Governor's Ball in October. If you want them, they're yours, and Frank Sinatra is the entertainment for the night!"

"Wow! Thanks, Father. I'm happy to take them. I know there are many others here who would love to go to the ball, and I really appreciate you thinking of me." Driving home, I wondered who I might ask to go with me. I didn't know it then, but my date would be a blind date, arranged for me by one of my friends.

September passed quickly and now that it was October, I had to get serious about finding a date. So, I checked with my friend Frank "Flip" McGeoy to tell him about the upcoming event, the free tickets, and to ask him if he wanted to go as well.

"Sure, that sounds great! Can I bring a date?"

"Yes, of course," I answered. "On that note, I haven't found a date yet, so there's a chance I might not be going at all."

Flip's date, Dallas, spoke with her roommate, Joan. Turns out she wanted to go too, so we ended up going on a double date. On the night of the ball, Flip and I, dressed in our best suits, went to pick up our dates. I rang the doorbell, and when the door opened, I just stood there with my mouth open. In the doorway stood my blind date, Joan, with what looked like a large empty orange juice can in her hair on top of her head! I had seen nothing like this before! I thought, *How am I going to go to a Governor's Ball with someone who has an orange juice can in her hair?* Like most guys, I didn't know that ladies used orange juice cans as hair rollers. Stupidly, I assumed the can was part of her hairstyle, which made me very nervous about this whole evening. Joan invited us in, but I declined. Instead, I said, "We'll wait for you on the porch."

I had a new plan. Once she closed the door, I would hit the road, fast. And I did. As I drove around the block, Flip pleaded with me to return. I agreed to go back only because I didn't want to ruin his night and date with Dallas. Fortunately, Flip convinced me we had no choice but to return to the porch before the girls came out to join us. When the ladies finally made their appearance, I immediately checked out Joan. *And oh boy, what a big mistake I nearly made!*

She looked terrific. Her long brunette hairstyle no longer included the orange juice can, and she was undeniably stunning. In addition, she was wearing a short, beautiful, black velvet dress that was very flattering. The second thing I noticed, after her hair, was her laughing green eyes. I'd never seen green eyes like hers. Standing there in awe, I kicked myself again for almost passing up this fantastic woman.

Early in the evening, I felt self-conscious about my left hand. To conquer my concern, I deliberately hid it in my suit jacket pocket, hoping I could conceal my injury. I don't know how Joan knew what I was up to, but she had noticed my left hand as I was driving, and she wasn't about to let me get away with hiding it in my jacket pocket all night. Instead, she surprised me in a way that I never could have expected; a moment branded into my heart for all of time. When we arrived in Newark, I parked the car and as we walked to the Armory, she reached out and gently drew my hand from my pocket as we headed into the ball. She smiled brilliantly at me and continued to clasp my hand as we walked companionably along.

Although we were on time, we missed the ball. Once we arrived at the Armory, we learned the fire marshal had ordered the doors closed because the size of the crowd already in the building had exceeded the capacity of the ballroom. That turned out to be something of a twist of fate that worked out to our benefit. Instead, the four of us spent a quiet evening getting to know each other while dining in a very nice Italian restaurant near Princeton, New Jersey. All I knew was that I wanted to see her again. But, when I asked her for her phone number, she said to me, "Bob, I'm moving to another apartment tomorrow, so I don't have a phone number to give you at the moment. If you give me your number, I'll call you."

Yeah, right, I thought to myself. *Don't call me, I'll call you.* It seemed like the classic yet polite way to give me the brush-off. I uncertainly gave her my number. Truthfully, I thought I'd never see or hear from her again. I wracked my brain trying to think of something I might have done or said to screw up the evening, but nothing came to mind. I really felt like we all had a great time and that Joan and I had made a special connection. Regardless, I moped around waiting for the phone to ring. Thankfully, three days later, she called me as promised. "Hey there, Bob. I'm finally settled, and I would love to see you again." Not wasting any time, I invited her to join me for dinner that night at Diamonds, a fabulous Italian restaurant in the Burg. It was to be our first date alone.

AFTER DINNER ON the way home, I felt that something special was in the wind. I had an urge to tell her that I had almost messed this up when I had left her doorstep and drove around the block before returning on the night of our blind date. Instead, I just thanked my lucky stars! It wasn't until New Year's Eve, three months later, that I summoned up enough courage to confess what could have been the mistake of my life, on the night of our first date. At first, funnily enough, she thought I was kidding, then she laughed at my version of our first date.

Determined to tell the truth, I reiterated what I'd said and then held my breath while waiting for her *real* reaction. I was relieved when she laughed, even harder this time, and said she didn't know how anyone could be so ridiculous. I tried to explain that I had never seen an orange juice can hair curler before. I had only seen the small, pink, spongy ones Mom and my sister Joan used in their hair. We were both laughing so hard that I knew she wasn't mad at me, and I would get to *stick around...for now*!

She had let me off the hook but continued to razz me for almost walking away from *the best thing that ever happened to me*, especially since I ended up proposing to her on our third date! Her response to my first proposal was, "Are you crazy?!" My big moment arrived on a sunny day in August, when I found the courage to propose again. This time properly, with a ring, and this time she said yes.

Joan has been my biggest fan and most ardent supporter since the day we first met. Among the lessons she has taught me was one that has kept me out of trouble throughout the years: *It's not what you say that matters, but how you say it.* Her love and acceptance helped me understand that my accident was not the end of my life, and that I could become successful by focusing on my remaining potential and looking *forward* instead of dwelling on the *past*. She never let me get away with feeling sorry for myself. It was exactly the right attitude I needed to make a new beginning.

Joan continued to encourage me to internalize the belief: *The only thing preventing your future success is worrying about what you can no longer do, instead of focusing on what you can do.* I applied this wisdom to our growing relationship and to my career aspirations.

That year, I had met the woman of my dreams and enjoyed a fulfilling, wonderful year as part of the Trenton Catholic High School faculty, and felt fortunate to receive an invitation to be a part of and reconnect with this terrific group of talented educators. But now, in the best way, the time to move on had arrived.

*

As a youngster, with my left hand intact, my ultimate dream had been to be a baseball player. After my accident, the replacement dream was to coach college-level basketball. Being a coach would at least bring me back into the world of athletics. I knew I had to coach first at the high school level, so I looked around to see what was available in our community. In April 1962, I learned that my friend and Rider College teammate John Wnuk had left his teaching position at Morrisville High School. That news interested me a lot because the teaching position included being the head basketball coach. Here was the opportunity I had been looking for. I applied for, received an offer, and accepted the vacant position. At Morrisville High, I would teach accounting and economics only, and I would be the head basketball coach!

The following June, Joan and I married at Saint Mary's, the parish where I had grown up, gone to grammar school, served Mass, and years before rang the exact church bell that rang at our wedding. It was a beautiful wedding, and almost one year later, we returned to Saint Mary's for yet another joyful event: the christening of our first beautiful little girl, Sharon.

Over the next four years, I taught and coached happily at Morrisville High, where I had the good fortune to mentor a fine group of young men, some of whom I still chat with on Facebook.

*

Then, out of the blue, in 1965, Father William Capik, the athletic director at Notre Dame High School in Trenton, recruited me to teach and become their head basketball coach. It was exciting because accepting the job meant staying in sports, as a professional, in my hometown, where I had gained a reputation as an athlete in my youth.

The lure to go back to Trenton to coach was strong because it had remained the hotbed of high school basketball in the entire state of New Jersey. It was still the same competitive environment it was when I attended Trenton Catholic from 1951 to 1955. After Trenton Catholic unexpectedly closed its doors in 1962 for economic reasons, the Notre Dame High School basketball program inherited the winning reputation once held by Trenton Catholic athletes. I knew that if I was ever to coach on the college level, I had to display I was a better than average high school coach. Notre Dame's ambitious basketball schedule included some of the best high school basketball teams in New Jersey. The chance to be part of the excitement in Trenton was once again irresistible.

I took the job, and successfully coached the team to the semifinals in the state basketball tournament. However, ranking third in the tournament was just a temporary comfort zone. Joan and Sharon (now almost two years old) never missed a game. Much to Sharon's delight, the kind sisters on faculty at the high school created for her a tiny cheerleader's uniform exactly like the real squad wore. At halftime, Sharon's little dance always stole the show. She loved all the attention the girls gave her and couldn't wait for game night so she could wear her tiny blue uniform with the short, flippy skirt and the large, white ND lettering on the front. It was a busy and happy time for us all.

THERE WASN'T MUCH time to enjoy our success. In early September 1967, legendary basketball coach Dick Harter was the head coach at my second alma mater, Rider College. One day, unexpectedly, he called to offer me the freshman coaching job at Rider as assistant to the head coach. This offer was the golden opportunity I had been waiting for, and I excitedly accepted the position.

My world then took several rapid turns that left my head spinning. A few days following my acceptance of the Rider job, Harter resigned to accept the head basketball coaching position at the University of Pennsylvania. Dick soon called me to say that although he would like me to come to Penn with him, he felt it wouldn't be fair to Rider if he took me away. He asked me to stay at Rider to help John Carpenter, who would replace him and who would need an assistant coach. My head was still churning when I received, that very same week, a call from Jack Devine, who had recently accepted the head coaching position at Fairleigh Dickinson University. He asked me to come to Fairleigh to become *his* assistant coach. I was rendered speechless. While coaching at Morrisville for four years, no one had ever approached me with a new job opportunity, let alone offered me a coaching position. Then, after two years at Notre Dame and the race for the state championship, I received two coaching job offers in the space of two days!

I spent the next several days thinking about my two unbelievable options. At Rider with Carpenter, I would once again work full-time at my alma mater...but it would be for someone I didn't know. At Fairleigh Dickinson with Jack Devine, I would work with somebody I knew and liked, but there was still one problem – the coaching position at Fairleigh was part-time, which meant I needed an additional part-time job to make ends meet. I accepted my friend Jack's offer of a part-time coaching position, along with his promise to get the position reclassified to full-time.

I thought that if I continued to teach at Notre Dame, where I had been so content, everything would work out as planned.

Father Coffee, our principal, told me he was happy with my performance as a teacher and would like me to stay.

In this chaos of opportunity and quick decisions, Pop would just say, "Okay, I wonder what's next?" It wasn't long before I knew the answer to that question. My sister Joan, Trenton State Prison's business manager, called to tell me that Professor Sidney Meth, the prison's director of Education, resigned. She suggested I apply for the job. This was unbelievable. Three jobs all at the same time. I felt lucky and overwhelmed.

I called my old boss, Warden Howard Yeager, to inquire about the position. He said he was happy I called and that he enjoyed following me during my career at Notre Dame in the local media. A short while later, we met at his office to discuss the job at the prison and my present situation. My problem was that, in my mind, any job I took could only last until I found a full-time faculty-level coaching position. I told Mr. Yeager that a full-time job at Fairleigh was hopefully in the works, so I might not be with them for very long. Obviously, this was not what a prospective employer would want to hear. Then I told him what I expected would be a deal-breaker, "Warden, the university is about a one-hour drive from the prison. Practice with my freshman team would be from 6 to 8 p.m. Monday through Friday. That means my workday at the prison would have to end at 4 p.m." I asked him if it was even possible for my work hours to be from 8 a.m. to 4 p.m. He surprised me when he said, "Bob, if you think you can handle that schedule, then it's okay with me."

After I left the meeting with the warden, I thought about how I had grown up living in Chambersburg, and basically in the prison's shadow. From childhood I'd had a strange fascination with the prison, and that curiosity remained, as once more I was drawn back. I knew the prison had a violent past, but there was still much more to learn before I could officially accept the job offer. I went to the state library to read everything they had in their archives, including their microfiche and microfilm files. Joan and I also read all the local media about the prison and learned it was indeed still an extremely violent institution. Many considered it as being largely out of control.

Among the many materials we read was a story written by *Trentonian* newspaper reporter Jon Blackwell. The title of his story was "1952: The Powder Keg Blows." It described conditions at the Trenton State Prison during the 1950s as being the most violent in the prison's long history.

Blackwell writes:

> "The State of New Jersey called them sexual psychopaths, passive homosexuals, aggressive 'wolves' with long records of fights and stabbings, escape artists, agitators, and incorrigibles of all ages. They called themselves the scum of society.
>
> "They were the hardest of hard-core prison inmates, and on three occasions in 1952, they placed the Trenton Prison under siege, destroying everything they could find, taking hostages, and resisting every plea to surrender.
>
> "It was the most violent, tumultuous year in the history of New Jersey prisons – a generation before uprisings at Attica and Rahway Prisons made inmate violence a raging national issue."

This left me wondering why so much violence occurred at this prison. Did this portend the future? After finishing my research, we still didn't have an answer to that question. We only knew that Trenton's sporadic violence, since its beginning two centuries earlier in 1798, was still dangerously rampant now in the 1960s.

Conversations at our house were predominantly focused on a *to go or not to go* decision. Joan preferred I stay at Notre Dame, but she also believed that if I chose the prison, as director of Education, I wouldn't be involved in security issues that could put me in any danger. I loved the kids at Notre Dame and would miss the hubbub at school, but I felt I could do more to help the education department at the prison.

As we weighed the options, my enthusiasm noticeably grew. Joan agreed it was time to try something new and we finally made the decision that we would go to Trenton. I met again with Warden Yeager and told him I would like to accept the job there, temporarily, until Jack Devine reclassified the position at the college to full-time. He replied, "Bob, that's fine, but I hope we can persuade you to stay with us in the end. We're going to work at it."

*

I don't know why this job seemed to be challenging me in a way that I couldn't refuse. *Is it possible that I could use my past trials, and the hard lessons I have learned, to somehow contribute to a positive change in this raging, perilous environment?*

There was really no question that I was destined to *try*. I clearly understood that I had a great deal to learn about prison management and institutional security. Still, I would enter the scene as an educator, someone who teaches, instructs, and gives practical vocational, social, and moral direction. In no way would I have anything to do with running the prison.

Looking through this alternate prism, I could possibly make a difference. But, as a family, we wondered what the significance of this new change in the course of our lives would be.

CHAPTER 7

School Daze Behind "The Wall"

Bob Hatrak, Director of Education, Trenton State Prison

"Adult education can pay rich personal and social dividends — not twenty years from now, but immediately."

— *National Advisory Council on Adult Education*

The crucial role of adult education is to allow adult workers to both develop their skills and to gain new ones.

In the wake of an economic crisis, it's essential for adults, especially those needing to work past pension age, to have the opportunity to undergo retraining and learn a new role. Why not offer this helping hand to men who will need all the help they can get when they return to society?

*

October 23, 1967 was the first day of my new job as director of Education at Trenton State Prison. I arrived early, as advised, to have a little time to scope things out.

Accustomed to the usual din of scholastic environments – teenagers in high school, athletic locker rooms, and campus life at college – the startling effect of that second sallyport gate slamming shut behind me, sealing me off from the outside world, was an unexpected shock. It was a disconcerting sensation of finality that I hoped would normalize over time.

Having worked here in the business office during the summers of my junior and senior years in high school, and again in the mailroom following my accident while I was in college, this prison wasn't new to me. It was clear, now that I'd be working inside instead of in the safety of the front house, that this time would be different.

For twenty minutes I stood in the busy hub of the institution known to inmates and staff alike as "Center" – an area full of hectic foot traffic going in all directions throughout the day, until the prison quieted down around 9 p.m. and lights went off at 10 p.m. Standing next to the "star" officer, who stood purposefully on the brass star embedded in the floor, I silently watched as he successfully directed the crowd with brisk commands and precise arm signals.

"Center" dominates the area to the right of the star officer and serves as the prison's nerve center. It sits protectively surrounded by bulletproof glass, with gunports strategically positioned at intervals out into the rotunda. The armory shares the Center. Its weapons and security equipment occupy the space behind the officer stations.

As the star officer blithely ignored my gestures to continue to my destination, I impatiently wondered if he was being deliberately rude. Now that the morning movement had started, I had to remain in place until the mass movement ended. *Why was I not told to arrive before or after this confusion began?*

I soon realized that my old friends here heard I was coming back and purposely set up this "delay" to launch my return. They planned for me to walk into the middle of this spectacle and have me stand, waiting for everyone else to pass, until the brass band finished playing. So, this was my welcome back – nice going, guys!

There was no mistaking their grins and creative hand signals as they whizzed past, escorting their inmate work details to their assignments and appointments. Smiling back at them, I thought how difficult it must be for the inmates to begin every day by rote and end them in the same structured way.

Nearby, the jarring and commanding sound of an ear-splitting bell signaled something was about to jump off or had already happened. These shrill whistles meant either a medical or security emergency. Slamming metal doors and sharp voices reverberating off unyielding concrete and steel surfaces punctuated the day's beginning events. *Would these recurring sounds become familiar to me?* While the bell continued to shriek, masses of inmates silently appeared and assembled at the entries to their housing units. *Where did they all come from so quickly?*

In all this controlled commotion, the band suddenly began playing. Once the center keeper announces a wing number, inmates normally trek in pairs to or from their wings to the mess hall, work assignments, recreation, school, and library destinations. As they entered Center, their muffled footfalls changed, and they quietly marched in step to the cadence of a loud and off-key rendition of "Stars and Stripes Forever." It was the band's job assignment to regale everyone daily with Sousa marches. The toiling musicians evoked grimaces as they did their best to create a paramilitary environment. Instead, it inspired grins and lightened the mood of the captive parade of inmates as they filed briskly past Center.

When the movement ended and regular foot traffic resumed, I finally got waved through and found my way to the school area.

*

When I worked at the institution before in my first part-time experience, my job was to supervise two inmate projectionists in a small projection booth. Their job assignment was to show the current week's movie to the general population seated outside in the auditorium. There was only enough room in the booth for two projectors and four chairs. Both men were serving life sentences for murder. One of them was the notorious New Jersey Duck Island murderer, Clarence Hill. Now, heading the Education Department would be a far different situation and involved managing dozens of men operating in a much larger space.

While walking along the narrow upstairs balcony, I thought once more that the end of every workday would be in reverse of the morning routine as inmates returned to their respective dreary wings. I imagined when the last bell signaled lights out, and everyone was tucked in for the night, I could almost hear some wise-guy inmate on some tier, imitating Bugs Bunny, and smirking, "G-g-g-good night, folks!"

Now, standing at the drab school entrance, feeling my enthusiasm return, I opened the door and stepped inside. Once again, my enthusiasm waned when I unexpectedly felt a feathery brush of a spider web against my ear! *What have I gotten myself into?* Tempted now to turn around and leave, I saw that the day's surprises were not over yet. The area was much smaller and more abandoned than I had expected. The only general illumination came from a few dimmed overhead fluorescent fixtures whose bulbs were mostly burned out. The stale, lingering smell revealed that heavy smoking had been a popular activity here.

Seemingly never washed, the two double-hung barred windows offered only minimal daylight. In addition, years of accumulated grime and cigarette smoke created a frosted appearance on the glass, canceling their effectiveness as a light source.

Glancing around, I made some unexpected and discouraging discoveries. The area included three classrooms, two offices, and two empty storerooms. All were in shabby condition. The staff's old metal state-issue desks begged to be replaced. There were no desk lamps. Rickety bookshelves made by the prison's maintenance department were dust-covered and half-empty. The bare, colorless walls were shedding layers of thick lead paint, and the total area was in disarray. Joan would tell me to wear gloves while working in this mess. Most surprising, I found no school records for previous years! I would need to begin from scratch.

At spotless Notre Dame High School I reported to school each morning wearing a suit and a tie. Here, I would need to wear old work clothes until I could create order. At Notre Dame our principal, the Reverend Father Tracey ("Big Red"), would have turned beet red and commanded that I bulldoze the entire area.

When I looked through the schoolbook inventory and saw the meager materials used in the Adult Basic Education and the High School Equivalency programs for the previous year, I understood why attendance had been so low.

I saw books I remembered reading in the first and second grades. Books about Dick, Jane, Sally, Spot, and their orange cat, Puff! Also, I found dozens of old, outdated, and faded Reader's Digests. How discouraging that would be to adult students. Someone purchased them as basal readers instead of searching for, and acquiring, more appropriate material for beginning adult readers.

I learned later when these materials were distributed to new students, most handed them back. It would also have offended me had I received children's books, and I would have returned them too. *How demoralizing*, I thought, and again, *what have I gotten myself into?*

The school year hadn't begun a month ago in September, as it always had. There was a tremendous amount of planning and organization to do before we could even think about being up and running. So instead, I rescheduled the first semester to start in early February 1968. That only bought us four months to create a clean and efficient workplace, hire staff, develop a curriculum, and order new books and supplies. Our only asset in this administration was our own enthusiasm.

After replacing the two full-time civilian instructor counselors I inherited, I hired Jake Wig the following week. Jake taught with me at Notre Dame and I could depend on his native intelligence, common sense, and loyalty. He performed well as the second in command of the Education Department and I could always count on him to handle difficult situations capably.

I recruited Notre Dame's head football coach, Walt Porter (RIP, Walt), as our first Recreation director. Walt turned around a "ho-hum" program in need of reorganization with ease, competence, and good humor.

I interviewed the previous year's teachers, kept all of them, and hired two more. Among the best, Walt Dabrowski, was an experienced and excellent history teacher at Hamilton High School West, who later taught history at Rider University. Paul Medwick, a science teacher at Notre Dame, was also a welcomed addition to our new team. They were all talented and well-seasoned educators who contributed significantly to the new Adult Basic Education and High School Equivalency programs we developed from the ground up together as a dynamic and inspired team.

There can't be many teachers who have never dreamed about the opportunity to re-imagine their school, to play district superintendent, and to put together their own version of a "perfect and new" Education department. We were all in high gear and full of inspiration, so this was everyone's chance to do just that!

I didn't want to go back to failed conventional teaching methods of Adult Basic Education. I remember reading that Abe Lincoln had once said, "I am a slow walker, but I never walk backward." This was precisely how I felt. I needed to find better ways to motivate and present basic education to our teachers and adult students.

THE SCHOOL YEAR got off to an excellent start. Our teachers began the year organized, well prepared, and raring to go, but the students were clearly less motivated.

In previous years, restless students had attended school to keep from getting locked in their cells early for the night. Signing up for classes provided a cover to visit with like-minded friends, play cards, and smoke cigarettes. The school had become a popular hangout. Students this year were in for a big surprise! This year, we would function effectively in an efficient and vigorous school environment.

The school nights flew by. Our new teachers were not calling in sick, nightly student attendance was high, and Dick and Jane's replacements didn't get returned to us. Better yet, one hundred percent of those taking the High School Equivalency Exam passed.

Soon, graduation was upon us, and we held the annual school banquet in early July. I served as the master of ceremonies and guest speaker. Warden Yeager and Chief Deputy Edmonds were the honored guests. Everyone was in high spirits and broad smiles were everywhere. The inmates' chosen menu included half of a fried chicken, mashed potatoes, vegetables, and a giant bowl of ice cream. Hands down, that meal was the men's favorite. I enjoyed seeing how proud each student was. There was a noticeable improvement in their attitude and demeanor. Their accomplishments gratified everyone.

Inmates accomplishing an eighth-grade reading level received Achievement Certificates. Students passing the state High School Equivalency Exam earned Equivalency Certificates. The General Educational Development (GED) tests were four-subject tests that provided certification that the test taker possessed high school-level academic skills when passed. It was an alternative to a high school diploma.

Following the ceremony, as the inmates proudly filed out of the mess hall, I gave each student, including the three inmate clerks, a carton of cigarettes. Cigarettes were a big deal because they were the official medium of exchange inside the prison. They were the same as cash in this closed society and highly prized by smokers and non-smokers alike.

Now that our first class of inmates graduated, they and others in the general population with high school diplomas needed an option to continue their education. Why couldn't they take the next step? College-level classes seemed to me like a real possibility.

Our new school program pleased Warden Yeager, and I was sure he would support an effort to offer college classes to inmates.

*

I devoted time to looking for a college with a progressive president. I imagined inviting professors into the prison to teach college-level classes to qualified inmates. *How sad would it be if we lost the enthusiasm and momentum of the past school year?*

My problem was the prison had no budget for college classes. Traditionally, college credits for inmates would have been unthinkable. But without exception, every inmate I spoke with about college classes told me he would gladly pay the per-credit cost with personal funds, using the twenty-six to forty-nine cents he earned per day on prison jobs or with the help of the GI Bill of Rights benefits.

Eagerly doing additional research, I learned, "Claimants incarcerated for a felony conviction can be paid only the costs of tuition, fees, and necessary books, equipment, and supplies."

*

A friend, Dr. Fred Price, learned about what I was attempting. Fred suggested I contact Dr. Richard Greenfield, Mercer County Community College president, noting that "Greenfield enjoys a reputation as a progressive college administrator with a vision. The president may work with you to develop this idea."

MCCC was established in 1966. The 292-acre West Windsor Township Campus opened in 1971 to serve the needs of Mercer County residents.

I met with Dr. Greenfield and explained my idea. He offered to assign Dr. John Connelly, his assistant, to the job of helping me make college courses available at the Trenton Prison. Together, we designed a program that offered a one-year certificate and a two-year Associate of Arts degree in educational and community services, accounting, general studies in humanities, and social sciences specialties.

To garner prison staff and local community support and avoid political criticism, we permitted prison staff to attend college classes on their own time. They, too, paid all per-credit costs they accrued to MCCC. In addition, private citizens living in the neighborhoods immediately surrounding the prison could also attend courses if they paid their own fees.

College-level programs would be new in New Jersey's prisons and reformatories. Our experiment would be the first school of its kind in a maximum-security facility anywhere. Formal college classes at the institution began on July 10, 1968.

A newspaper story appearing in the *Philadelphia Inquirer* dated March 13, 1969, carried the headline "State Prison Inmates are Given a Chance to Gain College Credits."

On April 30, 1969, the *Daily Journal* (Vineland, New Jersey) ran a story about our new college program for inmates. The reporter interviewed Warden Yeager, several college professors, prison teachers, inmate students, and me.

Elbert Hubbard once said, "If you want work well done, select a busy man – the other kind has no time." In the year of 1969, the Education Department staff was "burning the candle at both ends" and still running on collective enthusiasm. We were at the beginning stages of pioneering the first-ever college degree program for inmates and a second program using an electronic bridge linking MCCC with the Trenton, Rahway, and Leesburg State Prisons. Using this network, inmates and students on campus would take college-level classes together electronically.

*

In the midst of this beehive of activity, Director Wagner tasked me to implement a work release program for inmates recently signed into law. A statewide work release program for inmates would be established at the Trenton Prison first. Our staff was pleased that we were chosen to be the first prison in New Jersey to put this work release program into effect, even though we would be frantically busy implementing a college program statewide simultaneously.

We were also thrilled to see an article in the *Philadelphia Inquirer*, on September 24, 1969, titled "Outside Jobs Ease Transition for State Prisoners". The article stated that though the program was new to New Jersey, it had been successful in many other states and in Europe. The article quoted me saying how excited my staff and I were to be coordinating this program and how pleased we were with the response we were getting from the community. We all saw this as a significant step forward in actively helping inmates "get off on the right foot."

*

Time flies when you're having fun and accomplishing goals. Along with the development of the work release program, we'd completed another year of school and produced our first class to graduate with college degrees. On Sunday, June 20, 1971, the first five inmates from Trenton's maximum-security prison would receive an Associate of Arts degree. Interestingly, Trenton inmates behaved themselves exceptionally well on that day: Not a single disciplinary report for any breach of the prison regulations was written, something that no one on staff had ever seen before.

THE PRISON AUDITORIUM, an old, dingy, and musty room that dated back to the turn of the century, had been a silent witness to stabbings, rapes, brawls, gang wars, and one-on-one inmate fistfights. Yet, this well-worn space comfortably hosted a festive and uplifting ceremony full of joyful people witnessing this ground-breaking event.

Our Education Department inmate clerks did an excellent job setting up the room with four hundred rented folding chairs. The proud graduates had extended invitations to their families and friends to attend the unprecedented ceremonies. We were expecting a standing-room-only crowd.

I asked the warden to excuse me from taking my assigned seat on the stage. The day belonged to the graduates, and I didn't want to steal any of their thunder. Instead, I sat like a proud "papa" in excited anticipation with the graduates' exhilarated visiting families.

At 1 p.m., the room became silent. Spirited and familiar strains of the well-known graduation song, "Pomp and Circumstance," filled every corner of the room. Everyone stood as the graduates marched confidently into the room, dressed in the traditional graduation garb of a cap and gown.

The graduates included Samuel E. Bynes (Honors), Kenneth J. Manley (Honors), Donald P. Leotta (Honors), Robert E. Melwig, and George D. Mills.

Each man took his designated seat on the stage. Seated alongside them was Albert B. Kahn, a member of the State's Prison Board of Trustees, who presided over the festivities and gave the commencement address.

Warden Yeager and MCCC President Dr. Richard Greenfield filled the remaining seats. Dr. Greenfield presented the diplomas to our five graduates.

The excitement was contagious, and I sat and cheered with everyone else when each man proudly received his diploma.

The thing I took away from Mr. Kahn's address was his acknowledgment of how unfairly the state treats ex-cons, let alone those now possessing college degrees. Kahn said, "We don't know what the future holds for you fellows. The degree entitles you to a better life. Still, unfortunately, you won't get state jobs because of your background. State law prohibits anyone with a prison record from holding a state job. Why should private employers hire ex-inmates when the state of New Jersey will not hire them?"

I never forgot his question, and many years later I made a small in-road into solving that state policy. I worked hand in hand with a supporter of mine, former world heavyweight champion, the late "Jersey Joe" Walcott. Joe was a progressive human being and the state boxing commissioner. He was very approachable, and he listened thoughtfully to my request. Despite the tradition Mr. Kahn spoke of, Joe took it upon himself to license qualified inmates who were part of the prison's boxing school. A good example is inmate Eddie Johnson, whom the commissioner licensed as the first inmate ever certified as a boxing referee in the United States.

I enjoyed reading the Associated Press story about our graduation ceremony on the morning following the graduation, It read: "The five men looked like any other group of college graduates this June, a little older than most but still attired in the traditional academic garb. The five Sunday graduates are the first under a program enabling inmates to work towards a degree at the two-year Mercer County College."

*

With graduation now complete, the Education Department staff needed to help the graduates find meaningful employment and/or continue their educations.

Our staff inspired one graduate, Sam Bynes, to earn a Bachelor's degree and then a Master's degree upon release. After spending a significant part of his past life incarcerated, he became an educated and productive community member.

My inbox overflowed with letters from inmates at our sister institutions, Rahway and Leesburg. They all contained the following request: "Mr. Hatrak, I have a GED and money to enter your college program. As you are a member of the Classification Committee, I'd like to ask for your help to get a transfer to Trenton."

In numbers more extensive than ever before, Trenton inmates refused to transfer from Trenton Prison to the other two state prisons. The reason they gave, in all cases, was that they wanted to enroll into our college program before the start of the next semester. It was clear Rahway and Leesburg needed to be part of our program to accommodate the many requests I was receiving.

School enrollments for our regular school program also increased. At the end of the year, standardized testing scores offered exciting proof that the previous year's students had improved their skills – validating their hard work and the success of our new program enhancements and modifications. Everyone was satisfied and looking forward to the next semester.

I was devastated when I learned I would soon be hundreds of miles away.

CHAPTER 7 ½

Techy Times

THE VELVETEEN RABBIT

"...once you are Real you can't become unreal again. It lasts for always."

Velveteen Rabbit

"Education is the passport to the future,
for tomorrow belongs to those who prepare for it today."

– Malcolm X

I had to delay figuring out how to add Rahway and Leesburg to our college program. Our director, Al Wagner, selected me to represent New Jersey in a major national research project. Dr. T. Antoinette Ryan, a nationally renowned researcher at the University of Hawaii, secured a federal grant. It focused on training selected prison education leaders in pioneering and innovative methods for delivering basic education programs to prison inmate students.

I was excited to work with someone of her stature and couldn't wait to discuss our innovative pilot college program at Trenton with her. But Dr. Ryan's project was bigger and more comprehensive than any of us expected it would be. It would tie me up timewise, requiring my full-time presence in Morgantown, West Virginia for the entirety of one month.

MY SCHEDULE AT the prison had become overwhelming. I was struggling to develop the plan for our recently proposed school building within the prison complex while also supervising the current prison school system. Since the warden's heart attack, I was also helping with his incoming and outgoing correspondence, on top of my already ongoing projects with MCCC building our Prison Education Network (PEN) for inmates. At the same time, I was still traveling back and forth to Fairleigh Dickinson University to coach the basketball team six nights a week.

Dr. Ryan's federal project in West Virginia "tipped me over." There just weren't enough hours to cover it all. These new projects made it impossible to continue coaching part-time in the evening at FDU. Regrettably, it was necessary to resign from my coaching position. For now, my coaching days had ended—and my zeal to advance our residents and the Education Department increased every day.

*

Joan, always my best partner in life, had been a good sport about all that was going on during that hectic time. Everything at our house ran like clockwork because she had assumed many of my responsibilities at home, enabling me to maintain my ridiculous schedule. The decision to resign from coaching would free up my evenings from daily practice and our weekends from traveling to home and away games. Joan could finally stop mowing the lawn and shoveling snow from our driveway.

Driving almost every day of the week up and down the New Jersey Turnpike to FDU was the only way Joan, Sharon, and I could spend any time together. The first season went by quickly, and having their company made our trips north fun. When we all began to burn out, our driving adventures were less and less fun. Following the third season, it was time to take a break from coaching and to slow down. Stepping back into our "normal chaos" was very welcomed.

*

In 1971, Dr. Ryan selected thirty-six federal and state directors of Education, assembled in Morgantown, West Virginia, to undergo a training program, preparing us to become experts in Adult Basic Education in Corrections nationally.

This was the first time, since our wedding in 1962, that Joan and I would be apart overnight. It was going to be a very long month.

The first morning, we reported to our work site at the Federal Youth Correctional Center, a short bus ride from the Morgan Hotel, our home away from home in the city's downtown area for the next four weeks.

When Dr. Ryan bounced into the room, she surprised all of us. She looked exactly like her twin sister, Irene Ryan, whom we all knew from her role as Granny in *The Beverly Hillbillies*, a popular TV sitcom. As soon as she spoke, it was clear she was not a "granny."

It didn't take long to recognize that Dr. Ryan's renowned reputation was well deserved. We immediately determined she was brilliant.

But no one expected the masterful and assertive management style with which she conducted her sessions. She was a tiny, energetic woman with a sense of humor that could put you in your place, and you didn't realize until much later you'd been thoroughly admonished.

She quickly shaped us into an informed and skillful working unit, and she did it all with a smile. She and I shared a friendship that lasted almost twenty-five years until we lost touch.

A few years later in 1975, the United States Department of Justice, through the Office of Justice Programs, described the Model of Adult Basic Education In Corrections that I co-authored with Dr. T. Antoinette Ryan and four others as:

"A conceptual model developed for providing a rational approach for planning and evaluating prison education programs.... The model provided dynamic instructional systems that provide continuous improvement and modification of educational delivery systems to meet changes in offender populations and changing social and economic conditions."

It was the most demanding and rewarding undertaking of my career so far. We worked twenty-four consecutive days, with sessions starting at 8:30 a.m. and ending at 4:30 p.m. After dinner, we couldn't wait to get to sleep, only to start all over again in the morning.

At the end of four weeks, we finished the training sessions. Dr. Ryan then narrowed down the group and selected six participants to make up a model design team, of which I was the chairperson. We met in Oak Park, Illinois, every two weeks, working through the weekend, ten hours a day, from Saturday morning until Sunday afternoon for the next six months.

During this time, I learned the flowcharting language system, Language Optimizing Graphically Ordered Systems, referred to as LOGOS as developed by Dr. Leonard Silvern. We used this system's language to build our model. Feeling satisfied that we had done a great job, completing this revolutionary project, I returned to Trenton, exhausted but exhilarated. With this newly gained expertise, I now felt prepared to continue adding Rahway and Leesburg prisons into our college program. I would introduce and advance the unprecedented alternative methods and systems we developed in West Virginia to educate adult prisoners in our newly proposed school building.

The timing was perfect!

*

From Joan: Sharon and I were excited when Bob came home, and very happy to have him back with us.

As we were unpacking later, we looked for presents Bob had hinted might be in his suitcase. We found a copy of The *Velveteen Rabbit* with a lovely note inscribed on the front pages from Daddy. It quickly became Sharon's favorite book. (Today, it still sits as a prized possession on her bookshelf.)

A tiny little metal dump truck popped out of Bob's overstuffed suitcase. Sharon immediately assumed it was for her. Bob naturally played along and showed her how the back end of the truck lifted and dropped its cargo.

Truth be told, that didn't honestly explain the tiny truck's presence.

It seems that back in Morgantown Dr. Ryan decided Bob should be the chairman of this group. He took this charge seriously and everyone worked very hard.

On the last day, as everyone was saying goodbye, one of the men in the group, J.C. Verl Keeney, director of Education at the Oregon State Prison, whipped out the little truck and very formally announced it was a gift for Bob from the entire group. They had named it DT after him! After much guessing they told him DT stood for dump truck, in recognition of his special skill when delegating endless work to them.

A small group of six continued to meet monthly in Chicago, Illinois for the next six months to write a book. It was named *The Model for Adult Basic Education in Corrections.*

DT made the journey every month. It sat on the table in front of Bob to remind everyone of the hard work they had all invested in this project, and to "keep on truckin'."

*

Preparing to go back to work, I decided that the most logical solution to merge Rahway and Leesburg into our college program required that we identify a community college near each prison to do the same thing MCCC was already doing for our Trenton inmate students.

Someone suggested that I approach Dr. Greenfield, asking him to reach out to the presidents of colleges located closest to the two prisons. I hoped he would encourage them to meet with me to discuss implementing a pilot project like ours. And he did.

Warden Yeager encouraged me to pursue the idea but asked me to run it past Director Wagner first. He made it clear that I would need his "OK" before getting involved with our sister institutions. He also wished me "Good luck."

DIRECTOR WAGNER ASKED, "How do you propose to accomplish this?"

"I'm not sure, sir, but I would like your approval to pursue all of my options."

"Go right ahead. However, don't commit the division to anything. Please keep me informed whenever you make serious progress. Please don't speak with anyone in the other two prisons without talking with me first. We both know anything experimental must be introduced cautiously. Let's get all our ducks in a row before announcing anything. What's your first step?"

"I'm going to make an appointment to meet with Dr. Greenfield at Mercer College."

"Let me know how that meeting goes."

*

Dr. Greenfield asked Dr. John Connolly, his assistant, to meet with me. He then suggested we involve one of his professors, someone with a robust educational technology resume, to brainstorm with me.

I wondered if we could connect electronically with Mercer County Community College. Why wouldn't it be possible to link up electronically with the other institutions? Could two-way voice communications accomplish what I wanted to do? What technology, beyond the telephone, was available to help me? Was anyone, anywhere, doing anything similar?

*

This was 1971 and many years away from the development of the iPhone, text messaging, fax machines, or the World Wide Web.

The major challenge I faced was imagining the yet-to-be-developed technology to create an electronic bridge that included two-way voice communications with several prison locations. I knew what we needed, but I didn't know how to create it, or if it was possible at all.

I contacted the technology professor and shared my idea about electronically linking the college with several facilities.

He told me the college had recently purchased a piece of equipment called the Victor Electrowriter and showed me a picture.

He said, "The manufacturer has already shipped the Electrowriter, but it has yet to arrive. Looking at it, I was unimpressed. It appeared simplistic, but sometimes the most primitive and straightforward solutions are the most effective. For example, the Victor Electrowriter uses an especially manufactured piece of sheet metal, about eight and a half by eleven inches. An attached burning pen is used to write on the piece of sheet metal. This is what some people call writing electronically. These specially developed pens complete an electric circuit that helps etch similes into the metal sheet.

Etched images appear on a receiver, and then they project to far-away locations.

"I was told it's possible to add two-way voice signals to all locations. This is called tele-lecturing."

I sat there, speechless.

Once I recovered from the explanation, I said, "I can't imagine any of that!"

"Don't worry, Bob. Since I've yet to see the equipment, I'll ask the Victor Electrowriter folks to send someone here to demo it to both of us when we receive our writer."

*

Later, at home, I excitedly told Joan, "This could be an answer to my prayers! If the combined equipment can meet my expectations, we may be on the verge of seriously creating something fantastic!"

On the day of the demo, I saw, with my own eyes, handwriting etched into the metal sheet being transmitted from the demo room to three other remote locations! It was too good to be true!

Next, the two-way voice, recorded or live, had to be added to the handwriting and transmitted simultaneously. We had reached the limit of our expertise and were stumped temporarily.

I contacted Bell Telephone Laboratories and told them we needed their help to add two-way voice communications to the Electrowriter data transmissions we had combined.

Bell Laboratories quickly responded enthusiastically. They worked hand in hand with the Teletype Corporation and the Victor Comptometer Corporation. Finally, what I dreamed of doing could now really happen!

*

I envisioned a professor standing in front of a class of college students on campus lecturing to them as inmate students in remote prison classrooms took part in the lecture.

Other demos had to be arranged before I dared talk about our profound accomplishments. First would be Director Wagner, Warden Yeager, the Rahway and Leesburg superintendents, their Education directors, a Mercer County Workhouse representative, and their warden.

Innovation and creativity are not characteristics one would usually find in a maximum-security prison. As a result, they seldom get encouraged or supported. I was fortunate that both of my bosses, Director Wagner and Warden Yeager, were by now as enthusiastic as I was to move forward. It seemed important that we include a few carefully selected inmate students to attend the demo. Warden Yeager had always supported my endeavors, and he again approved my request to include inmates at the demo.

After we all saw what the equipment could do, everyone unanimously decided I should do everything in my power to be ready to move forward. If we could find the funding, we would begin using our groundbreaking experimental system the following fall semester.

THE NEXT DAY, Rose Newell, the telephone switchboard operator, called to tip me off that Director Wagner was on his way up to my office to see me. I was shocked because other than the wardens, he never went to any other office. Concerned and curious, I wondered what was on his mind. The director knocked on the door, entered, and as if he were a regular visitor, plopped comfortably into a wing chair in the corner of my office. I swallowed hard and listened as he thanked me graciously for my efforts on behalf of the division.

He continued saying, "I'll help cut through any roadblocks you run into. However, there is a funding obstacle I never expected. I honestly didn't believe the technology you needed really existed. I'm sure you didn't either."

"Bob, I have several contacts at the Higher Education Department who might help find the money we need. How about if I arrange a meeting for you with them?"

I said I'd be ready for them. "I'm working on a draft of a tentative budget and a comprehensive implementation plan. It will take several hundreds of thousands of dollars to get the model off the ground!"

Several days later, I received a call from one of Mr. Wagner's contacts. We set a date and time for a meeting that following week.

The technology professor from MCCC and I attended the meeting with our begging bowls in hand. We explained our proposed system. My immediate thoughts were, "Are we now on a fast track?"

We waited only several days before receiving a call following a successful demo.

"Good news, Mr. Hatrak. Please send someone to pick up a Pell Grant application. Then fill it out and submit it to the federal government."

I learned Pell Grants are grants and not loans. My immediate question was: Can they support college programs for inmate students with a Pell Grant's help? The answer I received was yes.

Dr. Greenfield and I agreed that because his college would administer the program, it made sense the college should prepare the grant. The completed grant had Mercer County Community College designated as administrator of the funds.

On June 1, 1971, we received word that our Pell Grant application for $300,000 was approved! It funded us for $247,625. We were all thrilled.

I set the official start of the Prison Education Network for Tuesday, September 7, 1971. Everyone enthusiastically supported the Prison Education Network (PEN). Students at the facilities were enrolling in numbers exceeding my initial projections. It pleased me that future graduation classes would far exceed the initial five Trenton graduates.

Director Wagner arranged for other institutions, at their request, to be included in the network. As a result, the Clinton Prison for Women, Annandale Reformatory, and the Yardville Youth Correctional Facility also joined the program.

On Tuesday, November 20, 1973, the *Asbury Park Press* ran a story with this headline: "Public's Education Is Urged By Graduating Ex-Prisoner." The article documented the network's growth and the success inmates achieved.

When we first began college-level classes at the Trenton Prison in 1969, the enrollment was twenty-seven inmate students as well as private citizens and correction officers, which helped us strengthen our relationship with the officers' union (PBA).

In September 1973, the network's enrollment increased to 187, with full-time inmate students and eighty-four part-timers taking part. When that article ran in November 1973, enrollment had grown to 359 full-time inmate students and 133 enrolled part-time.

*

One year later we were ready for our next challenge. We had been busy planning for our new $750,000 school building at the Trenton Prison, which was near completion. Our staff helped design and allocate the use of space in the new building. It was a struggle to move away from the traditional approach to teaching and learning. Determined to be more creative, we embarked on this more enlightened model, and decided to implement the curriculum developed in the book I co-authored, *Model for Adult Basic Education in Corrections*.

The new building included ten classrooms and fifteen staff offices. Gone were the sounds of loud bells, shrieking whistles, and the noise of slamming metal doors. Gone too was the musty odor that one could never escape. It was like any building on any college campus. We could barely contain our eagerness to get started.

The only reminder of the school's location were the big locks on the wire mesh doors between floors and the horizontal window bars.

We designated five rooms as learning laboratories where students worked alone in study carrels designed to seat one person. These students would learn at their own level (K-8) and at their self-determined rate of speed.

Everyone on staff was excited. We were advancing to a space-aged approach (the early '70s) to deliver education to inmates attending classes in the school. Inmates in lock-up status received tutoring one on one in their cells.

Our approach was novel to New Jersey and to everyone else. Dr. Ryan kept her contacts around the country advised about our progress. Eventually, over a hundred prison education departments—federal, state, and county—across the United States used our model to reshape educational services for inmates.

As in the past, whenever my life settled down, things would abruptly change. Everyone was aware Warden Yeager's health continued to deteriorate more quickly than we hoped it would. He soon left on extended sick leave. Before leaving, he made plans to promote me to the vacant director of Individual Treatment position created when my immediate supervisor retired. This was not the timing I would have chosen.

Being promoted to a new position and out of the Education Department just before the new building's grand opening was not in my game plan.

Preparing for the transition from the old-school system to a new one was richly rewarding. We had significantly enhanced New Jersey's prison education system, and I was looking forward to being part of its new innovative operation and its futuristic curriculum. However, the needs of the Trenton Prison came first before my own, and I reluctantly followed the warden's parting wishes.

I sadly understood it was likely we would soon have a new warden. Mr. Yeager had been my champion from the start. Of course, he took a little while to get over the incident when I nearly exposed the executioner's identity and almost caused a disastrous situation. He had always encouraged me. When he hired me, he told me, "I do hope you will decide to stay here with us."

I not only stayed, but I became totally absorbed in our new department, staff, students, and our groundbreaking contributions to education programs and systems in prisons throughout the United States. I would always be interested in the progress of our Prison Education Network. I looked forward to its future development in our state-of-the-art new school building.

*

Unhappily, as everyone expected, my friend and our warden, Howard Yeager, passed away. He was an inspiration to us all and he would be sorely missed, especially by me. RIP, Mr. Yeager.

I wondered now what my role as director of Individual Treatment would become when a new warden took over. There was much speculation as to who that would be.

**Sometimes you must set aside one dream
to pursue a new one.**

CHAPTER 8

Out of the Flames and into the Fire

View looking from the sally port into the Control Center

"...violence in prison is a function of its culture, the effectiveness of its management, and the political reality that excuses the mistreatment of prisoners..."

– Donald Specter

Currently, two major institutions – Rahway and Trenton – were operating without permanent leadership, and both were bubbling over with escalating daily violence. At Trenton, the acting chief deputy, Tom Driber, became interim warden.

I read that among the country's most stable maximum-security prisons, wardens devote time, almost daily, inside their prisons talking to both staff and inmates. Their discussions range from grievances and personal problems to answering all sorts of questions. Those wardens spend little time behind their desks. They don't rely on secondhand or thirdhand information about what's going on inside their facilities.

The Trenton Prison table of organization followed the traditional path upward through a conglomerate layer of security supervisors, starting with the correction officer until reaching the superintendent – if ever.

In August 1972, Bob Clifford, commissioner of the Department of Institutions and Agencies, ordered Division Director Al Wagner to appoint Bill Fauver, currently superintendent at the Annandale Youth Correctional Center, as Howard Yeager's replacement at Trenton.

Fauver's reputation as an administrator preceded him. Some said he had a low-key management style. Hopefully, he would bring much-needed stability to Trenton.

He reported for duty on Tuesday morning, September 5, 1972. My plan was to greet him at the prison's massive iron front door when he arrived. When the old brass doorbell rang, the front door officer, Harry Ibbs, a veteran of over 25 years, opened it to let in the new warden.

"Hey, Bill," I said, "I'm Bob Hatrak. Welcome to New Jersey's notorious heartbreak hotel!"

Fauver laughed and said, "Cut it out, Bob. That's no way to greet your new boss."

After escorting him to the warden's office and introducing him to his executive assistant, Evie Grover, I returned to my new office. I spent the rest of the day building a to-do action plan that would cover my first thirty days as the prison's newly appointed director of Individual Treatment. Of course, the plan was full of all my future projects that I was hoping to systematically activate.

*

The next day, not long after I arrived for work, Fauver appeared in my office doorway. "Good morning! Do you have a little time to talk to me?"

"Absolutely! But first, let me get you a hot cup of our world-famous prison breakfast blend."

"Okay, I'll take a cup, black."

"Thanks for the coffee, Bob. Let's move this down to the warden's conference room. We'll have more privacy there."

During a cordial discussion, the major subject was the rash of violence occurring here. I told Bill I read an article in the Asbury Park Press regarding the potential for continued violence at both Trenton and Rahway Prisons.

"Bill, I plan to read the report from the House of Representatives Committee on Crime, released in February. From what I understand, the select committee's report title is "American Prisons In Turmoil." The report includes New Jersey's prisons, and I'm eager to read what it said about us."

After a while, Bill asked me to accompany him on a walking tour of the prison. I didn't know what to make of his request. My immediate thought was that Acting Warden Tom Driber should be the one he talked to regarding the prison, especially about violence. However, it pleased me to be asked to accompany him.

We began by visiting six-wing, the infirmary, and the old death row, now vacant. While walking along on death row, Fauver said, "Director Wagner asked me to implement a contact visiting program for inmates. Is there an area we can use for this purpose?"

"That would not be an easy undertaking, Bill," I replied. "Every inch of space is being used to its most total capacity, except the spot where we are now standing. As you can see, death row is empty, and it is the only possibility. Because of its history, it's not a very welcoming place. But the inmate population would well receive contact visiting.

"Inmates often asked Warden Yeager to provide contact visits. He wanted to accommodate them but concluded a suitable space was unavailable.

"Current window visiting is not what the inmates want to continue. If we could replace the front house window visits with contact visiting someplace else, you could have some impact on the current tensions and ruthless environment here."

Fauver's answer was, "Let's work on it."

Continuing the tour, we headed to 1-left, the Administrative Segregation Unit. As we strolled along, inmates stopped us to ask questions, bitch, make requests, or just size up the new warden.

As director of Education, I spent a lot of time inside walking daily through the entire prison, attempting to develop a good rapport with my students and the general inmate population. Carrying a small spiral-bound notepad in my back pocket to make notes became a habit.

Typical comments made to me by inmates were:

"The Classification Department won't reply to my 'kites' (handwritten notes). All I want them to tell me is what my earliest parole hearing date is."

"My prison-issued shoes need replacement. Look at them. Can you help me get another pair?"

"Getting to the infirmary to see a doctor about refilling my meds is impossible."

"My teeth are rotting in my mouth, and I can't get to see a dentist."

I TOLD THE new warden, "A popular and effective captain, Jack Malkin, Sr., once told me it's the accumulation of minor issues, when left unattended, that lead to much of the unrest we experience here at Trenton."

"We have a few disruptive and influential inmate security threat groups fomenting unease. They make the staff tense and tyrannize vulnerable inmates."

Fauver asked, "What are security threat groups? And give me an example of one in existence here."

I thought there must not be threat group problems at the Annandale Youth Correctional Facility.

"Well, these informal groups include inmates involved in illicit activities such as rape, drug trafficking, retribution, stealing other inmates' personal property, burning inmates out of their cells and destroying their contents, strong-arming younger and weaker inmates, extortion, and intimidation. These activities helped separate and identify troublemakers from most of the inmate population over whom they wield consequential power.

"We have no sanctioned inmate social groups whose objectives would contrast from the covert factions. With no positive inmate organizations, there is no balance.

"By their very makeup, the security threat groups present a severe menace to the welfare of staff, other men, and to the steadiness of the prison itself."

Our tour ended in midafternoon, and by now I was starving. I suggested we go to the staff dining room where we could talk further over lunch. Bill shared some confidential information with me, explaining that his major charge upon being appointed warden was to reduce violence at the prison.

My thought was that it would be terrific if, at last, the notorious Trenton Prison came off the front pages of Trenton's two newspapers. I felt optimistic that he might have a different way of dealing with the strong-arm tactics customarily applied by our staff. There had to be a more effective method to control the outbursts we were experiencing here. Punishment invited retaliatory behavior and it was a vicious cycle.

*

I told him about an incident that occurred earlier this year:

One Saturday evening, my wife Joan, our daughter Sharon, and I were on our way to the 5 p.m. Mass. We turned left onto Cass Street and headed toward the prison. As we approached Third Street, we saw a line of ambulances parked with their lights flashing in front of the prison entrance door.

I remember thinking to myself, *here we go again, another weekend of violence at "the Wall"* (Trenton Prison's nickname).

I turned right onto Third and parked the car. Agreeing with Joan's comments, that the string of ambulances parked by the front door could only mean more trouble and that something terrible had happened again, I said, "Why don't you and Sharon go to Mass? I'll call you later when you get home to let you know what all this chaos is about, and if I'll be here again until Sunday."

Sprinting the rest of the block until I reached the first ambulance in line, I saw inmate Shultz on a stretcher, ready to be loaded into an ambulance. My God! My stomach lurched, realizing he had a thick, twelve-inch screwdriver sticking out of his neck, but still seemed to be alive.

Moving through the mayhem, I entered the prison and headed for the Control Center. Once there, the lieutenant told me what had happened. I groaned, "Theodore is at it again."

THEODORE GIBSON WAS a ruthless leader who controlled a large faction of the black population. His aggressive followers comprised our most pervasive inmate threat groups. Now, his soldiers summarily conducted a bloody attack on a Philadelphia mob boss, Anthony "Little Pussy" Russo, in the mess hall.

Gibson, John Henry Tillman (a stone-cold killer), and William Eutsey approached the table where Russo and seven associates were eating their evening meal. The attackers stabbed the men seated at the table without saying a word.

The reason for the attack on Russo and his cohorts was the inflated prices his mob was charging black inmates for drugs. Inmate clerks loyal to Russo stole most of these drugs from the prison pharmacy. White inmates paid far lower prices for the stolen drugs than did black inmates, and the black inmate population was not happy about it.

I said to Fauver, "This prison is full of angry inmates whose primary goals center on disruptive and violent activities."

Finally, I added, "I've witnessed the handiwork of at least one officer of the 'goon squad' operating in secret inside the prison. These squads administer retaliatory violence (to even a score) where the attacked becomes the attacker. This approach to prison control is counterproductive and contributes in part to the violence going on here."

We finished our quick lunch and headed off in separate directions.

*

I devoted myself to visiting with the department heads over the next few days, since they were now part of my extra responsibilities. Unfortunately, there was little interaction between departments because everyone functioned in their own small orbits. This had to change. My plan was to enlist their support to form a cohesive unit to prepare inmates for release.

THE FOLLOWING WEEK, on Monday morning, Helen Henry, my executive assistant, appeared in my office doorway to inform me that the boss wanted to see me as soon as possible. I of course headed straight to his office.

Bill stood to one side of the massive antique desk I had always admired when Mr. Yeager sat behind it. It seemed strange to see someone else standing there. He told me to have a seat. What he said next shocked me right down to my toes.

"I want to appoint you to a position that doesn't exist at this prison: assistant superintendent or deputy warden. What do you have to say about that?"

"Thank you very much. I'll gladly accept the position! After just rolling up my sleeves to begin my appointment as director of Individual Treatment, I never expected this. When do you want me to start?"

"Right now, he answered. "The first thing I'd like you to do is write your own job description. You seem to clearly understand the situation here and I'm curious to learn how you would approach our problems centered on violence."

"Bill, unless you tell me otherwise, I'm going to take the prison violence issue head-on. It has interested me, and I've been thinking about how to control it for a long time. Some ideas I've developed are ready to be implemented. My approach will include helping establish a straight-line relationship between you and the inmate population. Then, with your approval, I'll act as an intermediary to advance this line of communication to promote problem-solving. I've been planning to ask for approval to encourage the creation of several violence-control inmate social groups. If structured correctly, and with the guidance provided by a carefully developed group charter, they will go a long way in reducing the violence at this prison. As director of Education, I encouraged the theory to find a useful focus to help the men realize their full potential, assist them to get through their sentences, and then be successful upon release."

Fauver responded he planned to establish a close relationship with the Nation of Islam's inmate imam, Lester 2X Gilbert. "This move should reduce Black Power leader Theodore Gibson's influence on the black inmate population and establish equal recognition among all black inmates."

"Bill, I think good, respectful communication between staff and inmates is vitally important. Speaking in a calm and respectful tone, asking before ordering, and showing concern for an inmate's well-being are fundamental courtesies that can help anyone establish mutual respect."

"While assistant superintendent, I'll welcome, as I've been doing as director of Education, every opportunity to speak with an inmate in the presence of one or more correction officers. I intend to lead by example. I will instruct and expect staff to adopt my tone and manner when communicating with residents."

Developing the summary of my prospective role centered on the idea that spending a significant amount of my time inside the institution connecting with staff and inmates would best serve Bill Fauver. That would require spending full-time, 9 a.m. until 6 p.m. deep inside the bowels of the prison, observing operations, and solving problems, both large and small. This should happen before, not after, an inmate concluded he had to act out to get someone's attention. Besides interacting with staff and inmates, my daily routine needed to provide time to observe firsthand compliance or non-compliance with the institution's daily schedule. By the end of the week, I presented my job description to the warden for his approval.

His response to my plan of action didn't surprise me. "I think that's a great idea. I've operated somewhat the same way myself. Being attentive to small details, taking good notes, and being certain that reasonably swift remedial action will help make your efforts worthwhile." The warden added one more thing, obscurely, to my duties; I was to personally handle any important projects he thought necessary, even though he "didn't know yet what they would be, only that there will be some."

*

My first full day inside the prison as assistant superintendent went well, overall, even though staff and inmates alike didn't particularly understand, or welcome, my full-time presence inside. Some thought I was still the director of Education, and wondered why I wasn't upstairs in the school area. The director of Individual Treatment's office was in the front house, so why was I now on the inside?

Everyone was suspicious! Some men asked me, "What are you up to? Are you looking to harvest a truckload of snitches? How long are you going to continue this practice? Tell me, what wonderful things do you plan to do with the information you're writing in your little notebook? Will you be here on weekends? Do you plan to interview inmates? If I complain about something, and you write it down, will someone act? Will my kites (memos) to the senior classification officer now get answered?"

One notorious inmate leader, David "Guy" Baldwin, a Trenton native and local thug, sarcastically said, "What you're doing is such a load of bullshit! What do you think you're going to accomplish?"

My response was, "Guy, let's have this same conversation again six months from now."

"Okay, Hatrak, if you're still the assistant superintendent."

BALDWIN EARNED A reputation as an inmate leader because of his intelligence. He once served on the prison's Inmate Representative Committee and met with the state's governor. Baldwin was also a pathological liar. He was the only inmate I ever encountered who could defeat a polygraph examination.

He and six others escaped from a breakout-proof super-max facility, through an extension of the Trenton Prison known as the Vroom Building.

The *New York Times* ran a story, on September 22, 1972, chronicling David Guy Baldwin's well-executed escape titled "7 Convicts Flee Prison In Trenton". Baldwin, serving a life sentence for murder, and six other prisoners sawed through window bars and escaped from the Vroom Building on the grounds of Trenton Psychiatric Hospital, about three miles from Rahway Prison.

*

The months flew by, and I learned to be a good listener instead of a good talker. Repeating what the communicator said before responding helped establish that I was listening to what an inmate was saying.

The prison department heads, and security staff, were skeptical of what I was doing at first. It seemed obvious to some, less so to others, that I was on a witch hunt for the new warden. It didn't take long for their skepticism to turn into frustration. When none of their expectations materialized, here they were, being asked to resolve inmate problems that, in the past, they had ignored.

Many correction officers, and their supervisors, were doing a poor job supervising inmate-cleaning details and inmate housing unit porters. The prison was a pigsty. I had to be careful assigning cleaning projects because expecting a prison built over a century ago to look brand new would be an unrealistic anticipation.

The correction officer's union president, Leroy Jackson, a powerful influence and a prominent union leader, adopted a wait-and-see attitude. My mission soon became apparent to everyone. Once staff and inmates saw their problems resolved, they felt comfortable talking to me. Most recognized my priority was solving issues and not finding someone, or a lot of someone's, to hang out to dry.

My executive assistant, undoubtedly overwhelmed, did a masterful job keeping pace and researching each issue I had listed in the many spiral notebooks I filled. Thank you, Helen.

THAT FIRST WEEK was a whirlwind. On Friday night, as I headed home dead tired, my head was full of everything that happened and what I had learned during the handful of days I'd spent as assistant superintendent. My mind then drifted to what should happen next, which exhausted me even more. Although the issues brought to my attention in the following weeks seemed to be growing exponentially, I enjoyed that every day was different and the freedom of not being tied down sitting behind a desk shuffling paper. Meanwhile, the prison was becoming noticeably more stable.

*

In February 1973, all hell broke loose at the prison, and our violence reduction plan suffered its first significant setback. On that fateful day, I nearly lost my life in a two-alarm fire set by one of the black Muslim groups.

There were two different Muslim groups with ongoing turmoil at Trenton Prison. One was the Nation of Islam, with inmate Lester 2X Gilbert as their minister, preaching violence as the means to achieve his sect's objectives. The other was the New World of Islam, led by inmate Albert Dickens, who was fanning the flames of growing resentment. Dickens was fuming because Warden Fauver gave Gilbert an office and use of the entire old school area, so he believed Gilbert was being elevated to a status above any other inmate.

IN THE EARLY afternoon several inmates, armed with matches and a flammable substance, walked down the balcony leading to the school area toward Minister Gilbert's office. The office, once a storeroom, was at the very far end of the balcony. Once there, they started a fire in the office that had the potential to kill him and anyone else nearby. The fire was clearly arson. New World of Islam inmates were, allegedly, the cause. But we could never prove it.

Fauver's strategy to control prison violence was to buy peace with the Nation of Islam. It obviously didn't work. A match was being struck that ignited a fire, both literally and figuratively, as the warden and I took a well-earned lunch break in the officer's dining room just a short distance away. While devouring our piping-hot bowl of freshly made chicken soup, we suddenly smelled the sharp, pungent odor of smoke and knew there was a fire somewhere!

The warden and I hurried to the far end of the balcony. Before we even got close enough, we could see the black smoke. When we reached Lester's office, we saw the ancient walls ablaze. Flames were streaming over the many layers of thick lead paint accumulated there since this section, in the "Fortress Penitentiary," had been built in 1897. Looking over the open balcony revealed the downstairs hallway was also becoming smoke-filled. The smoke cut off the 6-wing housing unit, the infirmary, and Center Control. Residents and staff in those areas were being evacuated to the recreation yard.

Upstairs, the heavy smoke was billowing everywhere, concealing several Muslim "brothers" clustered at the far end of the room banging frantically on a window, attempting to break out a pane of glass.

One of them desperately used a paper stapler unsuccessfully as a hammer, while two others were frantically using their fists to break the glass to get some air. Loud, crackling flames almost drowned out their cries for help. There was far too much smoke to make out who they were. We didn't know at the time that inmate leaders speculated that the two Muslim groups would soon square off, and this would be just the beginning.

ONCE I SAW how serious the fire was, I told the warden that we needed help, fast. I suddenly realized that Fauver, being new to this facility, didn't know the physical layout of the prison as well as I did. My instincts kicked in, and I called out to him, "I'm going down to the Control Center to call the fire department! I'll tell everyone that fire trucks are not to be directed to the receiving gate per the normal procedure. Be careful while I'm gone!"

The receiving gate was located about one-half of a city block away from the Third Street front entrance, which then required winding through the length of the institution and was too far away from the upstairs balcony to get help up there in time. The quickest and most direct route to the fire was entering straight in through the Third Street front door! This seemingly reckless move would open the prison up to the outside world and render our security useless, and even though I knew it was the right call, all I could think was, God, help us.

Once down the set of concrete stairs, gasping, half running and half sliding through the billowing smoke, I reached the Control Center and told the lieutenant in charge of the area, "Don't send the fire trucks to the receiving gate! Instead, post an armed sergeant on Third Street opposite the front door. Instruct him to stop the fire trucks there! He is to direct the firefighters with their equipment to go to the front house sally port. The officer there is to open both grille gates simultaneously to permit easy access to Center. Have someone in Center ready to immediately direct firefighters up to the balcony."

Permitting firefighters entry through the front door would create an unprecedented high-security risk. However, I knew in my gut that we needed to bite the bullet and take that chance to save the lives of those trapped on the balcony and those about to be cut off on the lower level. Security must now be redirected and focused on the front house.

My assumption that the fire trucks carrying firefighters with firefighting equipment would be automatically sent to the receiving gate proved accurate, with the control center lieutenant planning to send them there just as the standard procedure required. Prison policy mandates that trucks enter the prison through the receiving gate one-third of the way down Third Street to be inspected, and its occupants identified and searched. Then, each truck would require a "truck walker" before entering the prison yard. There was no time for any of that this time.

The incredulous expression on the lieutenant's face was certainly justified. Knowing that until recently I was the director of Education and had nothing to do with security, I too would have wondered at my audacity to give him orders and why he should take instructions from me…. Here I was, a "civilian rookie," telling a senior lieutenant to do something that, in the prison's entire history, had never been done before.

Shouting over the confusion, I told him, "I understand we will break a lot of security policies and procedures, and I'll take responsibility for that. DO IT NOW!" I could see he was thinking…. It was beyond belief that every door from Center to Third Street would simultaneously remain open. This exposed the entire institution to the outside world and presented unbelievable opportunities for a mass escape right out the front door. No wonder this poor guy thought I was nuts. The lieutenant balked justifiably at my instructions. He knew this meant violating long-standing security procedures and he didn't want to be the one to do it. "Listen, if we don't do it this way, people will die! The flames and smoke already have men cornered and pinned down in the old school area."

Reluctantly, he ordered, over the PA, "All doors are to be opened from the Control Center to Third Street immediately." The lieutenant stared at me wide-eyed, and the officer standing nearby turned to face him, shocked by his announcement. Thankfully, the fire truck drivers got my message and parked their vehicles on Third Street opposite the front door and Tower 1. There was no need to have them searched. After all, if you show up with a fire truck, your identity should be apparent.

City police cars barricaded Third Street at both ends. The result was an open tunnel from the prison's secure area to the city street. I thought to myself, Holy cow, I'm in trouble now, big time! My mind kept racing. If smoke from the fire found its way into the inmate housing units, another more severe issue would emerge. Housing unit evacuations would be necessary because, obviously, those guys couldn't get out on their own. It was good to learn that our evacuation plan was already in place and ready to activate, thanks to Lieutenant Tom Stone.

A tall, commanding, and gray-haired captain named Alexander "Ike" Abbott (affectionally called "Machine Gun Abbott" by fellow officers) arrived on the scene. Quickly assessing the situation, Ike took command and efficiently formed two parallel lines of correction officers. Each man was handed an automatic weapon as they took their place in line. Starting inside at the Center Control, and stretching forward through the front house, out the only door, and down the four granite steps all the way out onto Third Street, they were armed with every automatic weapon available in the armory. Ike was rapidly barking orders to the officers, standing at attention in straight lines. Then, finally, he shouted, "No one escapes. Don't shoot unless I give the order to fire." There wasn't any doubt that Ike meant business.

Following me down off the balcony, Warden Fauver went to the Control Center. The first thing he did was call Director Wagner to brief him. I went back and stood at the bottom of the stairwell leading up to the balcony and directed the chaotic traffic to and from six-wing. From that vantage point, I heard a cry for help. Oh no. Now "someone" had to go back up again, into the inferno, to locate the frightened voice. Some firefighters were still on the balcony, but I didn't know where. The mounting fear in the voice drifting down out of the smoke left me no choice but to take a deep breath and retrace my steps back upstairs. Clinging to the iron handrail, shakily I started back up, utterly terrified.

At the top of the stairs, there was no visibility as I felt my way along the hot, textured wall until I reached the inferno. Walls were ablaze and everything was filled with heavy black smoke. It was difficult to see even my own hand in front of my face. The intense heat and stinging smoke made it difficult to breathe. My eyes were burning and streaming tears, and by now I was panting deeply, struggling to get enough air. At that moment I thought to myself, Hatch you're a dead man. The loud crackling sounds of the fire and the thickening black smoke made it impossible to locate the disembodied shout from nearby. The call for help took on a new urgency and became a series of frantic screams.

Not able to see him, I followed the voice through the acrid smoke and bumped into a doubled-over figure. Grabbing the man's shirt, it was then I realized in the heavy smoke I had completely lost my sense of direction. Which way was out? I dared not let go of the inmate because we might not find him again. I was sweating and coughing so hard that it felt like I wasn't much help to either of us. We moved slowly, unsure of the right direction while holding tightly onto each other and trying to avoid the flaming walls caving in on us. It was a tremendous relief when a firefighter grabbed my free arm and shouted, "We need to bail out, brother. Let's get going. Quick, grab my belt."

Gratefully, I stumbled along behind him, holding on for dear life, pulling the staggering man along with me. The firefighter led us, coughing and choking, to safety while telling us calmly the entire way, "Everything's going to be okay." I can't remember ever being so grateful. Some hero I was! My attempt to be a rescuer had become a life-threatening situation, and I, too, needed to be rescued. However, I was too grateful to be safe than to be embarrassed. A prison nurse examined and treated everyone for smoke inhalation in our prison infirmary. She didn't send anyone to an outside hospital, which indicated the inmate I pulled out with me was okay. We took good care of our own.

Once the incident was under control, Director Wagner arrived from Central office and demanded in a thunderous voice, "Who's the one who ordered all the security doors opened at the same time?" Holding my breath, I thought, Well, I survived the fire, and now I'm going to get fired. I replied, "It was me, sir." He looked at me long and hard. I couldn't read his expression, and he said nothing more. He didn't fire me. At that moment, an "atta boy" sure would have been nice....

*

The next morning the Trentonian had a front-page picture showing the cavernous tunnel stretching from Third Street to Center. I reassured myself, "No big deal, nobody escaped, and nobody died. Whew!" Either possibility would have been a disaster.

As I continued to make my daily "Walkin' and Talkin'" tours of the prison, my reception by the inmates and staff improved. Even correction officers, especially housing unit officers, specifically the segregation unit, told me how my presence in the institution took pressure away from them. Satisfied inmates whose minor issues are being resolved are less likely to pressure their housing unit officers or act out in frustration.

VIOLENCE WAS ON a downward swing and everything seemed to be going very well. I was handling special projects for Fauver that significantly reduced the amount of violence occurring in the prison. Things were going so well that shortly after

Thanksgiving, the boss cut way down on his prison tours, leaving them to me. Of course, I accepted that as a compliment.

I asked the skeptical senior classification officer to do a minor research project. "George, please look at the number of charges (disciplinary reports) written by correction officers since Warden Fauver arrived. I'll need the date, the inmate's name, the rule infraction, the disposition, and the penalty. Then do the same for the previous six months. Let's see what we find."

I was very pleased after reading his report. Inmate-on-inmate fights and assaults decreased by over 50 percent. There were no inmate assaults on officers, no suicides, no sexual offenses, no robberies of inmate property, and only three verbal assaults on staff! I wondered if this was just a coincidence or if Trenton Prison was actually a safer place to live and work now. And so, in part, my violence control plan was working. In addition, inmates now had a straight-line relationship with the warden directly through me.

Part two of my plan involved the use of inmate social groups to help reduce prison violence further. That plan finally began when we created Ayuda. This means "help" in Spanish. I allowed Ayuda to hold "rap sessions" with selected community members and inmate groups every Saturday morning. They helped Spanish inmates prepare for release and resume their position in their communities and their place in their families.

As inmate problems were resolved and new procedures began taking hold, my daily tours required less of my time. I found I had time to start the special projects added to my job description. When I told the warden this news, he asked me to first explore using the abandoned death row as a space for contact visiting. My first instinct was to reject the idea. It was a cold, sterile, small, and depressing area. It would take a significant transformation to accomplish this miracle, but I said instead, "Okay, boss, I'll check it out." He told me again, "Director Wagner had mentioned that area to him and suggested seeking you out because you would have some good ideas." He was sure it would please the director if we made that happen. I got the message. "Tomorrow, I'll tour the cell house with the maintenance manager, LeRoy Jackson (correction officer union president), Captain Tom Stone (the policies and procedures developer), and "Doc" Goss (chairperson of the Inmate Committee).

The next day, we assembled, and everyone took part in a discussion regarding the options for success. The tour of the cellblock itself took on a positive tone. Everyone sensed how important the success of this project was to everyone—from Director Wagner at the top, all the way through the institution, and to the residents, who would be extremely pleased to have contact visits with family and friends at last. Following the inspection, we adjourned to the warden's conference room. The discussion narrowed down the obstacles for renovating the space to accommodate inmates and their visitors, while still providing maximum visibility of the residents and their visitors by the supervising officers. When I reported our progress to Bill Fauver, I was told I had carte blanch to make it happen. Yes, sir!

Renovating the area required two correction officers with construction skills and the ability to get along well with inmates. I selected correction officers Frank Mitrosky and Jack Malkin to supervise. Both had civilian experience in construction work, and each had a good rapport with inmates. That seemed like a good place to start. The two inmates I selected to help us with the project were James Faison and Alan Gailes, with whom I had a good relationship. Both were burly, extremely strong, and more than willing to help. The four-man team didn't disappoint me. There were times I found the officers with their shirts off swinging sledgehammers or helping however possible.

Next, we needed policies and procedures to guide the operation of the new visit program. Captain Tom Stone, responsible for maintaining and training all policies and procedures, finished the job in less than a week. His finished product was outstanding. Everything was now in "go" mode. Contact visiting began without a hitch. The staff seemed satisfied, and the residents were ecstatic to have this program at last. After a long time, Trenton State Prison received positive publicity, a big difference from the days spent reading about inmate violence.

*

On December 6, 1972, the New York Times published a story about the conversion of the old death house to a contact visiting area. I was disappointed that the officers and inmates who had made it all happen didn't even get a slight mention in the story. The work they did should have received significant recognition. Captain Stone didn't receive any praise either. This group of people, working together, pulled off what I called "mission impossible, made possible."

I didn't take part in the December 9, 1972, opening program, because I was busy driving Joan to Saint Francis Hospital to joyfully welcome our long-awaited nine-pound son, Robby, a wonderful baby boy! It was overwhelming to have this perfect little guy join our family. We were very proud.

I FOUND IT amusing that the political types seemed to always line up, seeking the press's attention. Unfortunately, I observed this phenomenon often throughout my entire career. My policy was to remain in the background and place staff and inmates and their accomplishments in the foreground. This type of acknowledgment could boost an employee's career or speed up an inmate's parole release.

We made certain that the efforts of those who made "mission impossible" possible received their well-deserved acknowledgment within the institution. Each inmate's classification folder included a lengthy report for use by the Parole Board, and we passed out cartons of cigarettes to say thank you. In addition, employees had letters of appreciation and recognition filed in their personnel folders.

Our next project was to renovate the old license plate shop ("The Tag Shop"), which provided the perfect space to use as a Self-Rehab Enterprise Group – a vocational training area, long nonexistent, that was so desperately needed. Once again, the same team that renovated the old death house once more produced a minor miracle. These improvements provided three vocational training work areas, each with separate classrooms. There had been no vocational training in the past, and this visibly helped boost the morale of the inmates who eagerly took part.

My most effective project involved moving the vulnerable pharmacy and its civilian staff to the second floor in the secure front house, where the classification department staff worked. Inmate clerks were having a good time stealing controlled medication from the prison pharmacy located inside the prison proper and selling them to other inmates. They developed an inmate-controlled "black market" inside the institution right under our noses. When inmate presence and involvement were eliminated inside the newly located prison pharmacy, the black market, and the problems that went with it, quickly disappeared.

We were gradually decreasing violence at the Trenton State Prison. There is no doubt about our accomplishments. Daily life for residents and staff was now much safer.

The inmate population honored Fauver and me during a special assembly they prepared and paid for themselves. We each received a plaque recognizing our individual efforts. I was especially pleased and honored to be part of the plaque presentation ceremony arranged by the Inmate Committee.

Tara Jay Frank once wrote:

"People don't get promoted for doing their jobs well. They get promoted by demonstrating their potential to do more."

CHAPTER 9

Under the Dome

The dome over Rahway State Prison

"No one ever steps in the same river twice,
for it's not the same river and he's not the same man."

– Heraclitus

On Friday, April 26, 1973, The Daily Register (Red Bank, New Jersey) announced Bill Fauver's appointment as New Jersey's director of the Division of Corrections and Parole. The newspaper stated about Fauver: "The man credited with easing tensions at the Trenton State Prison became the next chief of the state prison system."

Two months later, on Friday, June 22, 1973, a warm and humid June midafternoon, I was in the prison storeroom when the telephone rang. It was Rose, the switchboard operator.

"Bob, I have Mr. Fauver on the line. I'll transfer the call to you."

"Hey. Bill, how's my favorite director on this muggy afternoon?"

"Okay, don't be a smartass! I'm calling to tell you the Civil Service Administration has at last approved Sam's [Vukcevich's] request for disability retirement. So, he is no longer Rahway's superintendent. Thus, the reason for my call. I want to appoint you to fill his vacant position!"

"Wow, I'm speechless! How long have you been kicking this idea around?"

"Wouldn't you like to know!"

Fauver continued the conversation.

"Don Thoms (Rahway's acting superintendent) has more on his plate than he can say grace over. He's worn out and never wanted the superintendent's position. His current plans are to retire as soon as possible and look for a house down the shore [any New Jersey beach]."

"I want to get you up there ASAP! Talk it over with Joan and take a little time—just a little, however—to think it over. Then, tell Joan to call Ilena [Bill's wife] to speak with her about what life is like for the wife of a prison superintendent."

I tapped the phone cradle button several times until Rose picked up.

"Rose, will you get Joan on the phone for me, please?"

"Hi, honey. I just got off the phone with Bill. You won't believe this."

Hanging up, I thought I would need to decide soon: change jobs or stay in place. I also realized I would be Rahway's third superintendent in less than two years if I took the job.

*

Sam Vukcevich replaced Superintendent Warren Pinto, and in his sixteenth month in office, his career ended when Rahway exploded into a major riot. It occurred two months following New York's Attica State Prison uprising. Both riots captured the full attention of the national media.

The job was no dream job. How long could I last?

Thinking about my tour of Rahway Prison with Warden Yeager after the rebellion, I recalled seeing the destruction of property and the cell in four-wing where several inmates concealed the superintendent while the riot raged.

I grimaced as I remembered cautiously picking our way through the rubble and destruction of state property. Then, finally, we reached the abandoned cell where inmates held Sam hostage. Then empty, except for open, discarded cigarette packs, food wrappers, soda cans, remnants of bloody rags, and the improvised implements used on Warden Vukcevich to stop the profuse bleeding and stitch up his wounds. The inmate who performed this "on-the-spot surgery" saved Sam's life. As a result, the governor commuted his sentence and sent him home.

I remembered the feeling of disgust for the brutality that had occurred there and the apprehension for Trenton and Rahway's future I had felt. It was undoubtedly an emotional and gut-wrenching experience to look back on, much like a movie documenting the horrible remnants of a war scene.

A voice in my mind reminded me of the promise I made to myself: "What I'm seeing would never happen at a prison where I was the warden—not on my watch!"

Before accepting the assistant warden's position at Trenton one year ago, I attempted to learn everything I could about the history of the Trenton Prison. Knowing full well I knew very little of Rahway's background before the 1971 riot, I returned to the state library, as before, to pour through the archives. This time to research Rahway's history.

I FOUND HUNDREDS of news stories at the state library describing the preceding three decades of the 1950s, 1960s, and 1970s. I found articles that dramatically documented the violent history and instability I would inherit if Joan and I accepted the challenges Rahway Prison would present.

One last thing left to do before we made a final decision was to learn of the changes made at Rahway since the 1971 riot and the action taken to resolve the inmate riot demands. Also, I needed to know what was happening before and if we accepted the transfer. Again, I visited the Division's public information officer, Jim Stabile, at the Central office to sort through the press clippings he had on file within the time frame I was seeking information. It was the same due diligence I had done before I began working at Trenton.

I expected to find significant improvements inside the vast twenty-one-acre blockade. Instead, I learned that violent conditions and tensions persisted at the same or even worse levels now, two years later, under the massive and deteriorating copper dome.

And so, in 1973, as I was weighing my options about a transfer to Rahway, I understood that currently this prison differed from the one I had visited with Warden Yeager following the 1971 riot, and that I, too, was now a different man. I had experienced and learned many important lessons, having seen more than my share of violence at the Trenton State Prison. Also, I had gained confidence while successfully producing and implementing several important projects as the director of Education.

As the assistant superintendent at Trenton, I developed some intestinal fortitude and the positive philosophy that the bigger the problem, the more opportunity to improve. I wasn't in a hurry to move to the next level. I had only logged seven years at the Trenton Prison, and I was still in my mid-thirties.

Amid dozens of press clippings referencing the facility and its significant incidents, there was only a brief mention of the daily inmate-on-inmate assaults, murder, inmate-on-officer assaults, rapes, or suicides. So, why wasn't the press learning about Rahway's inmate threat groups, and why wasn't Rahway's present situation brought to the public's attention?

Assembling the news clips in chronological order, I soon realized there wasn't anything reported in them I couldn't handle. For most of the situations, I had already dealt with and resolved them at Trenton, including the daily violence.

The Daily Journal reported on the April 1952 Rahway Riot titled "Eleven Convict Leaders At Rahway Riot Switched To Trenton Revolt Ends". It talked about how the Rahway Riot was started by five prisoners who had been transferred from Trenton State Prison, where they had been ringleaders of previous riots. They also reported that there were initially nine correction officers taken as hostages. There were thousands of dollars in estimated damages. As a result, eleven convicts were then sent to Trenton State Prison. A lack of a segregation unit at Rahway was cited as the reason for the transfer.

In January of 1961, *The Courier-News* ran an article about three guards who had sustained injuries during a 90-minute disturbance in the Rahway mess hall, where 150 inmates were throwing dishes and metal food trays at each other. A "launched" metal food tray can cause serious damage. After the event, Rahway's warden, Warren Pinto, asked Dr. Lloyd McCorkle, the director of the Division of Corrections and Parole, for aid by sending the goon squad from Trenton to Rahway.

I thought about the quote that speculated, "No one ever walks in the same river twice because it constantly changes." Acknowledging that I too have changed, I wondered what future issues would have to be grappled with, for whoever took the job, during their first year as superintendent and how things would get prioritized.

Goon squads needed to comply with prison policies and procedures. Sometimes they did not.

Later, after the men quieted down, McCorkle ordered twenty-two men removed from their cells, describing them as ringleaders. Later, they were transferred to Trenton. But I'm aware there is yet another, more detailed version of this event never reported to the press.

*

Ten years later, during breakfast in the Trenton Prison officers' dining room, several old-timers, over a second cup of coffee, told me about their firsthand account regarding the transpired events of January 6, 1961. While sitting with the group of correction officers who had been present in 1961 and who took part in that incident told me, that McCorkle wanted to send Rahway's inmates a message. So, he sent Rahway correction officers to each wing to round up Rahway troublemakers and escort them to the Tie-To. Once there, the officers told them to strip naked and line up.

Meanwhile, he ordered the Trenton officers he had brought with him to assemble in two parallel lines and wait in the rotunda while carrying their batons. McCorkle ordered the first inmate in line to enter the rotunda. Once there, he told him to run through the gauntlet of Trenton's goon squad as fast as possible to the opposite end of the rotunda. While inmates raced past, officers beat them from both sides with their batons. No body part was spared; they hit them everywhere. Gauntlets during this administration were not infrequent.

In the '60s, physical punishment was still the primary method used to establish prison control. In the late '60s, a high-ranking corrections supervisor proudly shared with me another story of physical punishment used to extract information from an inmate. They took an inmate who refused to provide information they wanted behind the Control Center, out of plain view. First, they instructed the inmate to strip naked and told him to get down on all fours and do push-ups. Then, holding a long baton, the supervisor flailed it beneath the inmate's private parts as the inmate neared the floor. It wasn't long before the supervisor got the information he sought. Once again, punishment was used without mercy as the means to establish control.

The New York Times reported on the 24-hour rebellion at Rahway that took place on November 25, 1971, in the article "Guarantee By Cahill Ends Rahway Prison Uprising". The convicts took Warden Vukcevich and nine guards' hostage. They set fires, broke windows and displayed bedsheets with the words written on them, "Remember Attica". The Governor, wanting to avoid loss of lives, like those (43) in the September riot at Attica, negotiated the release of the hostages, received a list of grievances from the prisoners and agreed to negotiations with no reprisals once they gave back control of the prison. The warden suffered head and back injuries and a few guards had some minor injuries. Immediately following the disturbance, forty-three inmates were relocated. Two, who were hardened criminals and had taken a leadership role in the instance, led a future riot at the Yardville Youth Correctional Center where they were transferred.

The *New York Times* did a follow-up story 2 days later stating that seven of the inmates involved were transferred to the Trenton Psychiatric Hospital because it was the closest maximum-security unit available. Two of the inmates had been able to break out of their cells at Rahway due to a faulty locking mechanism. Governor Cahill had quickly brought together a panel to look into the grievances submitted by the prisoners. They reported that about 500 inmates took part in the rebellion. There was a group of 5 prisoners formed to meet with the state's panel. The grievances included, inadequate food, poor medical care, high prices in the commissary, racism abuse by guards, a lack of vocational training and high prices in the commissary. The prisoners said that they had been unable to bring about changes in the system in any other way. They told the panel that all they wanted was to be treated as human beings.

Following the riot, the newspapers were full of stories about the aftermath. Most were negative.

On December 12, 1971, *The Record* in Hackensack, New Jersey ran an article titled "Wall of Silence Shields Truth About Rahway."

During the ongoing investigation of the riot, the prison grounds were closed to visitors while speculations about the causes circulated to include jail-brewed liquor (hootch), a Dear John letter to a convict, and parole frustrations. The Rahway inmates filed civil complaints about the prison being understaffed with filthy conditions and unusual punishment. The article stated that the Rahway annual budget was $1.7 million, with $1.3 million for care and treatment with $220 thousand for administration.

There were many more news stories to read about the 1971 riot: too many to list. My hunch is most of the stories had the same facts based on the author's interpretation of the information.

I read articles in papers about the prison in 1972 that included one about a correctional officer who had been assaulted with a trash can and received eight stitches in the head. Another was about someone shooting at the warden who was recuperating from his injuries from the Thanksgiving Day riot. There was also one that detailed an escape at Yardville by ringleaders (Inmates Hollinger and Ravenel) of the Rahway riot. Inmate Ravenel had also been accused of assault and battery on a correction officer and had allegedly made plans to kill the Warden if the state stormed the prison.

Ravenel once threatened me with bodily harm. I was Trenton's director of Education when I first met Ravenel. I thought of him as a psychotic sociopath with an extremely violent streak.

One of my least favorite daily duties was sitting as a voting member of the "Court Line," which served as the prison's disciplinary hearing board. One day Ravenel appeared before us to defend himself against a disciplinary report written by an officer, who described a very violent physical assault Ravenel perpetrated on a young inmate. Before the hearing began, Ravenel turned to me and said: "Hatrak, what in the f **k are you doing here? Your job is to educate convicts and not be part of disciplining them. Mother fuc**r, you better get out of here before someone hurts you!"

It was the first and only time an inmate threatened me. And worse yet, one who could make it happen.

The stories about the riot and existing conditions, such as further inmate disturbances, murders, suicides, escapes, at Rahway continued into 1973. The famous boxer, Ruben "Hurricane" Carter, who was an inmate at the time of the Thanksgiving Day riot wrote about the terrible changes that Warden Vukcevich brought to Rahway that in his opinion sparked the riot, in his book The Sixteenth Round.

EVEN BEFORE I finished reading the clips, I knew it was time to decide. Having gathered and studied a massive collection of information, I felt fully informed. I was confident in myself, and knew, in my heart, that I could do it. I had both the vision and the plan to meet the challenge of creating hope and order.

My plan was modeled after the successful one I had developed and implemented at Trenton, so I knew it would work again at Rahway. I intended to significantly reduce violence with my "do-it-yourself rehabilitation" programs, using inmate groups. These groups were intended to replace and redirect the inmate threat groups I had inherited.

There were many lengthy discussions between Joan and me over the following days. Finally, on Sunday evening, we sat before dinner with a glass of wine and weighed the pros and cons of us transferring to Rahway. My head was full of the many improvements and potential stability I was sure I could bring to the institution, and the more we talked, the more my enthusiasm grew.

Joan had strong objections to the move and felt this dramatic life change would negatively affect our family and could threaten our safety and serenity. After much deliberation, she surprised me by saying: "Your confidence and vision for change at Rahway is so strong it has become tangible! I don't like it, but I really believe you can make a difference and carry out all of what you are imagining. You know I would prefer not to do this. After all, I married a not-so-humble teacher/coach. I never dreamed we would raise our children on a fifty-two-acre maximum-security prison campus!"

She jokingly added, "But, if someone were to escape, they would hopefully not head for the warden's residence. Instead, if they are smart, they would take off in the opposite direction!

"But I know how capable you are, and, listening to your plans, I can feel your confidence. Sooooo, I believe you deserve the chance to present your ideology to resolve the prison's problems.

"I know you will do everything you can to keep us all safe, so against my better judgment, I will support whichever choice you make. Although I've known from the very start what your choice will be. Congratulations, Superintendent Hatrak!"

*

Rahway's needs were almost insurmountable; any change would be an improvement. My confidence came from our success at Trenton and the reality that I already had a successfully tested plan to turn things around and reduce the violence at Rahway.

Still feeling sure about my decision, the following day I called Fauver and told him, "If you want me, you got me! I will take the job. Thanks for the opportunity."

Once I decided, I began developing my goals. There were fourteen. Here they are, outlined below:

1. Immediate implementation of my unique "hands-off policy." ("You don't touch us, and we don't touch you.")
2. Chokeholds are forbidden.
3. Reduce the daily violence and prevent a repeat of the 1971 inmate riot.

4. Develop and publish a code of conduct for inmates, so everyone knows what to expect.
5. Revise the table of organizations to include two new violence control management units.
6. Control and expand the inmate furlough program.
7. Implement the maximum-security prison violence control methods I developed and tested when Trenton's acting assistant superintendent.
8. Review and remedy any unresolved 1971 inmate riot demands.
9. Reduce current runaway overtime expenditures by implementing a revised correction officer scheduling system to the greatest extent possible.
10. Revise and control the procedures on the use of inmate classification folders containing confidential inmate information.
11. Create an inmate locater system, making basic classification information available to staff in real time. (Updated daily.)
12. Enhance and expand the academic and vocational training opportunities and other programs and services offered to inmates. The goal was to have more square footage devoted to these programs than was designated to the existing square footage of all cells.
13. Determine the feasibility of using boxing, and the sport's related trades, as a legitimate vocational training program supported by the State Department of Education and the State's boxing commissioner.
14. Find meaningful work for inmates serving life or life equivalent sentences.

When I discussed these goals with Fauver, he said they were proper, "but maybe a bit too ambitious." I thanked him and asked, "When do I start?"

Bill said, "I'll be in touch with you soon, Bob, and thanks for helping me out."

ON A THURSDAY, October 18, 1973, Dr. Maurice Kott, acting commissioner of the Department of Institutions and Agencies, asked the Prison Board of Trustees to approve Fauver's choice of me as Rahway's third superintendent in less than two and a half years. The board voted unanimously to approve Dr. Kott's request.

First, I called Joan. Next, I called Mom. Pop had already died. Had he still been around, he would have been prouder than all of us. He was always my number one fan.

During the rest of October, I reviewed the goals I had set, and developed a first thirty-day tactical action plan. I knew that in New Jersey, the Patrolman's Benevolent Association (PBA), Local 105, is the correction officers' union and wields much political power. At Rahway, I would have one of the union's most powerful leaders, Correction Officer Frank Genesi, to contend with; and contentious is precisely what he turned out to be.

Once we got the violence under control and improved the facility's climate and environment, I could turn to inmate programming. But, again, I was still determined that inmate violence control/community groups would play the most significant role in this endeavor.

I felt ready "to get going" when I reported for my first day as superintendent on Monday, November 5, 1973.

The only thing I needed now was the tenacity to do it all.

CHAPTER 10

Forging a Path Never Taken

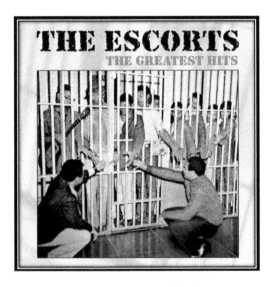

The Escorts: Rahway State Prison's first self-rehab enterprise group

"America is the land of the second chance, and when the gates of the prison open, the path ahead should lead to a better life."

– President George W. Bush

On Monday morning, November 5, 1973, I woke up early to prepare for the seventy-five-minute drive to Rahway Prison for my first day there as warden. Planning to leave home at 7 a.m., I felt unsure about the ability of "Molly," our red Ford Mustang, to make the daily round-trips to North Jersey.

At nearly 8:45 a.m., I approached the sharp curve in the road on Avenel Avenue, just as the prison came into view. Here it was again, the old and stately copper dome that would become so familiar to me.

Pulling into the parking lot, I said a silent prayer. I asked the Lord to help me be faithful to my new mission. I suddenly felt the weight of the responsibility I had sworn to assure for the life, health, and safety of 1,500 inmates and 600 staff in a warlike setting that most will never experience.

Walking across the parking lot, I was thinking that here in New Jersey, the Patrolmen's Benevolent Association (PBA), Local #105, is the correction officer union at Rahway and wields much political power. I knew I had to form a peaceful working relationship with Frank Genisi. He was one of the union's most powerful leaders I would have to contend with—and contentious is precisely what he turned out to be.

When I reached the entrance, Myrna Horner, my new executive assistant, greeted me and handed me the key to my new office door. I looked around and then sat down at the desk, planning to wade through the mountain of mail covering the desktop. After a brief time, retired Warden Sam Vukcevich, now recovered, buoyantly entered the office. He graciously offered to show me around and asked, "Are you ready to tour the prison?"

I really wanted a cup of coffee after my long drive, but I said, "You bet, Sam, let's get going!"

WE FIRST STOPPED at the drill hall (indoor recreation area). Upon entering the room, I spotted Rubin "Hurricane" Carter. He was now serving his time at Rahway. I remembered Rubin and the dark cloud surrounding him at the Trenton Prison years ago.

In the movie The Hurricane depicting Carter's life of crime, his character (portrayed by Denzel Washington) wasn't the same Rubin I had known a long time ago at Trenton.

The movie was presented as a factual representation; however, many scenes were fictional and seemed to portray an elastic understanding of the events. I know better because I was there too.

Once in the drill hall, I turned to face him and called, "Hey there, Rubin."

He turned his back to us. His behavior surprised me because previously we had a distant, yet civil, awareness of each other. Typically, he would have exchanged my hello with his usual monosyllabic grunt in passing.

Continuing the tour, I was aware that both staff and inmates were avoiding us. Why? I don't remember anyone saying hello or good morning. It seemed very odd. Even the inmates I recognized from Trenton ignored us, making me very uneasy. Why were they not approaching us?

I soon figured out why. As we neared the rotunda to exit the facility, an inmate approached us. I later learned he was Sam Williams, chair of the Inmate Council. He handed me a business-sized white envelope addressed to me.

I thanked him and said, "I'll read this and get back to you."

As soon as Williams walked away, Vukcevich offered me surprising advice: "Accept nothing inmates hand you. Williams knows the correct procedure here at Rahway to communicate with the superintendent!"

That told me a story!

Vukcevich continued, "He's required to send you a 'kite' (written message/memo) requesting an interview." The problem was that's not how I operated.

The rest of the morning passed quickly, and Sam bought me lunch at the Merchants and Drovers Tavern, in downtown Rahway. He seemed to be known and well liked there. Many patrons, including the manager, stopped to speak with him, calling him by his first name.

*

Returning to the institution after lunch, I first wanted to arrange entry meetings with staff. My top-ranking security officers had priority.

I asked Myrna to set up four fifteen-minute, one-on-one meetings with Captain Bob O'Keefe, acting chief deputy (head of security), Captain John Hassall, Captain Bob Eder, and Captain Jim Ucci.

When the last meeting ended, I concluded these were all good men. But before building the Table of Organization I had in mind, I needed to ask Captain Richard Curran to consider a transfer from Trenton Prison to Rahway to head the Violence Control Unit I wanted us to create together here.

The rest of the afternoon, I attacked my overflowing in-basket. Its contents puzzled me, loaded with mail addressed to many other people and various departments. There were also several sample-sized products and a plastic egg containing pantyhose!

I paged Myrna and asked her, "Myrna, why am I getting everyone's mail?"

"Mr. Hatrak, the procedure the previous superintendent established was all incoming mail was to be placed in his in-basket, after setting aside all personal mail. Then, after looking at each piece, he opened and read those addressed to the various departments. Following his inspection, I delivered it all back to the mailroom for distribution to the addressees."

Processing this volume of incoming mail could take all day! He must have taken it home to work on in the evening. Otherwise, I really couldn't understand how he could have done anything but process everyone's mail! This procedure wouldn't work for me. My priority was to work inside the prison, interacting with my staff and the inmates to learn firsthand what was happening there.

Okay. "Myrna let's change the procedure. Ask the mailroom sergeant to give me only the mail addressed to the superintendent, or me personally, and forward all other mail directly to the addressees."

My planned daily routine would resemble the one I followed at Trenton, which served both Warden Fauver and me. Here, when able, I'd spend no less than one-half of every workday (sometimes on Saturday or Sunday, too) walking and talking to staff and inmates. I would also attempt to drop in on every department and inmate work area from time to time. This routine would help reduce tensions inside the prison and give me a chance to develop a personal relationship with both staff and residents.

The only change I intended to make, personally, was to visit occasionally during the graveyard shift, and stay until the shift changed at 6:20 a.m.

On my first day, it was somewhere near 5:30 p.m. when I left for home, so I still had a long drive ahead of me during rush hour traffic. Joan worried about the daily ride to and from Rahway. (Little did we expect I would make this tedious commute between Morrisville and Rahway for eight months until mid-June when finally, Sam Vukcevich moved out of the warden's residence.)

*

On Tuesday morning, I arrived at work shortly before 9 a.m. I had a quick cup of coffee in my new office and entered the prison to begin my first full day of management by walkin' and talkin'.

This time, unlike my tour with Sam Vukcevich, the familiar reverberant noise level was what I considered normal, and I began to feel at home. Inmates by the dozens swamped me. Now, I thought, maybe they didn't stop to talk with me because I was with Vukcevich! I realized they weren't supposed to approach him when he was inside the prison. Phew!

When I continued my rounds, many inmates told me they were happy to see me, and they hoped Rahway would change for the better the way Trenton had while I worked there. Without question they were well informed about my record at Trenton and probably even knew what I had for breakfast that day. This felt like a good beginning.

I ate lunch with several officers in the staff dining room and returned to my office; every minute of my afternoon was fully scheduled. Later in the day, I met with Assistant Superintendent Ron Grooms, and the meeting went very well. We had a long discussion about my entry goals, objectives, and the first thirty-day plan. Ron liked the "Hands-Off" policy best as my first step in combatting violence in the institution. Also, he agreed, writing a policy prohibiting the chokehold was something long overdue.

I told him these two policy statements were not the end of our violence reforms; they must be only the beginning. I asked Ron to continue assuming the duties he performed for Sam Vukcevich, and he agreed.

*

It was Wednesday before I knew it. I planned not to tour the facility today because I had a critical 9:30 a.m. meeting with the labor union. The results of this first meeting would set the tone of my relationship with the membership.

Parking "Molly" in the spot reserved for the superintendent's vehicle, I spotted Captain Hassell waving his arms at me as he bustled in my direction.

"Boss! Boss, all uniform staff are out of uniform! No one is wearing a necktie today!"

I felt sure this was my first challenge with Mr. Genesi.

"Thanks, John. I'm meeting with the union this morning, and I'll discuss the matter with them." I thought to myself, It looks like Frank is attempting to set the agenda! But it didn't matter because I was ready.

Two men dominated Rahway's union leadership. The first was Frank Genesi. Frank was among the most powerful correction officer union leaders in the state. Even more influential than the elected state president of the union. Rumor had it Frank could meet with the governor without an appointment. I suspected this just might be true. The second was correction officer Jack Rafferty. Jack seemed antagonistic toward inmates first and superintendents second. I'm pleased to remember we became friends. I recognized Jack's ability and took him under my wing. Years later, briefly, he too became the superintendent at Rahway.

The union meeting agenda I developed the night before included several items. Of most significant importance was my "Hands-Off" policy. Next came a brief introduction to my alternative approach to maximum-security prison violence control, followed by a brief discussion of the brand new "Violence Control Unit." I would start operationalizing all of this within several weeks.

Last, and certainly not least was the high cost of Rahway's correction officers' overtime pay. I reminded myself this was a "sacred cow" and would create much friction. I could already imagine hearing the officers "ensuing mooing" over the assault on their sacred cow. I recall Director Wagner cautioning me, "Changes should be introduced cautiously and slowly." Whoops.

I ENTERED THE auditorium right on time for my meeting. I didn't climb the steps to take the stage. I wanted to be on the same level as the officers and not stand above them. Instead, I found a chair in front of the stage, and sat facing center front, a short distance from Frank Genesi, who had already positioned himself facing me in the center seat of the first row.

Before I spoke, the corpulent Genesi, with an unlit cigar hanging out of his mouth, leaned forward and said loud enough for everyone to hear, "So, you're the young schoolteacher sent here to fix all our problems! I'm Frank Genesi."

He didn't extend his hand, and neither did I.

As the room grew instantly quiet, I realized he had gotten the reaction he wanted.

I replied, "I know who you are, Frank. Nice to meet you."

Looking over the sea of officers' faces, I decided not to take the bait and allow Genisi to set the agenda. Instead, I didn't acknowledge the absence of their neckties. I began the meeting.

"Good morning, gentlemen. Let's get started."

Before I could present my plan, Officer Genesi spoke up again and challengingly asked, "What are you going to do, boss, about our decision not to wear neckties today?"

Undoubtedly, Genesi had orchestrated this silly test. However, I had to diffuse this situation without alienating the instigator, since I would need his cooperation and political power to achieve the changes I planned to bring to Rahway. He was counting on me being the new kid on the block. What he obviously didn't expect was that already I knew about the Central Office meeting recently held to determine officers' dress code statewide. But, most significantly, I also knew Genesi was present and served on the committee when the committee decided that a full uniform required a necktie during the winter months… Ha!

I told Frank that the Division's official decisions concerning the correction officer dress code were made by the Central Office through a committee, and the director decided what the dress code policy would be.

"Frank, since you were present at that dress code policy meeting, you need to raise this issue with Director Fauver, who, as you'll remember, since you were there, chaired the committee. Call him today, and I'll wait until tomorrow to process disciplinary charges for every officer out of uniform today."

Following a long and uncomfortable silence, during which Genesi's cigar traveled with uncertainty from one side of his mouth to the other, he answered arrogantly, "Let's talk about this disciplinary hearing process for officers."

He asked me, "Who will represent the administration at each disciplinary hearing? Jack Rafferty and I will be on the union's side of the table. Who will represent your side?"

I answered, "That would be me, Frank! I alone will represent the administration."

Silence followed my comment.

Since the meeting was now mine, I raised the next issue.

"Moving on, I'm concerned about the violence which has been part of Rahway's landscape for decades."

I told the group about the press clippings I had read concerning recent correction officer strikes at Rahway. The primary concern expressed was from the union about poor working conditions and the daily violence everyone, not just union members, endured.

"Men, you need to know my primary aim here is to reduce violence. Our efforts will apply to both staff and residents. I am issuing the directive I will distribute now to the union first. Next, I'll discuss the matter with the Inmate Council."

I handed a packet of policies to the nearest officer to pass around.

"I call the new policy 'Hands-Off.'" Then I read it out loud:

"Effective at once, everyone must keep their hands to themselves. Placing one's hands on another inmate, or any member of Rahway's staff (fighting, pushing, and shoving, for example) is a hands-off wrongful act. The disciplinary committee shall administer penalties to inmates, and the warden shall administer penalties to the staff. Repeated violations of this policy by an inmate will cause his transfer to the Trenton State Prison. Staff will be disciplined as required.

"Inmates must understand the policy applies only to routine and not extreme or emergent situations (for example, to restore control and order). Staff will keep hands off inmates.

"I will never tolerate unprovoked assaults on an inmate by staff. Instead, I prefer staff attempt to head off violence through skillful thinking, verbal communication, and other non-coercive preventative measures to avoid using physical force.

We will offer In-Service Training (IST) in these skills areas soon.

"So, there will be no misunderstanding I am saying: 'Mutual respect for everyone under this dome will be the practice here from now on. We will show high regard for our brother officers and the prisoners alike.' I believe mutual respect is missing here, and it is the key to calming down and reducing the violence here at Rahway."

"However, everyone here understands there may be times when physical restraint will be necessary. We will use the minimum force needed to restore order in those cases. I will never allow chokeholds."

WHAT FOLLOWED WAS a spirited discussion. The officers asked many good questions. I ended the conversation by informing the group I would wait a week before implementation.

"But men, we will implement this policy!"

Then, I distributed copies of the new Table of Organization I had developed and which the director had already approved. Next, I discussed the new management units included in the table: The Control and Operations Units and the Self-Rehab Enterprise Groups. Again, this generated a lot of discussions. My last comment was, "This new alignment of our organization will take effect as soon as I discuss it with the department heads on Friday. Regarding future meetings, I will reserve the last Friday of every month to meet with you. If you prefer a different day of the week, let me know."

There was not enough time left to discuss what would have been a time bomb—the $2+ million unbudgeted overtime expenditures of the previous year.

At the end of the meeting, I said, "If we work together, we can minimize runaway violence and improve conditions here for everyone."

*

When I got home, I had a beer to celebrate what turned out to be a successful day. I enjoyed both the combat with Genesi and the beer!

*

The first thing Thursday morning, Captain Hassell met me at the front door again. He exclaimed, "Everyone is in uniform today, boss."

I couldn't resist calling Genesi to tell him, "Hey there, Frank, everybody looks sharp today." He quickly changed the subject. Frank had suffered his first defeat at Rahway! I figured I won that round, but I knew it was only the first of a fifteen-round fight.

"Just because you got the monkey off your back, it doesn't mean the circus has left town!"

– George Carlin

*

The first item on my Thursday morning agenda was to meet with the Inmate Council. The meeting went well. They supported the Hands-Off policy.

Our discussions centered on the same things I discussed at the previous day's engagement with the union. The most popular question was: "Will we have personal TVs like they do at Trenton?" I told them, "First, we need to determine the ability of our electrical system to carry the added load. If the existing power is adequate, the answer is yes."

The rest of the meeting we discussed any unresolved demands presented by the rioting inmates at the end of the 1971 riot. I agreed to hold monthly meetings with them and devise workable solutions. Everyone seemed pleased, and the meeting ended on good terms.

On Friday morning, I had my usual cuppa coffee and thought about the morning's upcoming meeting with the prison department heads. The meeting would be the last entry meeting and the end of my first week! When we finished introductions at the meeting, I distributed the Hands-Off policy. The group's consensus was this policy should be in place right now.

So far, so good!

Next, I distributed copies of two organization charts, current and revised.

TRENTON AND RAHWAY CURRENT TABLE OF ORGANIZATION

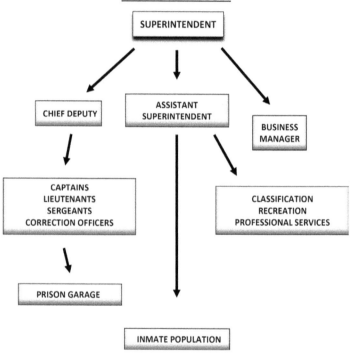

The table of Organization I found when I arrived at Rahway could not accommodate the three new management units I would implement.

"Let's review the current chart first."

Discounting scheduled interview lines, or meeting by accident, the distance between the superintendent and inmates is far too great.

"Inmates suffer when the prison's warden does not maintain direct control of the prison."

The warden gets disadvantaged because someone often filters the information he receives second and thirdhand.

"We need an organization where the warden is always in direct control of the prison. The revised Table of Organization supplies the required command structure."

What followed was a brief discussion. Most department heads recognized for the first time what I was saying.

Next, the discussion centered on the revised Table of Organization. The dotted lines on the table mean there is communication and coordination and not direct-line supervision. A solid line shows direct supervision responsibilities.

SUPERINTENDENTS REVISED TABLE OF ORGANIZATION

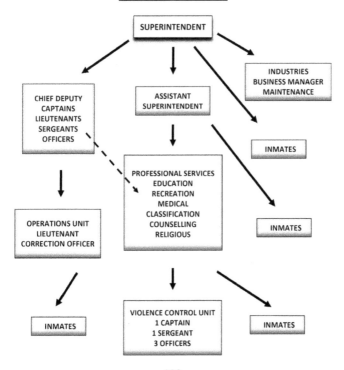

Ken Hamner, the regional laundry manager, raised his hand and asked, "Warden, looking at the first chart you distributed, is this how Trenton operates?"

"Yes, Ken, it is. I redesigned Rahway's chart to include and reflect two new management units: a Violence Control Unit and an overtime control unit named the Operations Unit."

"As you can see, the chart creates a straight-line reporting relationship between the inmate population and me. I'll be talking more about each of these new management functions as we begin implementation."

Bill Pendergast, Rahway Sex Offender Treatment Unit director, asked, "Do you really believe this will solve maximum-security prison violence? During the 1971 riot, general population inmates savaged the inmates in the sex offender unit. Since then, I've seen only a minimal change in the level of violence here."

I replied, "Yes, Bill, we did it successfully at Trenton. The inmate committee recognized the many changes we made in less than one year and acknowledged the improvement by presenting Bill Fauver and me with plaques at a banquet they held in our honor."

Next, I asked each department head to make a brief presentation, including their department's mission, along with any pressing issues needing my immediate attention or that may affect other departments.

I Informed them that I planned to have a department head meeting every month and encouraged them to interact with me on my daily prison tours whenever I was in their area. To make it clear, I also told them I preferred an open-door policy, and most times, an appointment wasn't necessary to see me. My door was always open.

There were no other questions, and I adjourned the meeting.

*

In a memo, I alerted everyone, with the need to know, that every Thursday at 7 p.m. I would hold inmate interviews (one-on-one) in the attorney's visit room off the Tie-To. To schedule a consultation, inmates would drop requests in either dropbox outside the rotunda.

To help me manage my enormous amount of daily mail, I drafted Mike Power, a young civilian teacher assigned to the Education Department, to process the in and out baskets, the same job I had performed for Warden Yeager at Trenton. Mike turned out to be a gem. His competent help enabled me to get out from behind my desk and into the institution. Mike became one of my protegees, and many years later he became Rahway's superintendent.

I always suspected that Warden Yeager was grooming me at Trenton and I did the same for talented youngsters I encountered. As a result, six of my trainees became superintendents—some at Rahway, one at Trenton, and one in the Iowa Department of Corrections. One of the six, Howard Beyer (RIP), became a deputy director.

Things were getting organized, and this first week was a very productive one. I was eager to implement our new organizational structure, staff the new organization chart, and activate the new Violence Control Unit. As I designed it, the unit should make significant inroads to establish effective violence control.

On Saturday, Joan and I would relax before I toured the prison on Sunday with Captain Hassell.

*

My second week at the job began on Sunday, November 12. In a show of support, Captain Hassell volunteered to take me on a tour of the entire physical plant. He told me it would be better to tour on Sunday because we would be uninterrupted.

We met early on Sunday morning at his home in Rahway.

We talked about the recent gubernatorial election on the drive to the institution. The citizens of New Jersey elected Brendan Byrne as their governor. The election occurred on November 4, one day before I started working at Rahway.

Out of curiosity, John asked if I had heard any scuttlebutt about who our new boss will be.

"I'm talking about the commissioner's job."

"I don't have a clue, John. But I'll bet the current director, Bill Fauver, is wondering too."

What an ambitious tour we took. The captain walked my legs off. We toured every shop, industry, the Rahway Treatment Unit (for sex offenders), the school area, the drill hall, the inmate dining room, the tuberculosis ward, the dental laboratory; we sat through part of an inmate visiting period, the prison garage, the recreation yard, the Rahway minimum-security camp located outside the wall, and I even climbed up into a tower! The tour lasted until 4 p.m. I wondered how many acres were behind the wall. It seemed there were at least twenty acres. This place was humongous! Poorly maintained, it was shabby, smelly, and dirty. These would be the most straightforward problems to correct.

I excused myself early because I planned to arrive at work the following day sometime around 5 a.m. I wanted to see some of the graveyard shift (10:20 p.m. until 6:20 a.m.) and the next day's shift briefing from 6:05 a.m. until 6:15 a.m.

*

On Monday morning, I arrived at the prison at 5 a.m. As I entered the empty Front House, all was eerily quiet. No one other than John Hassell was expecting my pre-dawn visit.

I first went to my office to call the prison's center keeper, Lieutenant Richard Carstens, to inform him I was on campus and would soon begin a quick early morning tour of the facility. The sally port officer recognized me while looking through the small bulletproof window cut into the heavy security door and admitted me. Once I entered the sally port, he locked the door behind me. I spotted Hassell speaking with the center keeper.

Here, I was pat frisked. Even though I was the warden, I required the officer to search me and to request I empty my pockets. This was a new procedure for Rahway. I wanted to establish there would be no exceptions for anyone to be entitled entry because of their rank.

I had issued a directive about this procedure soon after I arrived, stating: "All visitors, all employees, including the superintendent, will get pat frisked and be required to empty all pockets upon entering and exiting the rotunda sally port." This procedure will remain in effect, even after our new metal detector is delivered and installed.

When the officer completed searching me, he opened the grill gate leading to the ninety-foot tall circular and barred area beneath the dome known as the rotunda. He then locked the door behind me when I passed through.

The Tie-To officer opened the second of two rotunda grill gates. Once I walked through, he locked it again. Now I was in the area known as the Tie-To. The Tie-To is a fifty-foot secure hallway connecting the secured portion of the prison to the outside where shops, industries, the sex offender unit, the receiving gate, regional laundry, and a large communal recreation region were located.

I turned left to begin my abbreviated tour of the facility. Singing was coming from under the steps leading to the auditorium… The voices stopped me dead in my tracks. What was I hearing? Was it a radio? I walked toward the sound. What I saw next startled me. There, under the staircase, I saw seven inmates huddled together, harmonizing.

I stopped and stood motionless. The men were as surprised to see me as I was to see them!

I asked, "What's going on? How did you guys get here so early in the morning? The institution is still in lights-out lockdown."

I thought to myself, someone is violating a significant security policy.

The group's leader spoke up. "Sir, we are a singing group known as The Escorts, and because of overcrowding, we can't find a better place to practice other than in a bathroom."

I asked, "Practice for what?"

One man said, "Well, about seven months before your arrival, we made a record album right here at Rahway. We're hoping to do another. And so, we need a place to practice."

"Okay, guys, stay put. I'll be right back."

The prison still being locked down meant that someone allowed this severe violation of security procedures. The Center keeper should know what was going on. I returned to the front of the Control Center and asked Captain Hassell to explain how something so dangerous could occur. He said he would find out.

"John, get back to me before lunch."

Returning to the inmates, I said, "You can return to your wings for now. We'll work this out."

Deciding my tour could wait until I learned how and why these men were out of their cells at 5 a.m. before the institution opened. I processed back out of the rotunda, and I returned to my office.

My planned focus for the rest of the day centered on determining the first steps to implement the Violence Control Unit. It was the keystone of my comprehensive plan to reform Rahway.

Just as I reached for the phone, Tom Hundley, the Recreation director, appeared in the doorway to my office.

"Come in, Tom. Have a seat."

"Sir, I understand you met The Escorts this morning singing under the staircase near four-wing."

"Yes, I did. We surprised each other."

"Mr. Hatrak, didn't anyone tell you about the inmate talent show the Recreation Department sponsored before your arrival here?"

"No, Tom, please tell me about it."

"If you have time, I'll tell you about the group, the inmate talent show, and the record album they cut here."

Listening to Tom, I learned that inmate Reginald Haynes created the singing group in 1968 at the Trenton State Prison. Reggie had sharpened the group's smooth singing style right here at Rahway under discouraging circumstances. From Alithon Record Company, George Kerr attended an inmate talent show here as a guest of an inmate's sister.

Following two years and many unsuccessful attempts of seeking the previous administration's cooperation, Kerr contacted the commissioner, Robert Clifford, who at last approved the project.

What followed was the recording of their first album.

I thanked Tom for the information he shared with me. He suggested I request press clippings from information services to learn more about the group and their album. I now understood and agreed that The Escorts required a place and time to practice. But not under a staircase at 5 a.m.

I reached out to George Kerr from Alithon Records to introduce myself. Also, I wanted to assure him I was available to help him and The Escorts.

"George, I'm very interested in allowing inmates to prepare for release to society possessing a set of self-determined skills, helping them make it in the outside world. The goal is one I believe in; I call it Self-Rehabilitation." I briefed him on my "brainchild," regarding inmate Self-Rehab Enterprise Groups. "My work with The Escorts will be the first step to establish this endeavor."

*

Captain Hassell got back to me to tell me he had investigated the morning's incident and concluded it was an honest mistake. "Hmmm." "Okay, John, please arrange for The Escorts to practice in the auditorium. The sergeant assigned to that section of the prison will periodically check on them. Tell them their practice time is from 9 a.m. until 11 a.m."

"Since nothing unseemly resulted from this adventure under the stairs, I'll not pursue the details, but you tell whomever you're covering for: "It Better Never, Ever, Happen Again!""

*

The Escorts deserved some support at last, and I was excited to change the auditorium's negative vibrations into other, more positive ones. Opening the space up to The Escorts could be the start of using the area for constructive endeavors, removing the stigma of the 1971 riot that occurred there. And boy, did it ever work! The auditorium quickly became a busy place, hosting the newly formed inmate program, the Self-Rehab Enterprise Groups. The Escorts were the perfect group to be the first to participate in the program.

Before being interrupted again, I wanted to get back to my planned focus for the day, setting in motion the groundwork for the Violence Control Unit.

To begin, I called Albert Grey, Trenton Prison's recently appointed superintendent. As a courtesy, I wanted to talk to him before speaking with a captain of his, Richard Curran, to ask him to consider a transfer from Trenton to Rahway. Rich Curran and I worked together at Trenton, and we were an excellent team. I trusted him and felt confident about his abilities. We had already implemented violence control procedures together at Trenton that had nearly eliminated threat groups there. Warden Grey agreed to my request, and I called Curran. After a lengthy telephone conversation, he enthusiastically requested a transfer to Rahway to lead the Violence Control Unit for us.

Rich arrived at Rahway within a couple of weeks. My Friend and The Best Captain In New Jersey.

*

I occupied much of my time, now that Curran was on the team, structuring and completing my detailed plan to implement the Violence Control Unit and monitoring the impressive progress of The Escorts.

The Escorts practice sessions were occurring without a hitch. I scheduled their leader, Reggie Haynes, to see me on one of my Thursday night interview lines. I planned to tell him I had spoken with George Kerr, and that I gave him my commitment to work with him and The Escorts. Upon leaving, Reggie spoke up and said, "Thanks, Warden! We appreciate your trust in us! The Escorts will do nothing to embarrass you or Rahway Prison."

And I believed him!

*

November and December were productive months. However, the holidays and my birthday, on Christmas Day, interrupted December.

The day before Christmas, I got a joyful surprise when Margaret Yavor, the switchboard operator, asked me to go with her to the front house. I saw it packed shoulder to shoulder with dozens of civilian and uniform staff members when we arrived there!

"Margaret, what's going on? Has something happened?" It overjoyed me when they sang "Happy Birthday" to me! They overwhelmed me! I thanked everyone and told them they all deserved a coffee break! Everyone enjoyed our coffee together in the front house, chatting and visiting like old friends. I couldn't believe that only one month before I didn't know any of these warm and welcoming people.

Things were progressing well. The Violence Control Unit planning activities were on schedule. The security staff accepted the revised Table of Organization and the proposed Violence Control Unit.

It looked like the new year would begin on a high note.

Inauguration Day for the newly elected governor, Brendan Byrne, was on January 6, 1974. His first appointment was to name Ann Klein to a cabinet-level position, as commissioner of the Department of Institutions and Agencies. Now, everyone was waiting for her announcement regarding the appointment of a Division of Corrections and Parole director. It pleased us to learn she would keep Bill Fauver as director.

In the middle of January, George Kerr approached me about the possibility of The Escorts performing live in the community. "George, you're asking me to do the impossible!"

As usual, word leaked to the staff and inmates alike, and the rumor flew through the prison.

George had already selected a location for the performance: New Jersey's Symphony Hall in Newark, New Jersey.

"Fat chance!" I laughed.

He would not get any encouragement from me.

But I soon realized that I could use the same revised furlough rules created at Trenton by Warden Fauver, and then work out the details for The Escorts.

The more I thought about it, the more I asked myself: Why not? Why can't I work with the same escorted furlough rules used already at the Trenton Prison?

EARLY ONE MORNING, Tom Hundley stopped by my office to tell me the betting odds out in the inmate population were ten cartons of cigarettes to one that I wouldn't agree to permit the live concert. And if I did, there was no way in hell I could make it happen.

The betting odds were correct. A live show in the community at Symphony Hall meant I'd have to release The Escorts from prison for at least half a day, and all the group members were maximum-security inmates. But, of course, it helped that such a furlough had already occurred, and it was my boss, Bill Fauver, who granted it to a maximum-security inmate. I got busy and found I could indeed work out the details, enabling a live performance for The Escorts at Symphony Hall!

There would be a significant major difference in the details of our Rahway escorted furlough. Unlike at Trenton, I'd select the escorting officers and not allow the inmates to ask for officer volunteers. At Trenton, I always said, "Using volunteer correction officers provided a temptation for them to look the other way, allowing inmates to violate the escort furlough rules." I didn't want any of that. Our officer escorts would be handpicked by me.

At Rahway, I ordered that the Classification Committee had to approve each escorted furlough individually for each inmate. So, first, I briefed them about Trenton's escorted furlough program. Then I told them it was their choice alone to approve or deny each furlough separately.

Committee members voted for approvals for every inmate except Steve Carter, who served a life sentence. I made it a point to meet with Carter to explain why the committee denied the request for his furlough. Steve was unhappy and disappointed, but he appreciated my visit to explain why he didn't get approved.

The reality of a live performance at Symphony Hall was settling in. Inmates were saying to one another, "Hatrak seems to be the 'real deal' and maybe now things will change for the better at Rahway."

I hoped other inmate groups we created in the future would follow the example of The Escorts and assume responsibility for their Self-Rehabilitation. That way, it would become a reality and not just a concept.

Handpicking the escorting officer team took little time. I chose Officer Charles Butler to be the team leader. Butler could appoint four officers, with me being the sixth member of the team.

If I ever needed to have someone knocked out, it would have been Charley. While in the United States Navy, he won the Navy's light-heavyweight championship. Charley received an invitation from President Richard Nixon to take part in an event held at Camp David. President Nixon invited all the US Military boxing champions as his guests. As time passed, Charley became one of my closest friends, and Joan still claims him to be the nearest to a big brother she ever had.

*

And then the big night of the performance arrived. It was terrific to see Rahway Prison so abuzz. Even the dome sitting at the top of the prison seemed to glow more brightly than usual.

Two short years after the 1971 riot, and five months since I assumed the superintendent's job, The Escorts, seven excited and well-dressed young men, all maximum-security inmates with long sentences, brought down the house at the renowned Newark, New Jersey Symphony Hall!

What a long way they have come, I thought to myself, from the time they huddled practicing under a staircase at the prison."

The Escorts had top billing, which meant they were the last group to perform. In the middle of their performance, The Escorts asked the jubilant crowd, "Are you on our side?"

Every person in the crowd responded with a boisterous "Yes! – and so did I!

George Kerr, the show's producer, seemed ecstatic.

After the performance, Mr. John Kralovich, co-president of Alithon Records, presented a plaque to the WNJS radio station representative in appreciation for their support. Mr. Kralovich surprised me when he invited me to join him on the stage. He gave me a handsome plaque reading: "For Your Outstanding Contribution and Achievement In Rehabilitation."

I had never stood on a stage before and received thunderous applause. It was terrifying! Looking out at two thousand smiling faces, and four thousand clapping hands, I realized mine was the only white face in the crowd! What a high!

I swallowed hard. I thanked them for their support and enthusiasm and said it thrilled me to have played a part in making this event possible, and I hoped it would be the first of many more. The grin on my face lasted for days!

The Escorts were the first inmate group to make pop music history. They were also the only incarcerated group to produce and sell over 300,000 recordings, singles, and albums from behind the bars of a maximum-security prison. In addition, theirs was the first live performance in the community while on escorted leave. Everyone, staff, and inmates alike, were extremely proud of their accomplishment.

In the early '90s, The Lifers rap group also joined the music world and became a box office sensation while still incarcerated.

Helping inmates discover their personal self-rehabilitation goals and then developing them to the fullest extent did help minimize violence in the prison as inmates redirected their focus on the groups and their own personal development.

Later that night, it occurred to me that good things were in store for the Rahway State Prison. As I drifted off to sleep, I wondered why neither Bill Fauver nor a division representative had attended the performance....

THE NEXT DAY, someone handed me the New York Times story dated February 17, 1974. It praised The Escorts' electrifying performance at Symphony Hall the night before.

Many other inmates would benefit from the success The Escorts enjoyed. Overall satisfaction caused working and living conditions to improve for everyone. In addition, future inmates in large numbers would enjoy the advantages of new and meaningful "release preparation strategies," and discover they were "not the same men leaving prison as they were when entering Rahway Prison."

At the end of February, Jim Ucci, Richie Curran, and I were ready to operationalize the Violence Control Unit. The next step for us was to dig in and begin working to get things started.

*

Before I knew it, March came in like a lion, and so did Ann Klein, the newly appointed commissioner of the Department of Institutions and Agencies.

She contacted all wardens by mail, return receipt requested, mandating their presence at a warden's meeting in Trenton she scheduled for mid-March. I looked forward to the meeting, expecting this would be the time for Ms. Klein to tell us about her plans for the Corrections Division. And she sure did.

Little did we know, this introductory meeting would set all the wardens assembled there back in their seats!

CHAPTER 11

Correction Officer Scheduling and Overtime Control

The balancing act

"People who are chronically tardy never understand the many ways in which they screw up the schedules of people who are punctual.

– Lauren Kate Fallen

Following The Escorts' live performance at the Symphony Hall in Newark, New Jersey, I turned my attention to operationalizing the Violence Control Unit. At the end of February, Jim Ucci, Richie Curran, and I began operationalizing the Violence Control Unit. The next step for us was to dig in and begin working to get things started.

*

Before I knew it, March 8, 1974, the day of Commissioner Kline's first wardens' meeting, had arrived. Expecting today to be a good day, I started early from home in Morrisville, Pennsylvania, and headed to Trenton. The meeting would include wardens, Director Fauver, and all bureau chiefs. When we were all assembled, there was standing room only in the small, nondescript meeting room.

For as long as anyone remembered, the department had existed as the Department of Institutions and Agencies. Tucked protectively under this umbrella were the agencies of Mental Health, Prisons, and Welfare.

Now assembled at the meeting, waiting expectantly to meet our new boss, most of us were seasoned superintendents. Some were good old boys, and there were a few of the often-arrogant corrections professionals. I was the only rookie in attendance. It would be fair to say that not everyone was happy to welcome our new commissioner, a social worker, a politician, and the first woman to our historically male fraternity.

When he won the gubernatorial election in 1973, Brendan Byrne appointed Ann Klein as commissioner of the Department of Institutions and Agencies. Ms. Klein, a graduate of Columbia University with a degree in social work, had been president of the Woman's League of Voters and elected to the New Jersey State Assembly. Now, she was the first woman and non-corrections professional to become the department's new commissioner. None of us knew what to expect.

Suddenly, the door opened, and through it strode a tall, attractive, dark-haired, confident woman in her early fifties. She wore a black dress with a bright red jacket and bright red lipstick. She looked animated and raring to begin. Accompanying her was a small cadre of what "we guys" called the "commissioner's smiling bow ties."

The meeting began promptly at 9:30 a.m. Ms. Klein introduced herself. She surprised everyone when she mentioned the live performance The Escorts gave at Newark's Symphony Hall a few weeks earlier! It was nice to hear her acknowledge them and their success since no one else from the division thought to attend and congratulate The Escorts.

Then, she dropped a bomb! Standing at the podium, and without the benefit of a microphone, Ms. Klein pointed a manicured finger out toward the assembled group and said, "I will fire one, or all of you, this year! Any one of you who does not reduce overtime expenditures, beginning today, at your institution, will lose their job.

"In the past, the Division of Corrections and Parole had its chronic and massive overtime spending resolved when the commissioner raided the budgets of the other agencies. I will not do that. History will not repeat itself."

My immediate thought was, *Oh God, I don't know how to do that!*

There I was, a newly minted superintendent, having to think about the possibility of my job vaporizing!

After a long, uncomfortable silence, one voice sarcastically asked, in a heavy New Jersey accent, "Shall we do that ta-day or ta-morrow?"

Commissioner Klein shot back, "Not ta-day and not ta-morrow...but ta-now!"

After her alarming declaration ended, I paid little attention to anything else during the rest of the meeting. I was heavy in thought. My expected plan to activate a Violence Control Unit (VCU) designed to eliminate the activities of all inmate threat groups now had to take a back seat to streamline overtime costs! But no more delays after that; my project was next out of the box!

WE COULD STILL continue to develop the new VCU. Captain Richard Curran had already joined us, had selected staff, and started training security people he would work with within the new unit. Was it possible we could do two major projects at one time? I would need to consider what it would take to create an operations unit to satisfy the commissioner's directive to reduce overtime costs, while simultaneously structuring an internal VCU to deal with Rahway's violence problem.

Reducing overtime costs would be a weighty undertaking. There was no way we could eliminate the total amount of last year's overtime of two million-plus dollars. Some overtime would always exist. How much of a reduction would help keep me from being fired? Since I didn't have any experience managing employee shift scheduling or overtime expenditure control, I didn't know where to turn.

Then, I remembered that our past director, Al Wagner, had invited me to attend a superintendent's meeting in the late '60s with him. I was then Trenton's director of Education. I felt out of place because I was the only non-superintendent in attendance. I recalled the only item on their agenda was developing workable strategies to control the overtime expenditures at each prison and reformatory in New Jersey. Overtime costs had always been a problem.

At the end of the afternoon, after making a valiant effort, the division's best and brightest, the superintendents and bureau chiefs, all went down swinging.

Not one strategy worth pursuing developed. What I heard was one reason after another cloaking the obvious problem. The repeated justification was, "There will always be overtime. It's built into the labor contracts."

I thought to myself, *they're "going to skip go" on this one!* I was right! No one ever studied the problem, and here I was all these years later, in 1974, being told to solve something none of them then, and none of us now, knew how to fix.

When Ann Klein left the room, several superintendents wondered out loud if the commissioner was "for real." *Me?* I had no doubt she was "for real"—which made it even scarier.

*

When I arrived home, Joan saw how upset I was and asked, "What happened at the wardens' meeting?"

"Joan, it may be for the best that we haven't moved yet. Maybe we won't need to pack our bags after all. We may go nowhere!"

I told her what Ann Klein had said to open the meeting.

"What are you going to do about it?"

"I need to locate the best practices regarding overtime practices in corrections today. I hope I have enough time to get it done. Our next meeting is on the first Tuesday in April. Less than one month from now! *Holy crap!* It's back to the State Archives for me."

That night, sleep didn't come easy for either of us. In the morning, Joan supplied her expected expert advice, suggesting that we reach out to the friends I'd made when I took part in Dr. Ryan's national educational model development project in West Virginia.

Joan had an aha moment. "Bob, you need to phone Toni Ryan first. She likes you and would be more than happy to help. You may not have time to figure this out alone." She chuckled and said, "Do not begin vast projects with only half-vast plans." I didn't have a quick comeback for her quip, so I merely rolled my eyes.

EARLY THE NEXT day, I called Dr. Ryan. I summarized the superintendent's meeting, telling her I needed help to find the best overtime control and correction officer scheduling practices in the country. It was an impossible task for me, and I needed it in a hurry. "Ta-now!"

Dr. Ryan suggested I contact Sylvia McCollum. I met Sylvia several times during the projects I took part in with Dr. Ryan. She was a top administrator for the United States Federal Bureau of Prisons.

I told Sylvia when I called her that I needed information about the bureau's approach to correction officer overtime control and correction officer shift scheduling.

"Bob, I'm happy to hear from you. I remember you."

I was relieved and pleased to hear her say, "Bob, I'll share everything the Bureau has that can help you. In addition, I'll send you a box full of general information, policies, procedures, shift scheduling information, and much more about what we do regarding general overtime cost control. Finally, I'll send correction officer staffing plans using a correct relief factor and a correction officer scheduling system, which are key components to overtime control." I didn't know what she was talking about, but I thanked her profusely. I told her how much I appreciated her help and that I was grateful for her friendship.

I called Joan. "Hi, honey. As usual, your advice was spot on. I had two excellent telephone conversations this morning. First, I spoke with Toni Ryan at the University of Hawaii and then Sylvia McCollum from the Federal Bureau of Prisons in Washington, DC. Sylvia can help me with the overtime control problem Ann Klein dumped in our laps yesterday. She's going to ship me a box full of materials, which should help us big time."

A week later, Sylvia's care package arrived. I wasted little time devouring the information she'd sent and mentally correlated it with what little I already knew.

Given Sylvia's information, I realized it would take a herculean effort to design an officer overtime control scheduling system. To accomplish the task, it was apparent we had to revise Rahway's antiquated methods for scheduling correction officers by writing their names on a magnetic board, to something more sophisticated and hopefully effective.

Shift work is an employment practice designed to use or provide service across all twenty-four hours of each day of the week (often abbreviated as 24/7). The procedure typically sees each day divided into shifts, or set periods, during which different workers perform their duties. The term "shift work" includes long-term night shifts and work schedules in which employees change or rotate shifts.

I thought all this through and concluded we had an awful lot to consider when revising Rahway's eight-hour shift scheduling system. The current structure was a copy of Trenton's, and both were inadequate and, in many circumstances, fostered and enabled over time. Joan was right. "Half-vast plans" would not help resolve this situation.

I needed help, and Jim Ucci immediately came to the rescue. Rahway was lucky to have Jim in a ranking security officer position. When I arrived at Rahway, I quickly recognized that he was the best and brightest supervisor at Rahway. Approaching him, I asked if he was interested in helping me attack Rahway's large overtime expenditures. Without hesitation, he agreed to help.

Jim suggested I approach Lieutenant Bill Miller to determine if he was interested in helping us. Bill agreed, and so it was off to the races. I told them both about the ultimatum Commissioner Klein had issued.

"I've been trying to learn all I could about overtime control. Working with the information shared with me from the 'Feds,' I've developed an implementation plan."

I shared the end goal. "We need to make drastic reductions to last year's overtime spending, or else!"

I explained my recently developed implementation plan to each of them. "The first step we take will be to do what I now call a 'post-analysis.' I learned if post (duty station) scrutiny is evaluated incorrectly, the result down the line is managers will battle excessive overtime, compensatory time, dissension among staff, job dissatisfaction, resignations, potential injuries, and officers working stuck double shifts.

"The post plans shall document the absolute need for every post and the number of days and hours the post operates daily. Therefore, prioritizing posts and classifying each as mandatory (always staffed without exception is compulsory—*always*). Flexible posts can be closed for all or part of a shift."

"And so, guys, we need to challenge each existing post to determine its necessity. Individual duty stations that require multiple staff will need special scrutiny."

Since Ucci and Miller were veteran supervisors with many years of experience, they knew Rahway's post structure and physical plant far better than I did. And so, I assigned them each to a challenge reflecting their individual strengths.

This was a big, overwhelming piece of work to analyze and produce, and we needed to hurry. To be efficient, Jim split the workload with Bill.

"Consider recruiting two or three supervisors to work with each of you. Then, let's review your progress in the middle and again at the end of every week.

"Meanwhile, I'll gather correction officer and correction supervisor time and attendance records and information, otherwise known as 'non-deployable days.'"

"This will include reasons such as union business, in-service training, voting, funeral, sick, vacation, National Guard drills, among others, to be added separately to each shift and to each rank." (Family leave and maternity leave weren't available in 1975.)

Obviously, we needed to precisely evaluate where we were right now before changing anything.

Once collected, I used these statistics to calculate "shift relief factors" for each of our three facilities, applying Dr. McCollum's formulas to our data.

Without Dr. McCollum's knowledge about the relief factor and what to do with the information we collected and analyzed, we could have never succeeded or found a solution to the overtime problem.

When we finished with our calculations, the prison's overall factor turned out to be 1.8, but the division historically funded us using a 1.6 factor. The cost of a 1.6 relief factor represents the salary cost for one employee and six-tenths of a second employee's time to cover the days off for the first employee. Then one must consider that there were three shifts and three separate institutions. Multiply one and six-tenths times three shifts and the cost for correction officer coverage for one post around the clock is 4.8. Small wonder that overtime expenditures, statewide, were out of control, and now Jim, Bill, and I at Rahway had the solution.

For us, this was a "Eureka" moment and it felt pretty damn good. We were shocked when we realized that we had the answer to the multimillion-dollar overtime cost problem that Commissioner Kline was demanding to fix statewide. Jim, Bill, and I hurriedly rushed to the telephone to inform Director Fauver of what we thought was a monumental discovery. We were astonished when he said he had no interest in our solution to reduce overtime costs at the facility level. Years later, when he was the commissioner, statewide overtime was approaching $1 billion, and his boss, Governor Christie Todd Whitman, permitted him to retire.

I never did discover the origins of the division's 1.6 relief factor. They must have developed it in a vacuum. It routinely passed from one administration to the next. No one ever challenged its accuracy, and there was no effort to re-evaluate its relevance. My theory is that most managers in the department had little or no understanding of shift relief factors. I think most didn't know a relief factor from a hand grenade! Until recently, that also included me.

WHEN WE APPLIED the adjusted factor to Jim and Bill's revised post plan, I understood why Rahway's overtime expenditures were high. The staffing requirement for one hundred posts on one shift using 1.6 is 160 positions (people). Conversely, the same calculation for one hundred posts, but with a 1.8 current factor, demands 180 positions. The difference is twenty officers for every 100 posts on all three shifts or a total shortage of sixty officers. The overtime problem was apparent in the misuse of the relief factor and an antiquated scheduling system.

How was that shortage managed? To the greatest extent, overtime clearly made up the sixty-position shortage of the past.

Since Dr. Ryan had introduced me to Dr. Leonard Silvern's flowcharting language (LOGOS—Language Optimizing Graphically Ordered Systems), I taught its basics to Jim and Bill, and the three of us designed our new comprehensive manual scheduling system.

Now I could eliminate the reason Frank Genesi was constantly bending my ear about "stuck overtime": Officers not being allowed to leave when their shift ended contributed to overtime expenditures.

Frank once told me, "Boss, my officers spend two or three days a week working a double shift because of staff shortages. The result is officers working when burned out. This creates violence problems. Tired officers are short-tempered officers. Inmates, because they see different officers every day in their housing units, bitch about lack of consistency as every officer follows their own procedures, resulting in chaos!"

The primary facility, Rahway Prison, was the biggest user of overtime, so we attacked the "biggest alligator" first. Completing the Operations Unit required building a simulated schedule, applying the gathered statistics and then testing it. As Jim and I suspected, the solution required program managers to revise the administration of work scheduling and roster management practices.

In April, only three weeks later, we began implementing the new management unit, which we called the "Operations Unit." Jim assigned Lieutenant Miller to head the effort, and an old-time correction officer whom everyone called "Pappy" assisted him. Pappy was a valuable resource, and he knew how things worked now and in the past. We created two full-time posts for Miller and Pappy to prepare master and daily schedules for each of the three facilities: Rahway Prison proper, Rahway camp, and Marlboro camp.

So, the "Ucci, Miller, Pappy, and Hatrak system design team" rolled up their collective sleeves and implemented the new system, which helped Rahway reduce overtime costs. The reduction amounted to $1.6 million in one year! In the second year, the remaining overtime of $400,000 was reduced by $200,000. This remainder was due to requirements like shift overlap specified in past union contracts.

Once we completed the first schedule design, we tested it, selecting the worst six days in the recent past, which evidenced the most extensive overtime usage. Next, we adjusted posts, scheduled off-duty time, and learned that the new system outperformed the current "non-system" by far on any of the six days.

When run in parallel with the new system, the outdated, static method used a lot of overtime. In contrast, the new flexible system used none.

When Chief Ucci, Lieutenant Miller, "Pappy," the business manager, and the captains saw the test results, they gasped! I, too, was floored because I had expected some savings but not at the level achieved!

We needed to hold a union leadership meeting and convince the union leader, Frank Genesi, to agree to get out of our way, at least until the system had undergone the pilot test we planned to conduct.

Jim and I met with the union's leadership without heated discussions. The only agenda item was the prison's increasing overtime expenditures. Obviously, there were no budgeted funds to support overtime costs.

A lengthy discussion ensued. I told the group that the statistics I had gathered revealed that some correction officers were earning so much overtime their salaries were more than doubled! I also told them I understood that the expensive motor homes, foreign cars, costly vacations including cruises, vacation homes, and other extravagances they had become accustomed to were paid for with their overtime earnings.

"Hey, boss, you're kidding, right?"

I told them, "I am cold-blooded serious about making massive reductions in overtime pay."

It was vital for the union leaders to discuss this matter with their membership. Employees needed to be aware of potential reductions in take-home pay. In addition, the officers needed to be prepared for the possibility their overtime pay would substantially decrease, and that would happen soon.

The first thing every morning, Chief Ucci, Lieutenant Miller, and I met to review the previous day's schedule. Lieutenant Miller had to justify every hour, or portion of an hour, of overtime used. Interestingly, these morning meetings, though painful, helped us develop new overtime avoidance strategies.

Commissioner Klein noted Rahway's success at our next monthly meeting, which the team, who had worked so tirelessly, appreciated. But unfortunately, Commissioner Klein's glowing acknowledgment didn't help me keep the goodwill of the other wardens I had until now enjoyed.

At warden's meetings, she always placed me on "Front Street," when she would say to the room, "Don't tell me you can't reduce your overtime costs. Just look at what Bob Hatrak is doing. Visit Rahway to see firsthand how he does it."

I was pleased she championed our efforts at Rahway. Still, she was steaming up the other wardens and I didn't need any additional problems. I wanted to crawl under my seat before somebody punched me.

ONLY GARY HILTON, Trenton's Warden, had his staff visit Rahway to learn what we were doing. As a result, he adopted a revised version of our system and reduced his overtime costs using a newly calculated relief factor. In addition, he was the only other warden to take the commissioner's order as seriously as I did.

Our friendship went way back to high school when we competed against one another in baseball. He was a catcher for Trenton High, and I was pitching for Trenton Catholic. We were archrivals.

When Gary transferred from the Clinton Prison for Women to Trenton Prison, he gave our family his beautiful horse, Baron. Baron was an offspring of a Kentucky Derby winner (but we can't remember which one).

Distinguishing himself he became the acting commissioner of the Department of Corrections when Bill Fauver retired.

Now that the Operations Unit was humming, and Ann Klein was happy with us, we could finally direct our attention to controlling the violence that had plagued Rahway for years.

We began by crafting policies and procedures for our soon-to-be-installed Violence Control Unit. I was confident we would work with the same boundless energy we had summoned up for the overtime project. We were now in position and prepared to put inmate threat groups out of business and encourage the inmate population's participation in our future Self-Rehab Enterprise Groups. And finally, and certainly not least, we needed to resolve riot demands, not yet fully satisfied.

*

From Joan: On April 22, 1974, Easter Sunday dawned clear and sunny. Warden Sam Vukcevich had extended an invitation to Bob, the kids, and me to visit the warden's residence at Rahway. We hoped that meant he was recovered enough now to move out.

After our usual special Easter breakfast of blueberry pancakes, we attended Easter Mass. That was followed by our wonderful traditional Easter brunch at Mom's with all ten nieces and nephews gathered for an Easter egg hunt. We wish we could go back again and revisit everyone.

Midafternoon Bob, Sharon, Robby, and I left our home and began our ride to Rahway.

Traffic heading north on Route 1 was surprisingly sparse. Bob drove cheerfully along, anxious and excited to see the state-owned house we would be moving into.

Eleven-year-old Sharon and I were willing to move, but we were both apprehensive. Year-and-a-half-old Robby munched contentedly on the four carefully selected jellybeans he brought along with him, and he didn't care where we were going.

From the road, the sprawling Woodbridge Mall offered the only actual enticement for Sharon and me to relocate.

When we approached our suggested landmark, the Avenel Fire Station, Bob said we were nearly there. Suddenly Rahway's huge dome and the buff-colored institution walls appeared on our left. I was speechless! It didn't look real. It looked like a huge poster was placed against the distant view. I hadn't expected it to be so imposing.

Across the street from the prison, a long, circular driveway led to the back of the house, where a large bank of fuchsia azalea shrubs book-ended a small fishpond. Huge maple and evergreen trees punctuated the generous expanse of lawn. Here, the house and big trees blocked the view of the prison, and the property didn't feel institutional at all.

Warden Vukcevich and his wife, Ann, graciously welcomed us and invited us inside.

Eventually we toured the house, which unexpectedly was a lovely old Georgian Colonial, circa 1910.

It was huge with four bedrooms, three bathrooms, and servant's quarters above the kitchen.

The historical significance of this home was clear, but considering its size and obvious maintenance requirements, it was "a woman killer." There was no way I could physically maintain the large rooms on my own steam, nor did I want to.

Passing from the living room through the French doors we entered the sunporch. It was bright and cheerful with three walls of windows. I was thinking it would be a wonderful playroom for Robby, until Sam pointed up to the ceiling and called my attention to several short scrapes in the plaster. He said, "Those are the bullet holes left by my would-be assassins when they attempted to prevent me from testifying against them in the riot trial!"

There I stood with our toddler in my arms as Sam proudly displayed, above us, the grim circumstances of this home's very recent past.

Abruptly, the charm of this lovely antique house faded. Bob's pop would have asked, "*Jesus, Mary, and Joseph, what's next?*"

I decided "pretended bravado" was the only way I could deal with our future. Surely, my courage would kick in eventually. Until that happened, I would adopt a new mantra I had heard recently:

"Fake it till you make it, baby."

I tuned back into the conversation in time to hear Bob say to me, "Honey, it will be good to move in and end the daily commute to and from Morrisville!"

"Well, at least we certainly agreed about that!"

*

On the drive home, Joan and Sharon had a lot to talk about. Robby had exhausted his supply of jellybeans and so he fell asleep. I never imagined the challenges, opportunities, and adventures that lay ahead. The only thing I needed now was the tenacity to do it all!

It was time, at last, to focus on changing the climate and environment there under "The Dome."

"Violence control unit, you're up next!"

CHAPTER 12

Violence Control

Rubin "Hurricane" Carter.

"As long as people use violence to combat violence, we will always have violence."

— Michael Berg

Chief Deputy Ucci received information from a mob-connected inmate about an escape planned for Easter Sunday. Jim had an excellent rapport with the inmate population and staff and often received actionable information. He passed the "tip" on to the unit captain, Richie Curran. The chief authorized overtime for several of Curran's unit members, tasking them to conduct a surprise evening search of the entire prison, focused on finding specific contraband items and their location.

This all-encompassing search would require a total lockdown of the prison, and so we waited until lights out when the prison would already be buttoned down. Locking the prison down was viewed as punishment and so we waited.

As was always the case, the information Chief Ucci received was spot on. We found a treasure trove of escape paraphernalia in the exact locations provided to us. The chief, Captain Curran, and his men foiled the escape of three men, all serving life or life-equivalent sentences. They planned to scale a wall at the back end of the property and kill the correction officer in the tower to prevent him from reporting their escape.

Among the most interesting and disturbing things found were these:

1. A prison-made shotgun (test-fired by the State Police), and it worked as designed.
2. A twenty-five-foot metal ladder, crafted by inmate John Mahodnick, a mafia hitman. They discovered each separate piece, including the small plastic bags holding nuts, bolts, and washers, each hidden in a different place throughout the prison.
3. A homemade zip gun, concealed in an inmate's cell, hidden and disguised, as part of the toilet paper dispenser. The State Police tested it, and it worked just fine.

We learned several inmates planned the escape to take place during the graveyard shift scheduled to begin at 10:20 p.m. This gave us only several hours to locate the evidence.

The twenty-five-foot metal ladder Curran and his men found hidden was assembled using a prison-made version of an erector set. What is an erector set? When I was seven years old, my sister Joan gave me an erector set for my birthday. It included various lengths of metal pieces with regularly spaced holes. Included were nuts, washers, and bolts to assemble structures. The components of this ladder were much the same.

*

Without the "tip-off," these items would never have been discovered because of the ingenuity used to conceal separate parts of the same item all over the place.

According to the New York Times, prison riots increased steadily during the 1970s. They reported thirty-nine prison riots in the United States between 1971 and 1980. Their message was that prison violence went virtually unchecked. This violent environment reinforced the public's "anti-rehabilitation" attitude of the '70s and reflected that decade's point of view. But I believed that the four-pronged Violence Control approach I developed, and partially tested, while still the assistant superintendent at Trenton would be successful in helping to reduce and control violence. We knew we were rowing against the tide of public opinion and political reality, but we believed we could counter that reality, and over time we would prove it.

Bob Clifford, the Department of Institutions and Agencies' commissioner, and Director Bill Fauver, director of Corrections and Parole, supported my goal and the direction I wanted to take.

*

Establishing uninterrupted control at Rahway was not a simple task. It would have been impossible if we had not initially put in place two significant initiatives. First, a "Hands-Off and No Chokeholds Ever" policy had been introduced and routinely practiced, as we attempted to further develop trust and respect between staff and inmates. Second, crafting a new table of organization was imperative.

Our principal restructuring enacted a straight line of an uninterrupted communications network between every prison inmate and me.

In his book Close Control: Managing a Maximum-Security Prison, Nathan Kantrowitz took a position I agreed with. He wrote, "The warden of a prison is the key figure in prison control. The warden is engaged in a daily battle minute-by-minute, and inch-by-inch, over who is in control: either he is, or his prisoners and guards are...."

Rahway's Present Staffing Levels:

Superintendent	1
Chief Deputy	1
Captains	3
Lieutenants	5
Sergeants	7
Correction Officers	500
Medical Staff	3
Professional Staff	15
Other Civilian Staff	8
Total Number of Staff Between the Inmates and Me	543
Inmates	1,500
An inmate had to jump over hurdles to get to me!	543

Under this communications model, the superintendent didn't have a chance to be firmly in control of a prison. Notice the many layers of staff between the warden and inmates. The result? Years of repetitive violence, and the malignant degradation of inmates.

*

Transferring Captain Richie Curran from Trenton Prison to Rahway Prison was the first step I took to install the Control Unit. He was the obvious choice to head the unit. While at Trenton he enjoyed the respect of the inmate population, and he had earned my complete trust.

Rich Curran and Jim Ucci were Rahway's "dynamic duo," helping advance our newest improvements skillfully.

As Jim and I made genuine progress developing the Operations Unit, I began working with Captain Curran in the afternoons. Rich was actively staffing the new module; he had already selected one sergeant and three correction officers to staff his section.

As soon as the proficiency of the Operations Unit was apparent, Ucci moved over to work with Curran and me. This was vitally important because the captain and the chief deputy would need to work closely together once the VCU was up and running. So Chief Ucci, Captain Rich Curran, and I were joined at the hip as we "moved the ball downfield."

When we were ready to operationalize the VCU, we planned to do it in two phases. To begin the process, we installed the enforcement and investigative piece, followed by the people and the communications module. That required coordination with the offices of the Attorney General, the County Prosecutor, the State Police, and the local police. It wasn't long before the fundamental parts were in place; we were ready to activate our newest unit. The prior Rahway Prison administration established control by installing iron gates and wire mesh barriers in parts of the institution designed to slow inmate foot traffic down and limit access to recreational areas. Punishment as a means of control was routinely doled out.

Some observers back then said it was "only a matter of time before, lacking diversions, the inmates would explode." I had a flashback to early in the new year when staff triumphantly removed all iron gates and wire mesh barriers. This immediately eased tensions and lightened everyone's spirits—mine included.

It was obvious we needed an effective pass and movement control system to improve an inmate's ability to get to medical appointments and other services. It also provided perfect inmate location control and kept inmates away from places where they could prey on other inmates.

When planning our inmate travel pass system, we divided the prison into zones and assigned each zone a different color. Soon, a rainbow of yellow, red, blue, green, and orange walls boldly announced exactly which zone an inmate was in. If he didn't have a pass or his pass was the wrong color, he was out of place. Out-of-place inmates received a disciplinary charge and were confined to their cells for one day. These charges were considered seriously by the parole board. It was soon recognized that "out of place was not a good place to be."

We printed colored inmate travel passes to synchronize with the colored zones in the exact locations of the appointment.

Next, we designed an inmate travel pass system listing inmates on a published and widely distributed schedule, helping them pass through specific security checkpoints at their scheduled appointment time.

The result was positive, with inmates now having access to better care. In addition, staff could control inmate movements at scheduled times.

If an inmate's pass was the wrong color, he was sent back to his housing unit, thus eliminating opportunities to be where he didn't belong.

*

We quickly recaptured the momentum we built for the Control Unit's development before Anne Klein redirected our mission. We began by creating the unit's unique in-house small police department. We staffed it with responsible correction officers who preferred to be police officers. These men were biding their time until they could transfer to a city government police department. Until then, my strategy was to keep them at Rahway by offering them a tempting challenge.

They would be our internal police force performing the work of a cop on the beat. This move took away some of the workload correction officers were already doing informally.

This experiment proved to be an instant success. The staff responded well, and it sent the message I hoped it would deliver to all. Without robust violence control, meaningful inmate programs and services had no way of succeeding. Our drug problems would flourish, and the inmate threat groups would continue to thrive.

The VCU's internal police force was the first and only such unit of its kind in the corrections department in New Jersey, and maybe anywhere else.

I viewed Rahway Prison as a small city with all of a small urban city's inherent problems and needs. Having our own internal police force that kept us informed and positioned to deal with the many problems we encountered daily became a significant advantage. But our headaches were so numerous that the Control Unit was soon overwhelmed, and we lacked the authority to resolve many problems. We contacted those members of our staff who were waiting to join a local police force. We asked if they were interested in additional training that would certify them as police officers. The answer was a resounding "Yes."

I contacted the State Police and spoke with Colonel Pagano. He graciously offered to accept our officers as candidates to be trained and earn certification as police officers at the State Police Academy! At first, the guys couldn't believe what I was telling them, and then every officer in the prison was elated and wished to become involved.

We sent twelve eager men off to the academy, and when they returned to us, they were each fully trained, and certificated, by the New Jersey State Police Training Academy as police officers. We were so proud of all of them. As we hoped, most of them stayed with us at Rahway as officers, now with official police authority. Having our own internal police force, trained and certificated by the New Jersey State Police Academy, helped us enhance the safety and security of staff and residents.

In this percolating environment, it would be pushy to suggest yet another squad for our over-tasked Violence Control Unit. But several officers began requesting the formation of a SWAT team. That would add more demand to an already overburdened Deputy Chief Jim Ucci and Captain Richie Curran. But I learned Jim could handle "burning the candle at both ends, and in the middle too."

Do we really need a SWAT team? I asked the chief. This is SCO (Senior Correction Officer) James Lee's recollection regarding the start of Rahway's emergency response team: "I took the idea for the formation of our SWAT team to Lieutenant Bill Miller. He took it to you [meaning me] and the chief deputy, and the rest is history."

I believed we had all the security we needed, and I had no interest in a SWAT team, but Officer Lee's boundless confidence convinced us to reconsider.

Following several weeks of additional appeals from Officer Lee we finally agreed: If he could assemble and train a volunteer team, on their own time off the clock, we would view a trial of their proposed squad.

Officer Lee set up a demo of the team in action for the chief and me. We watched in awe as these self-assured young men propelled off our building's roofs and, in mid-air, kicked in windows to perform hostage rescue simulations I never expected to see. I was breathless. They honestly blew me away. Jim and I readily agreed to support and enable their impressive project.

We soon found their program to be as needed and important as any emergency plan we had, even if we didn't need it until there was an actual emergency.

Captain James Lee was very active and a firm supporter of our boxing program, the Lifers Juvenile Awareness Program,

The Escorts, and other inmate groups, including the Ayuda toy drive group.

IN FEBRUARY 2022, Captain Lee reminded me of the time I had the business manager purchase a small food truck for the recreation yard. I wanted it stocked with ice and cold drinks that inmates and staff could purchase (during the summer months) using script. Among the advantages was that commissary sales increased, providing additional funds for the inmate welfare fund.

Captain Lee was among the top staff contributors to the programs that received national attention from the media. However, it's important to note that it took a lot of captains, lieutenants, sergeants, and correction officers to help Rahway Prison reduce violence by some sixty-three percent.

*

Our small police force conducted and reported on all internal investigations and liaised with the county prosecutor and the local police and State Police. They made criminal referrals too and fulfilled the required official police training and certification at the State Police Training Academy to legally do this.

The Commission of Investigation of the State of New Jersey, in their April 1977 report to Governor Brendan Byrne, included the following in its report (page 95):

The Control Unit Concept

During the commission's investigation, and prior to the May-June 1976 public hearings, Rahway State Prison introduced the Violence Control Unit and locater board concepts into the state penal system [sic; only] at the Rahway State Prison.

At Rahway, the Violence Control Unit is composed of a select few correction officers who are specially trained and have responsibilities in intelligence gathering, inmate discipline, investigative technique, and prison control technique.

The unit maintains its own polygraph capability and regularly delves into areas, including the importation of contraband into the prison and work release and furlough related checks.

The unit monitors actions of prison employees and inmates.

Through the efforts of this unit at Rahway, many narcotics and weapons-related arrests have been made and "no show" work release positions were discovered.

Just before word went out about the establishment of our new unit, the New York Times printed an article on December 17, 1976, about drug sales and possession, (mostly marijuana being brought in by visitors) within the prison. I was quoted as saying, "Behind the walls of Rahway there is a city with crimes going on, and we had no way to cope with the problems." A couple of days later, when our initiative reached an editor's desk at the same paper, they officially introduced our police force to the public in an article titled "Rahway Struggles". They acknowledged the start of our private internal police back in March of 1975, to expose drug users and determine the extent of the problem. The article also pointed out that correction officers had been sent to the State Police Academy to be trained to deal with the situation, as well as prison officials were liaising with local police units in an attempt to cut off the supply of narcotics.

Now we were ready to attack our drug problem. I sent a letter to federal, state, and local law enforcement agencies, inviting their participation in a drug trafficking task force the VCU was organizing.

*

At successive committee meetings, the broad range of recommendations included a urine monitoring system. As a result, hundreds of inmates provided samples of urine for analysis to determine if there were narcotics present in their systems.

We also used narcotics dogs borrowed from a local police department to search inmate cells while the men were in the recreation hall. I am proud to say no inmate ever saw a dog. Eventually, we bought two staff support dogs trained explicitly for narcotics detection. We purchased the dogs in Canada and had them shipped to us.

Senior Correction Officer Anthony Amicuchi proficiently formed a small team of dog handlers. Frank Landers and his vocational training students built two kennels to house them. On visiting days, we moved the dogs to other kennels in an area where visitors passed, enabling the dogs to sniff out and detect visitors attempting to introduce drugs to the prison.

*

Beyond the security services provided by the VCU, we also needed to counterbalance that focus with skillful inmate interactions.

Captain Curran, excellent in custody and security services, was also adept at working with inmates. In addition, everyone viewed him as fair. He was the logical "counterbalance" needed to establish a needed rapport with the inmate population.

The most crucial programs installed were the inmate disciplinary procedures and how we meted out inmate discipline. Why? The main reason is that following the 1971 riot, inmates filed a list of demands that remained unsatisfied. One of them read: "Guards work out their frustrations on prisoners in a kangaroo court-type atmosphere." This had to be corrected ASAP.

In 1974, Commissioner Ann Klein, then also recognizing the problem, ordered a revision of current procedures for managing inmate infractions of prison regulations and transferring inmates within the state prison system.

We grabbed the bull by the horns at Rahway and began revising our internal inmate disciplinary program before Anne Klein issued her directive. But the division blithely ignored her directive, as they had previously ignored the overtime order issued by Klein. As a result, Rahway's carefully crafted policies and procedures, prepared with the expert help of Sylvia McCollum from the Federal Bureau of Prisons, had been developed and up and running long before the division issued its own revised standards. When finally published, sections of their new standards mirrored Rahway's work.

ANOTHER SIGNIFICANT TASK performed by the new VCU was the development of an inmate grievance process new to the division. I decided that inmates should have an alternate vehicle to bring issues directly to me, by submitting written inmate grievances. That became a valuable supplement to my "listening to and acting on" inmate grievances, which I heard daily.

Soon, the operation of these invaluable programs provided the evidence needed to refine and revise the current inmate pass-and-movement system.

Prison control breaks down when pass systems do not dependably facilitate inmates reaching appointments for services they need—like medical care. In addition, poor movement control allows inmates to enter areas they should not be in. Violence occurs when this happens.

BACK ON THE second morning here, I stood waiting to be passed through to the Tie-To. I noticed uncontrolled traffic descending on the "star" officer, making his job incredibly stressful. A pass system would control and bring order to all that inmate movement. If inmates were not at work, school, medical appointments, the law library, or recreation, they should be in their cells.

It had been impossible to know the whereabouts of every inmate, and that was my challenge. In addition, it became apparent that the lack of an inmate movement control system led to chaos. However, after much trial and error, everyone welcomed our new pass system—staff and inmates alike. Happiest of all was especially the day shift star officer, Senior Correction Officer Gagliano ("Gaggs"). His job was finally manageable.

Once again, Director Fauver didn't show an interest in our progress at Rahway. This was the opposite of the encouragement to pursue my new ideas when we worked together at Trenton.

What changed? Innovation and improved prison control had been a good thing at Trenton, but now that I was at Rahway doing the same things, it was no longer recognized as improvement or even as a good thing to do. This indifference created confusion.

Since I no longer received feedback from the director, I decided if we were to accomplish anything at Rahway I would move forward on my own as I did when working with Bill at Trenton. If he didn't approve of what we were doing, I felt sure I would hear from him. I never did.

*

Our progress remained in zoom mode. In the upcoming pages, I'll give a few examples of the outstanding work performed by the unit...

ON ONE OCCASION we responded to an incident that could easily have gotten out of hand. A group of fifty-eight inmates suddenly descended on the staff dining room, where they didn't belong, because of the vulnerability of the weak pass and movement control system we inherited.

In the room on his lunch break, Sergeant Bobby Martin (among the best I had) saw the nefariousness headed their way, and discretely asked the officers and staff still dining to "Leave the area now! Don't ask questions!" before telephoning Chief

Ucci. Based on the chief's instructions, he quickly removed the knives from the kitchen and dining area and was able to get out while locking the inmates inside. He reported back to the chief, whom I was now next to, and gave us the updated situation.

The chief and I determined we would not lock down the institution. Instead, we ran work, school, law library, recreation, and other movements on schedule. We planned to run the institution right past them. They could watch inmates going about their normal business by looking through the small windows at the top of the dining room wall. And that's just what they did!

The instigators stacked dinner tables one on top of the other to reach and look out of the top windows. From that shaky vantage point, they could see the short hallway leading to the dining room and the end of the Tie-To walkway. There, they could observe inmate movement as everyone else went about their usual routine.

I made several trips to an outside dining hall window during that night to communicate personally with the troublemakers. On one such trip, I asked "Mean Joe Green," an inmate I spoke to often and enjoyed trading banter with, "Are you in there?" No response!

"If you're in there, Joe, you need to help me get this thing over with." Again, hearing no response, I promised, "I'll see you guys later as you're being escorted out of the dining room."

It was a freezing night, and we had turned off the heat, water, and electricity in the dining room, hoping the protestors would be cold and uncomfortable enough to give up peacefully.

It took until four in the morning, and then with the help of the local fire department we hosed the troublemakers down through the window the firefighters had broken. Within a few minutes, they were soaked to the skin. I worried their dripping clothing would soon stiffen in the cold.

I hollered to inmate Joe Green, "Hey, Joe, ready to talk?"

His response was, "Yeah, boss, we're ready to come on out."

Once they surrendered, Lieutenant Bill Miller supervised our recently formed Emergency Response Team officers as they strip-frisked each man. Once searched, each shivering man was escorted back to his cell by two officers. We videotaped the entire process for the record. There were no hands-on incidents. Our Hands-Off policy was by now working routinely.

Commissioner Klein called me at 5 a.m. to say, "Thanks for a job well done." It pleased her that the whole thing went down without a single bit of violence. We were also pleased.

I asked Commissioner Klein to loan me the department's ombudsman, Don Tucker, to sit in on all disciplinary hearings to lessen the possibility of civil suits. As a result, there were no appeals, grievances, or inmate lawsuits afterward. Thank you, Don.

The inmates faced disciplinary charges, and after an investigation, Captain Curran referred some to the county prosecutor's office.

The news story that ran in *The Millville Daily* on December 23rd describes what occurred and told about the hearings scheduled for 58 Black Muslim prisoners who had barricaded themselves in the dining room for 18 hours, and then peacefully surrendered, in protest of the transfer of two inmates to another institution.

*

When investigating inmate crimes, violence, inmate grievances, disciplinary reports, incident reports, and other communications, "my word against his" always presented a problem. When I informed the director about our adding a polygraph program to Rahway to the VCU, I was pleasantly surprised when instead of his normal indifference he supported our purchase of polygraph equipment from our budget. As a result, I sent a corrections sergeant to New York for thirteen weeks to train as a polygraphist. One of the country's leading professionals trained him. Rahway's inclusion of this program and purchase of the right equipment and accessories was among the best investment I made for the institution.

ANOTHER INSTANCE OUR internal police force investigated was the murder of an inmate in four-wing. Only one murder occurred during my entire tenure as warden. An inmate murdered another inmate because he stole the inmate's wife's picture from his cell. Our prison police responded to the murder, sealed off the area, and set up a crime scene. They then interviewed staff and inmates, and before long, they had a prime suspect—before the county prosecutor or even the county coroner arrived on the scene. We were once more grateful for the training the State Police Academy gave to our VCU officers. Without this, we would never have the authority to establish a crime scene or to interview witnesses.

IN YET ANOTHER incident, potentially an explosive one, Captain Curran and Chief Ucci did a masterful job helping us resolve a situation that could easily have led to another takeover riot like the one in 1971. It involved Rubin "Hurricane" Carter.

Rubin "Hurricane" Carter and Tommy Trantino were two of the most defiant, dangerous inmates ever confined in the New Jersey prison system. Both were Rahway inmates, and both were there at the 1971 riot. They were still there when I arrived.

After becoming a warden, I learned about Carter's ongoing subversive activities inside Rahway Prison. I remembered him, from Trenton, having an obstinately uncooperative attitude toward discipline and authority.

It all began when we received intelligence briefings from our internal police force concerning an insubordinate and surreptitious meeting Carter planned to have in the drill hall (indoor recreation area). Carter, an antagonistic disruptor, called his group the "Rahway People's Council." They were among some of the angriest and willful inmates we had.

We assigned several of our officers and a sergeant to the Drill Hall during evening recreation. They were to observe and supervise evening recreation for the next several nights.

If Carter had a meeting, we needed dependable security staff there. They were told not to interfere with the assemblage. The chief and I wanted a rundown immediately following the evening's recreations. Waiting impatiently in my office, the chief deputy, Captain Curran, and I received periodic reports via radio from the drill hall.

The intelligence information we had was correct. That night there was a meeting, and an emotional Carter defiantly led it. Some 200 to 250 inmates were present, for their usual recreation period in the hall, and most seemed uninterested in what Carter was saying. Some seemed curious, but soon drifted back to their basketball game.

Carter instructed the assembled group to refer all complaints or grievances, major and minor, to him and not to me. He referred to me as a "liar" several times during his angry tirade. He didn't say when I'd lied.

He stated, "From now on, I'll be the one to give the complaints to the committee Governor Cahill set up to hear inmate grievances!"

Carter's group included his recalcitrant appointees. As expected, he appointed himself as the group's chairperson. His second in command, cop killer Tommy "The Rabbi" Trantino, author of Lock the Lock, was present. Bill Grimsley, the group's inmate paraprofessional lawyer, was also there. I inquired if inmate Mastrapa, the duly elected chair of the Inmate Council, was present at the meeting. It relieved me to learn he was not in attendance.

At the end of the meeting, Captain Curran walked across the street to the superintendent's residence to develop a strategy to manage and control the situation. I called the chief at his home on campus and asked him to come over to my house to join the planning session. The usually low-key Captain Curran reported, "Boss, the meeting was highly charged and very inflammatory."

THAT NIGHT AT the 10 p.m. lights out, wing officers reported a lot of chatter in their housing units. I believed the inmates worried about potential violence when the prison opened for business in the morning. Many talked about not coming out of their cells for the breakfast meal. Most men wanted to avoid any problems.

Based on the information at hand, we determined that Carter, Trantino, Bill Grimsley, and three others had to be transferred from Rahway that night on a "night train." The night train was a caravan of buses and vans used to transport inmates safely in the middle of the night.

I called Director Fauver from my home office, giving him a full briefing, and asking for permission to transfer Carter and four other inmates from the Rahway Prison later that night. With no hesitancy and absent questions, the director approved my request. He said he would inform Trenton's warden to expect a transfer of several Rahway inmates.

In high-risk situations, we could use lethal force. In fact, the chief scheduled a security supervisor to ride in the "night train" with Carter. That supervisor was armed with a Thompson sub-machine gun just in case anyone attempted to interfere with the transfer on Route 1 and assist Carter in escaping.

The newly developed cell extraction and new transfer procedures designed and implemented by Chief Ucci prevented us from having to use force. It wasn't difficult to figure out that sending a large cell extraction team for Carter would display overwhelming force to discourage resistance from the start to the end of the transfer.

Officer Charlie Butler led the cell extraction team selected by the chief. The team voted to have Butler take the cell entry lead position to extract Carter from his cell. Someone shouted, "Hey, Butler! You go first because you were the US Navy's light-heavyweight champ. Then, if Carter wants to fight, you can knock him out!"

Once the men arrived at Carter's cell, Butler asked him to exit his cell peacefully when the cell door opened. Charley's order was, "Okay, Carter. Time to go. You are leaving for Trenton. The night train's waiting for you. Leave everything behind. Come out with your hands up in the air."

Carter complied with Butler's order. However, he made one request. He asked Butler if he could take his legal papers with him to Trenton. Charley said okay. He told the two officers assigned to pack up Carter's things and to treat them as if they were their own. At other facilities, they would not have been handled with respect and care. I was proud of the work performed by Charley and the team.

Chief Ucci directed Captain Bob Eder to write disciplinary charges for the men who conducted the unauthorized meeting.

When the population woke up in the morning, Carter and his cohorts were gone, but there was no reaction from the inmates to their absence! He clearly didn't have the influence he thought he had.

I MET WITH the Inmate Council the first thing that next morning, not knowing what to expect. Council Chair Augusto Mastrapa didn't complain about Carter and the others' transfer to Trenton. He not only didn't complain, but he also assured me that "we have no problem, boss."

Carter blatantly discounted the duly elected council's authority (which I had supported from the start), thus Mastrapa's indifference to the transfer. This was prison politics, and this time it benefited us.

Following a ten-minute meeting with the council, I left to begin my daily "temperature check" of the inmate population. It was a relief to discover Carter's surreptitious get-together of the previous night and the covert plan to set the administration aside and "run the show himself" had not become an issue. But I couldn't believe absolutely no one even mentioned his name. That told me everyone had decided they preferred the prison at peace.

Still, I was aware it was the elephant in the room that no one mentioned.

I believe Carter was a troublemaker through and through. None of his adverse claims about Rahway being mismanaged were true. Rahway was running better than it ever had. Staff and inmates alike appreciated our efforts to attack the problem of rampant violence so aggressively. Both sides saw progress being made and welcomed it.

Carter's actions were a prep for a coup. It would have sparked another 1971 riot if he had been believable.

The plan was to eliminate my influence and re-establish the violence that was on the wane, while putting threat groups back in business again.

*

Chief Ucci and Captain Curran performed yet another excellent job when they helped me resolve a 1976 hostage-taking incident at the Adult Diagnostic and Treatment Facility in Avenel, New Jersey.

It was detailed in an article in *The Morning Call* on November 26, 1976, titled "City Woman Held Hostage Is Freed By Prison Inmate". It described how an Allentown woman was held hostage for 8 hours in Rahway by a convicted rapist. The inmate, who was serving a 30-year sentence held her with a sharpened television antenna to her throat. He was demanding the transfer to a different facility, private psychiatric care, a review of his original charges and amnesty for the hostage event. He surrendered to me.

CHIEF UCCI AND I completed yet another major assignment. Commissioner Fauver ordered me to close the maximum-security sex offender unit inside our walls and open a new facility in the neighboring city of Avenel. The chief and I worked out how the facility would temporarily operate for the next few months until the commissioner appointed a new superintendent there. We had to operate two maximum-security facilities simultaneously, Rahway, and the Treatment Unit, with only Rahway staff available to us. We all breathed a sigh of relief when the new administration was finally installed there.

**But I learned that resolving one
problem only led us to our next adventure:
DEATH THREATS!**

CHAPTER 13

Threats and Promises

An assassin leveled a shotgun blast at my predecessor,
Superintendent U. Samuel Vukcevich,
through a sun porch window directly behind the trees

*"I tell the truth. And I know what I'm talking about.
That's why I'm a threat. When you're a threat,
you're always a target."*

— *Snoop Dogg*

The Violence Control Unit (VCU), Chief Ucci, and the State Police prison liaison, Lieutenant John Mazekian, helped my family get through the death threats we received that began shortly after we arrived at Rahway.

I guess officially, it began one morning before moving from Pennsylvania to Rahway, when on the way to work, Joan and I narrowly escaped having a serious car accident.

Traditionally, inmates assigned to the prison's garage supported the institution's fleet of vehicles. Their work was supervised by one civilian mechanic, Mr. Benedetti, who could not possibly supervise the work of so many inmate mechanics on his own. I wasn't surprised that someone seized the opportunity to sabotage the brakes on my state-issued vehicle.

We were headed north on Highway Route 1. Joan was with me, planning to restock the bookshelves in my new office at the prison. Traveling in the early morning work traffic, suddenly the foot brakes in the car fell apart. With lots of luck and a little skill, I maneuvered us at full speed onto a dogleg to our right and off Route 1. Once in the dogleg, I made a sharp left turn and piloted us up a steep grassy embankment, bringing the car finally to a stop.

The State Police crime lab inspected the brakes in the state vehicle and concluded someone had deliberately rigged them to fall apart. We never learned who had tampered with the braking system, but we changed the garage procedures and provided correction officer supervision, to support Mr. Benedetti, in the garage, pronto.

WE HOPED MOVING to Rahway and living on prison grounds would afford us more security, and it did. But, one Saturday morning, as I usually did, I went to the front porch to get the morning newspaper. It stunned me to see on the front page an article detailing how Joan, the children, and our dogs were to be beheaded and stacked up on top of each other on our living room floor, left for me to discover when I arrived home from work.

My entire family, including the family dogs—we had three—found ourselves on a hit list. To this day, I do not know why or who set up the plan. Captain Curran thought the death threat could pertain to my incident with the group of inmates who took over the officer's dining room. However, none of it made sense to me because I had never threatened or angered anyone. But it was apparent someone or some group of someone wished to get my attention—and they did.

I asked Fauver to check out this information. He reported back to me there was, in fact, a plot. We were under a death threat. Everyone took the threat seriously.

Chief Ucci had Joan taken to the prison rifle range and taught her how to fire a weapon. When away from home, she carried a handgun in her purse and held a two-way radio in her hand. She told me she avoided grocery shopping carrying the gun and radio. People would back away from her whenever the radio crackled with a message (remember, this was 1974, before cell phones). Fortunately, she never needed to remove the gun from her purse.

Armed guards drove our daughter Sharon to and from school or wherever she was going. She said she felt like she was Amy Carter, the then president's daughter, because the car that took her to and from school was an all-black security vehicle. The escorting officers, dressed in full dress uniform, and armed, made her arrival at school very conspicuous. There were no door handles in the vehicle's back seat, making it impossible for a passenger in the back to open the door for themselves. The officer needed to leave the car to open the back door from the outside for her to exit the vehicle. The kids at the school thought she was a celebrity. She didn't dare explain. It was all very embarrassing for her.

Our house had alarm buttons that connected to the Control Center, installed on the inside of each door jamb leading to the outside. In addition, a panic button was installed in the master bedroom on the second floor.

*

Years later, I learned that two good friends—a Rahway sergeant and a senior correction officer—paid an "unofficial visit" to the inmate they heard had ordered the hit on our family. I was told their grim message to him went something like this: "The warden's family is under armed guard. We want you to understand that if anything happens to any member of the family, or any of their dogs, there will be a 'rash of suicides' inside Rahway Prison. Spread the word. Understand, we'll be watching, and that's a promise."

Eventually, we were able to call off the armed guard support, and cautiously returned to "normal routine."

*

Was the VCU effective? Absolutely, yes. According to Captain Richard Gilgallon, who at the time was a correction officer at Rahway: "Got to admit, many of the changes made were pure genius. The Locator, Pass Office, and Operations Unit are examples. The Locator system at Rahway in the past was two or three Rolodex boards which inmates changed. No one could find the inmates. Wing officers transferred inmates from wing to wing and simply sent a wing change slip to Center."

Every officer had a passbook, and they sent inmates moving around unchecked. Operations was the shift blotter clerk (correction officer) deciding where each person was assigned. And if a change was made, they sent you a telegram at home (outside the prison). Giving credit where it's due, the new changes made long-lasting improvements to the system.

*

Reporting to the governor, the New Jersey State Commission of Investigation held major hearings investigating the Furlough

Program statewide. Unexpectedly, and beyond the scope of the investigation, the commission took time to heap praise on Rahway Prison's new Violence Control Unit.

The following was taken from the commission's full report on furloughs, statewide:

VIOLENCE CONTROL UNIT

During the commission's investigation and before the May-June 1976 public hearings, Rahway State Prison introduced the Violence Control Unit and Locator Board Concepts into the [sic; Rahway institution only] state penal system.

With the concurrence of Rahway Superintendent Hatrak, the Violence Control Unit has also devised and implemented a security system dealing with inmate records. The records are kept behind bolted doors and are accessible only to specified civilian prison employees.

Personal Information duplicative of that in the inmate's file is kept updated in connection with the Rahway locator system. This system comprised a wall-sized chart of the name and location of every inmate, including those on Pass in the institution. In addition, color codes and cards are used to show such things as furlough or work release status, escape or medical risk, narcotics history.

The inmate's movement in the prison is also consistently posted on the chart. Under the Locator System, information from the inmate's file—which is used as the basis for work release, furlough, [sic; parole] and other decisions. It is automatically cross-checked against the Locator material for discrepancies. Thus, at Rahway, two separate packets of material would have to be changed for an inmate to take advantage of misinformation.

The Commission commends officials at Rahway for their initiative in devising these necessary and useful systems.

We hope and trust that the Rahway method will soon be extended to all State Prisons.

*

I welcomed the commission's praise for the hard-working staff of the VCU. It was a good feeling knowing that knowledgeable corrections professionals recognized the success of our unique approach to prison violence control. We were excited to have improved the institution's image.

The Department of Corrections, however, never acted on the commission's "hope and trust" about expansion statewide. Once again, we at Rahway heard not one word from Director Fauver or his staff regarding the commission's acknowledgment of the VCU and their recommendation to implement the program statewide.

Inmates were not the only ones enjoying this more secure environment. One day soon after the report was made public, I was stopped on my walking tour by a rookie officer who was obviously enjoying all of the ongoing activity. He called out to me: "Hey, boss, what are we going to do next week?" His use of the word we indicated to me that he was part of our team and that there was unity within the staff. I called back, "Hey! Welcome to the team! Next week is an overdue surprise."

THROUGH OUR RECENT research for this book, I've learned that in the 1980s, the department's administration disbanded the Violence Control Unit. Unfortunately, this brought the resurgence of violence back to the institution. Once again inmate threat groups menaced the prison and the men living and working under its dome.

*

Besides describing our Violence Control Unit in this chapter, we hope this information serves as a vehicle and finds its way into the operations in some of today's maximum-security prisons. It can assist wardens in establishing direct and meaningful control of their prisons. As a result, they will observe significant reductions in the amount of prison violence (inmate on an inmate, inmate on staff, and staff on inmate).

With the support and praise heaped on the VCU, and its success within the institution, it was now time to turn our attention to what we had been working on in parallel with everything else…since my first month on the job…

Our unexpected inheritance.

CHAPTER 14

Unexpected Inheritance

Inmates hanging out on the tiers of their wing. Above is one of several results when an officer loses control of a housing unit

"Success occurs when opportunity meets preparation."

– Zig Zagler

Coming face to face with Rahway's problems, past and present, was like entering a colossal ever-twisting kaleidoscope. Long-festering issues were so obvious that I felt I was seeing them in brilliant technicolor.

Two years had passed since the 1971 riot when I arrived late in 1973. I realized little had changed since the revolt. One management problem I had not expected to confront was the lingering problem of unresolved riot demands. It bewildered me I could recognize very little headway after two whole years had passed and many of the same conditions lingered on.

During that same period, correction officers continued to stage strikes protesting low pay and violent working conditions.

At least two inmate work stoppages and one strike by correction officers called attention to post-riot conditions.

The article in The Central New Jersey Home News in June of 1972, titled "Inmate Strike Blamed On Stalled Negotiations" stated that conditions had really not improved since the Thanksgiving riot and that the work stoppage was the action of inmates who wanted to protest with non-violence. The story that appeared in The Record on November 18, 1973, titled "Inmates Bid Byrne Visit At Rahway" just thirteen days after I took over as warden, said that the Inmates Council was calling for Governor-elect Brendan Byrne to inspect the conditions of the prison because some of the conditions that caused the Thanksgiving riot still existed.

These newspaper accounts are just a few of many documenting the ignored conditions at Rahway.

The inmates who rioted handed over a list of demands to reporters as the riot neared its end. With that, they released the hostages, thus ending the violent disturbance.

*

This was the seething Rahway I inherited. The most essential unresolved items on the rioter's demand list pertained to life, health, and safety. Therefore, we worked on those issues first. Our strategy was to resolve those demands, one by one, as we simultaneously and systematically reshaped the operations of the institution.

Collaborating with the inmate council we prioritized the unresolved demands and took immediate action.

INMATE RIOT DEMANDS

1. RIOT DEMAND: INMATE MEDICAL CARE

"Aspirin" is the wonder drug for all ills at Rahway. The doctors do little "doctoring."

CONFIRMED CIRCUMSTANCES:

Referrals to the infirmary took days for doctors to schedule. It didn't take long to determine that we needed a trained infirmary administrator to manage infirmary operations. That person's first step was to prepare policies and procedures and retrain all infirmary staff.

Another circumstance presented itself early on. We needed a separate secure space at Rahway General Hospital to hold up to five inmates.

Inmates sick in their cells or injured on the job, in the yard, or somewhere else on the twenty-plus acres inside the prison walls waited a long time to receive what might be life-saving attention. Emergency help was only available in the infirmary or Rahway General Hospital.

An inmate or staff member needing urgent care had to walk or be carried to the infirmary. Occasionally, neither of these options were possible.

I learned our prison doctors' favorite procedure was to send sick or injured inmates to the Rahway General Hospital for treatment. That was unnecessary because the inmates seldom needed hospitalization, and their ailments could be handled at our infirmary. When I questioned the doctors regarding their unusual practice, they indignantly asked, "Do you know the cost of liability insurance?"

ACTION TAKEN:

Incredibly, no written policies and procedures guided the prison's infirmary operations. The only way to reorganize our healthcare program was to hire a qualified infirmary administrator. I moved money around in the budget to engage an administrator at no added expense.

It did not take long for daily infirmary operations to improve. We soon had a complete set of infirmary policies and procedures to follow, and all staff received training.

Another significant improvement in medical services occurred when, at my request, the Rahway General Hospital administrator assigned a separate secured ward for five "Rahway Prison inmate patients only."

I expected some resistance from the hospital administrator. But when I entered his office and explained why I was there, he readily accepted my proposal. In addition, he agreed it would be mutually beneficial for the security of his hospital staff and civilian patients to secure an area only for our inmates.

At our direction, our maintenance crew remodeled a dedicated area at the hospital with enhanced custody (inmate observation) and security features (locks and keys) in the separate ward. These renovations gave our officers better vantage points to keep their eyes on inmate patients.

We designed, trained, and implemented an emergency rescue squad staffed by inmates and civilian medical staff.

Our inmate volunteer squad was announced in an article on June 20, 1977 in The Central New Jersey Home News.

Not only was our inmate rescue squad unique, but it also responded to both staff and inmate emergencies.

To facilitate immediate emergency treatment "on the yard," in the shops, in school, or anywhere else on the property, I asked the staff if the emergency squad could respond in five or fewer minutes, in an emergency anywhere within the four walls of the prison, and they did.

Correction officers nearest a medical emergency received word as soon as the infirmary received a call for medical treatment. All officers were told to clear the way for the squad, much like traffic makes way for an ambulance in the community. Quickly opening gates and doors helped the team gain the speed needed to reach an emergency within our five-minute goal.

We now could access a doctor (if available), nurse, and two inmate technicians (all wearing properly equipped backpacks) to help save lives. One squad member carried a portable stretcher, and later we bought a portable defibrillator.

It was to our benefit that the Rahway General Hospital was a teaching and research hospital. I was enthusiastic about the continued training Rahway General offered to our rescue squad and with our new Infirmary administrator, Gigi.

In addition, hospital administrator Mr. Yoder volunteered his staff to train and license our staff and inmates as accredited emergency medical technicians (EMTs). A handpicked team of twelve inmates and civilian nurses completed a long course for qualifying as medical and surgical technicians.

After completing the course, the hospital certified each as emergency medical technicians, making them highly employable when released. This dedicated group formed one of our first Self-Rehab Enterprise Groups.

Without the total support and active participation in this program by the correction supervisors and correction officer staff, this effort would have failed. They helped assure everyone that the emergency squad was important not only to inmates but also to all staff.

The first emergency the squad responded to helped save an inmate's life. This pleased the correction officer's union (the Patrolman's Benevolent Association, PBA) and the inmate committee members.

Once alerted, our transport staff took the inmate to Rahway General Hospital.

Inmates at the prison complained it was almost impossible to see a doctor. When they saw one, instead of being treated, they got shipped out to Rahway Hospital. I checked our transportation records and learned their complaints were legitimate.

I interviewed our two doctors at the same time. The meeting went poorly. When pressed about the number of inmate transfers to the hospital, one of them angrily asked, "Do you know how much liability insurance costs us?"

I got the picture. There was no personal risk for the doctors when they shipped the inmates off to the hospital to be treated. That way, they could escape private lawsuits.

I said, "You're both fired!"

Shocked, one of the two asked, "How can you fire us? You'll be without doctor coverage!"

"You're right! However, until I hire two doctors that care, I can send inmates to the hospital myself! Just as you have been doing! Dr. Pepper would be more competent than you two."

We hired two new doctors (Dr. Pepper wasn't available!) and the situation improved with the help of our capable, new administrator. News traveled quickly on the prison's grapevine, and soon the population knew what we were doing. Changes we made relieved earlier tensions among the inmate population about health care. The "new guy" (me) gained credibility with the staff and inmates.

ANOTHER LIFE-SAVING event occurred when we used an unorthodox method to transport a critically injured inmate to the Rahway General Hospital.

At that time, we were in the process of a major remodel of our armory. But we needed a secure space to store our weapons and other security equipment until we completed our project. A staff member told us we could borrow a tank (Armored Personnel Carrier, APC) from a nearby National Guard unit for an indefinite period.

Captain Curran offered the inspired suggestion: "We should use the tank to store the equipment kept in our armory while it's under renovation."

When the Violence Control Unit checked it out, they reported the tank was an excellent secure space and would safely hold all our weapons and security equipment. Checking with the staff, we learned we had officers on each shift who belonged to the National Guard who were already qualified to operate an APC.

Senior Correction Officer Bobby Vasquez volunteered to travel to the local Guard unit to pick up our new on-loan tank. It attracted much community curiosity parked on our lawn in front of the institution and encouraged lots of lighthearted speculation.

Not long after the tank arrived, New Jersey had a major snowstorm. It was referred to as a "hundred-year storm." Not inches, but several feet of snow, had fallen. Checking with the State Department of Transportation, we learned the roads and streets of Rahway were closed. Because of the heavy accumulation of snow, the route usually traveled to the hospital had been entirely blocked. It wasn't simply an inconvenience for us; the storm paralyzed the entire town.

I worried: "How do we transport medical emergencies to the hospital?" Then a solution came to me. I called the chief, saying, "Jim, get one of our licensed officers to start the tank. Be sure it has plenty of fuel. Park it in the parking lot near the front entrance and leave it running."

The snow continued drifting lazily down all afternoon. Early that evening, my worry became a dreaded reality. An inmate suffered life-threatening stab wounds while eating in the mess hall. He needed to be transferred, at once, to the hospital. But unfortunately, we couldn't stop his profuse bleeding, and the man was barely conscious.

We had set up a command post in the conference room to monitor the storm and coordinate operations. From there, we informed state and local police that despite the street closures we would be on the city streets within minutes taking a seriously injured inmate to the hospital in a tank. He would undoubtedly die if we could not get him there in time.

We were hoping to get a police escort to guide us along the city's now impassible and hidden streets but were told they could not get to us. So, we were on our own. Senior Correction Officer Bobby Vasquez saved the day and remained on duty to operate the waiting vehicle.

We placed the inmate into the tank. Bobby struck out for the hospital in the blinding snow along the hushed and invisible streets.

We maintained continuous communications with the local police. They told us anxiously their switchboard was lit up like a Christmas tree. Great. They were getting frantic reports of a tank spotted roaming on a city street… We didn't expect that. Folks apparently thought an invasion of Rahway was taking place, and we were under attack! Whoops!

Our Violence Control Unit informed the hospital we were on our way to them with a stabbed inmate in a tank! It took a little convincing before they believed we weren't joking. When the tank arrived at the hospital, nurses and doctors were standing outside in the storm waiting for it. As the tank came into their view, they began applauding, waving, and cheering. Yes.

Chief Ucci, the Violence Control Unit, Officer Bobby Vasquez, a trained inmate medical/surgical technician (maximum security), and "the tank" saved the inmate's life. Everyone felt like Superman. We've been told this event has become a "Rahway legend!"

The Inmate Council made a big deal out of this, causing everyone's trust, hope, and confidence in us to soar. We were proud of ourselves too.

What a long way from the complaint of riot demand number one: "Aspirin was the drug of choice for every inmate's medical complaint."

We wondered: Would there have been a 1971 riot had inmates felt more secure?

2. RIOT DEMAND: MENU SUBSTITUTIONS

"Ninety-five percent of all inmates suffer from tooth and bone decay because of a lack of calcium in their diet."

CONFIRMED CIRCUMSTANCES:

When I took the time to examine the inmate dental records, I learned that 95 percent of all inmates suffered from tooth decay and it was true that it was mostly because of a lack of calcium in their diets.

As with other medical situations, inmates had difficulty seeing the dentist. I learned they attributed this to a lack of an inmate travel pass system. For this reason, it was nearly impossible for inmates to pass through Tie-To security and keep scheduled appointments promptly—if at all.

The highest number of serious complaints received from inmates on my daily walking tours of the prison was the excessive daily menu substitutions.

"Mr. Hatrak, why bother publishing a menu on housing unit bulletin boards? I made my decision about skipping meals based on the published menu. But I think I'm making a major mistake. Most days, the published menu differs from what really ends up on my tray."

Another complaint involved medical diets. Several groups of men required a doctor's prescription to meet their dietary and food preparation needs. These men included diabetics, cardiovascular patients, and those with other special medical conditions, including religious nutritional requirements.

Our internal kitchen and food services inspections and official assessments by the New Jersey State Department of Health routinely underwent scrutiny and found our food services program acceptable. Food services operations in the other state prisons were closed until they could pass an inspection. Luckily for us, the ongoing work on inmate riot demands allowed us to focus on the kitchen. As a result, and thanks to the hard work of Sergeant Bill Carter, we'd already made improvements that prepared us to pass random inspections.

ACTION TAKEN:

We distributed an administrative memorandum saying that the warden must approve menu changes. So, everyone now knew what to expect on the food line.

The Maintenance Department remodeled the Muslim fast food preparation area to meet their dietary and food preparation needs. In addition, the business manager bought all new cooking utensils and dinnerware for them.

On major holidays, we surprised the general population and served open buffet-style meals continuously throughout the entire day. This had never happened before. Inmates could help themselves and select from items on the serving line. Whatever the small additional cost, paying for peace on holidays was a small price. Just ask anyone who was here at the time of the 1971 Thanksgiving Day riot.

A state dietician conducted permanently scheduled three-month menu reviews to ensure we met dietary requirements.

The kitchen prepared medical diets ordered by a physician. Inmates picked up their meals on the serving line. It didn't take long to identify those inmates who had "scammed" a doctor into prescribing a special meal. They soon decided they preferred the regular meal everyone else was eating instead of the prescribed diet.

These changes satisfied riot demand number two, and we found: "Better chow equals better behavior."

3. RIOT DEMAND: INMATE PROGRAMS AND SERVICES

"Programs are inadequate, and there is no vocational training at all. We should teach prisoners a skill to help them get employment after release."

CONFIRMED CIRCUMSTANCES:

The director of Education I inherited was doing a poor job. He did not even try to visit the Trenton State Prison Education Department to observe school operations so painstakingly set up there by me and my faculty years earlier.

Rahway's school area was old, shabby, and much too small, needing remodeling or replacement. We required much more space to house the academic and vocational training programs we would soon begin implementing.

We replaced the director of Education.

We implemented two models for correctional education: A Model for Adult Basic Education in Corrections and another Model for Career Education. I had helped write both in Chicago in 1964 with Dr. Toni Ryan.

We made certain Rahway became actively involved in the Prison Education Network, encouraging participation, and granting college degree curriculums I had set up at the Trenton Prison in the 1960s.

Our Self-Rehab Enterprise Groups (SREG) would soon begin in the new inmate group center.

Sbnation.com published an article on March 12, 2014, some 42 years after I moved on, verifying I met my goal:

"… Under Hatrak's watch, there was as much space devoted to shops and classrooms inside Rahway as cells. He pushed hard to give inmates a shot at a life outside prison walls."

1. RIOT DEMAND: DISCIPLINARY SYSTEM

"Guards work out their frustrations on prisoners in a kangaroo court-type atmosphere."

CONFIRMED CIRCUMSTANCES:

The inmate disciplinary program was the source of many complaints I received on my daily walking tours.

ACTION TAKEN:

As described in Chapter 12, we put the Violence Control Unit in place, which significantly revised the inmate disciplinary program and created a brand-new inmate grievance program.

2. RIOT DEMANDS: DISCRIMINATION

"Blacks and Puerto Ricans are discriminated against. Blacks and Puerto Ricans make up 85 to 90 percent of prisoners and Puerto Ricans not able to practice their own cultural identity."

CONFIRMED CIRCUMSTANCES:

We discovered little support or interest to add Black, Hispanic, and Puerto Rican inmate programs.

ACTION TAKEN:

We helped create several inmate self-help groups. Among them were the Nation of Islam and Ayuda ("Help" in Spanish) and other Hispanic groups. We also formed an NAACP group supported by a local community chapter. Also, separate Narcotics and Gamblers Anonymous groups were set up. We maximized the availability of programs for Black, Hispanic, and Puerto Rican inmates. We involved local NAACP chapters in developing an inmate group to service alcoholics and drug users.

Once we closed the Sex Offender Unit, we used the entire building to develop an in-house drug abuse program. Here again, group members lived together and received treatment within separated communities. Pat Avonio created and managed the extraordinarily successful drug treatment program. Black, Hispanic, and Puerto Rican inmates heavily attended the program.

3. RIOT DEMAND: RELIGIOUS SERVICES

"Only certain religions can be practiced."

CONFIRMED CIRCUMSTANCES:

The only religious services and programs available to inmates were Protestant and Catholic religious services.

ACTION TAKEN:

We added Muslim, Spanish, Jewish, Catholic, and Protestant services and clergy. In addition, the Education Department offered Bible study groups for any inmate who wanted to attend.

4. RIOT DEMAND: MAIL SERVICES

"Mail is often delayed and often rifled."

CONFIRMED CIRCUMSTANCES:

Correction officers assigned to the mailroom read magazines and newspapers sent to inmates. We confirmed inmate complaints about package handling. Sometimes officers even helped themselves to the food too.

ACTION TAKEN:

We distributed incoming mail on the same day received. I handpicked a sergeant and assigned him to full-time duties in the mailroom. Together, we reviewed inmate complaints, acted, and, in short order, we eliminated 99 percent of all complaints. I stopped by the mailroom daily until the mail got distributed the same day received.

5. RIOT DEMAND: MANDATORY WORK ASSIGNMENTS

"Inmates not permitted to quit jobs they don't like, and wages are low."

CONFIRMED CIRCUMSTANCES:

The Classification Committee kept a priority list of jobs they were required to fill to maintain routine operations. However, they rarely gave inmates job assignments or transfers they requested. We had no authority over inmates' pay, as that was controlled by state directives.

ACTION TAKEN:

We took time, attendance, and pay record responsibilities from the hands of inmate pay clerks. Where it should never have been!

We found what could have become a scandal. Inmate pay clerks allowed a system of no-show jobs.

Paying cigarettes to inmate pay clerks resulted in an inmate's attendance records showing him present on a day when he was absent. This system developed when an inmate ingratiated himself to a civilian shop supervisor who rarely oversaw an inmate pay clerk's record keeping. The result was that fraudulent time and attendance information not only got an inmate paid money, but they also received work credits, which reduced an inmate's sentence. So, by manipulating "time served" records, inmate clerks covertly reduced the time inmates had to wait to appear before the state parole board.

I learned of this practice on one of my Thursday night interview lines. An inmate complained he "could not afford to pay cigarettes to have his work hours and workdays falsified." Had I not had the practice of weekly interview lines, I may have never learned how corrupt the inmate time and attendance systems were.

6. RIOT DEMAND: INMATE PROGRAM ASSIGNMENTS
"Programs cater to only a few inmates."

CONFIRMED CIRCUMSTANCES:

Space available for programs and services was at a premium, and not much space was open. Programs available to inmates were the same ones typically offered to prisoners in a maximum-security prison.

ACTION TAKEN:

I gave extra attention to accommodate the substantial increase in programs and services (psychological and psychiatric, for example) we were preparing to offer. To begin with, we closed the old school area and opened a new one in a reclaimed shop area that we remodeled to accommodate ten new classrooms and several staff offices. We took an old and unused boiler room and renovated the space to accommodate vocational training. Vocational Training Director Frank Landers did major construction in old and unoccupied space to enable our expanding visions. We maximized the use of the underutilized prison auditorium. We found one of the largest space additions in the regional laundry's unused basement and reclaimed it to add an enormous new contact visiting area! This was almost immediately followed by the addition of an outdoor visitor space to seasonally alternate with the warm summer conditions in the regional laundry area.

These newly developed areas all helped us meet my entry goal: "to have more program space than there was cell space."

7. RIOT DEMAND: INMATE REHABILITATION
"Rehabilitation does not exist."

CONFIRMED CIRCUMSTANCES:

This was an accurate statement. There was a short menu of programs and services we assigned inmates to, often without their concurrence. Inmate self-rehabilitation was not the policy.

ACTION TAKEN:

We encouraged and began a program of inmate Self-Rehabilitation. We called this Self-Rehab Enterprise Groups (SREG).

We tried to include ordinary daily activities everyone encounters into our release preparation programs.

We offered men opportunities to attend college classes live or remotely using existing technology.

Operating a commissary program, like a 7-Eleven grocery store, offered real-life experiences as a customer or as an employee.

Providing access to banking and postal services offered experiences with daily tasks. Normalizing an inmate's life wasn't "coddling." Instead, we showed the men how to function effectively in the current society to which they would return.

On May 25, 1977, our plan to give more than 1000 inmates at Rahway individual bank accounts was announced in the Asbury Park Press. The program was designed by myself and Lloyd Harris, president of Community State Bank and Trust Company. It was designed to exchange the current scrip system used for payments to inmates for work, into an experience that will help them manage their finances and save money for when they return to society.

*

From Joan: I had been watching Bob working with the men in the institution on the prison's side of Avenel Avenue. I decided I would participate from our home on the opposite side of the street and attempt to ease a situation I had observed here.

The warden's residence, which we were required to live in, was a large and lovely turn-of-the-century house. But its twelve rooms were far too large for one person to maintain. We solved this by re-starting the past practice of assigning a crew of four minimum security inmates and an officer, twice per week, to provide housekeeping services. This was needed, especially since the house was used frequently to hold meetings and dinners and had to be ready to receive unexpected visitors at the end of the day.

It was immediately apparent to me that the men on the cleaning crew were not at ease in these unfamiliar surroundings. They were afraid of breaking anything they touched and were so formal that I had trouble believing they were prison inmates. Eventually some relaxed and sadly told me that they had never sat together at home at a table and shared a meal with their family. Breakfast was whatever they could "snitch" at the neighborhood convenience store. This was usually a soda or the nearest unsecured cupcake or chips they ate on the way to school (if they went to school).

Feeling left out, passed over, or just plain feeling unprepared and uncomfortable can happen to anyone in many different scenarios. Their pasts had been difficult and limited, and often "family interaction" was rare. Since family life and feeding our kids was the main focus in this chapter of our lives, I decided to provide an example of a usual meal at "our house" for the crew.

I expected that eventually this big house and our family's normal chaos would seem more natural to them and give them a glimpse of a different way to do things. Some had been at Rahway Prison for many years and were now accustomed to living in an all-male society. There were no niceties or social graces observed in the mess hall.

Obviously, they were close to going home, otherwise they would not have been assigned a job on my side of the street. Knowing this, now was the right time to prepare them for the experiences they would encounter once they were released and rejoined their families.

The solution seemed simple, and the next cleaning day I told the crew that once every other month, on the first Friday, the cleaning crew, and the supervising correction officer, were invited to stay for lunch. Everyone sat at the large table in the kitchen and the men relaxed together and enjoyed a casual meal in a home and not in the mess hall.

THEY HAD LUNCH in the kitchen twice with our toddler son Robby circling the room on his variety of little vehicles. ZOOM ZOOM. He was determined that everyone saw his cars, but I was determined that his presence would remind the men what it was like to have a little one around. I could see the men enjoyed our little guy as they talked and laughed with him.

Now that I felt the men were more comfortable, I took the next step to normalize family routines by moving our "kitchen lunches" to "dinner in the dining room." I set the table with our very best tablecloth and crisp linen napkins. There were always fresh flowers on the table, and I used our best china and crystal glasses. These men were minimum custody so I could add knives and forks to the settings. I'm sure they hadn't used them for a very long time. It was fun doing this and everyone seemed to enjoy the chance to eat anywhere but in the mess hall eating prison-prepared food.

I'm sure they asked each other, "What's she doing next?"

All went well with the next couple of lunches until the day an extra crew member of only a few weeks joined us and sat motionless in his chair. Suddenly his shoulders shook, and he silently began to sob. As he left the room, we all felt his distress. The officer talked him back into rejoining the group and we warmly welcomed his return to the table. Everyone behaved as if nothing had happened. After dinner he told me he had "never sat with his family for a meal." He was afraid to touch anything and said he had seen nothing like the table we had prepared.

I wanted the men, each of whom had unfortunate childhoods, to know there were many different ways families chose to live. Mealtimes can be a highlight of the day when they are routine and can be expected and counted on by family members regularly.

My goal when they left Rahway was that they would remember our lunches and take with them the camaraderie they shared. Hopefully, they would continue to observe this experience regularly with their families in their own homes. This was not to be viewed as an example of "coddling the resident," but as preparation for new experiences.

Sitting at the head of the table with their families, showing their sons and daughters how "daddy" conducts himself in a variety of situations would help normalize family interaction and build harmony in their homes when everyone knew what to expect.

*

During Bob's tenure as superintendent, Rahway became a model for innovative self-rehabilitation. He began adding other inmate groups and new and challenging vocational training programs to the school's curriculums.

He focused on inmate programs and encouraged the groups' members to fulfill their most significant potential. The dedication of a highly skilled staff guaranteed their success. Providing educational preparation, mental health assistance, vocational training, sponsorship, and encouragement was new. Next, he turned his attention to the largest group of inmates at Rahway.

What could we do for the Lifers?

CHAPTER 15

Juvenile Awareness Program

Students are hard at work in an academic and vocational training program

*"It's amazing what someone can accomplish
so long as they don't care who gets the credit."*

— Anonymous

On day one at Rahway State Prison, I brought along with me my many daydreams about improving prison management's historical methods. Just as I had been eager to redesign the Trenton Prison's Education Department, I was now impatient in continuing to pioneer new, innovative, and improved violence management systems at Rahway.

As at the Trenton Prison, Rahway Prison had its share of clandestine inmate "crypto" groups. These groups had a secret and hidden agenda—violence in all forms. Although they operated in the shadows, their perverse incentives caused the maximum amount of distress as was possible for the average inmate simply wanting to do his time. It was my contention that it was structured inmate Self-Rehabilitation Enterprise groups that could replace these menaces.

I did a quick survey of the inmate population. What I learned surprised me. The number of inmates serving life or life-equivalent sentences (twenty-five or more years) was substantial. So sizable that the combined sentences of this group totaled over 1,300 years! This group wielded a lot of influence with younger inmates, who needed something constructive for their specific segment of the population to focus their attention on—something more meaningful than just hanging out and getting into trouble. They needed help to do the vast amount of time still ahead of them.

The significant inmate and public support that The Escorts generated in February 1974 exhibited the proof I had been searching for all along. It was now clear to me that my inmate Self-Rehab Enterprise Groups (SREG) concept had obvious viability. It encouraged us to hurry and install the third part of my violence reduction plan and offer a positive focus to 1,500 bored, restless, and angry men.

While waiting in a small office in the Tie-To for my next Thursday night interviewee to arrive, I sat in an uncomfortable captain's chair listening to soft jazz on the radio.

My friend "Sarge," the second shift Tie-To officer, was on duty. Although forceful, the inmates liked and respected him.

An ex-Army drill sergeant, his gruff demeanor hid his polite and respectful personality.

Sarge knocked on the door, entered, and announced, "Boss, inmate Rowe is next in line to see you."

"Send him in, Sarge."

Once Rowe introduced himself, he told me sadly why he was there.

"Warden, my young son will soon be one of your inmates. He thinks prison life is glamorous. I would like to prevent him from believing in such foolishness. I know better, firsthand."

He asked, "Will you consider allowing him to tour the prison? I want him to see firsthand the reality of prison life."

We talked about his son and the trouble he was getting into with the authorities. It didn't take long to decide Rowe was a sincere, worried dad.

"Rick, I'll get back to you soon; I need time to think about this. But I understand your concern. There may be something we can do."

A FEW WEEKS later, while again conducting Thursday night interviews, I just finished a follow-up with inmate Rowe, and I was finishing up with my notes. Once more, the radio was playing softly in the background. Suddenly a news bulletin interrupted, and what I heard was beyond shocking.

While I was talking with inmate Rowe a few minutes earlier, Patrick Curran, warden at Holmesburg Prison in Philadelphia, and his deputy warden, Robert Fromhold, were stabbed to death while conducting an evening inmate interview line. They were doing the same thing in Philadelphia's Holmesburg Prison as I was doing here, but now they were both dead.

I went to the door, opened it, and motioned to Sarge to join me. When I told him what I had just heard on the radio, he at once said he would clear the entire Tie-To area and send the porter back to his wing.

When Sarge returned, and we were alone, I told him: "Sarge, I think I'll call it a night. Please send the inmates waiting to see me back to their housing units. Ask the Star officer to stop all inmate traffic from entering the Tie-To and call the Center keeper to inform him what I am ordering. Keep all inmate traffic from entering the Tie-To from the back. Every inmate here has a TV or radio and has already heard what I just heard. We don't need a copycat caper here tonight."

With my remaining interviews now canceled, I headed out of the room and turned right. I walked toward the officer controlling the Tie-To grille gate leading to the rotunda and headed for the Control Center to speak with the Center keeper, Lieutenant Carstens, to tell him about the murders in Philly.

In the evening, the rotunda was usually quiet, and you could hear the low buzz of easy inmate chatter in the distant housing units. But now there was only an eerie quiet. Some messages in prison arrived in silence. It was a spooky feeling. I realized most inmates were aware of what had taken place at the Holmesburg Prison. The prison grapevine would have seen to that. Everyone knew that every Thursday evening, I was in the institution conducting inmate interviews in the Tie-To.

The surrounding silence might cause some concern for my safety, or it might be regret for missing an opportunity to make tonight's interview line also my last. I guess I'll never really know...

"Lieutenant, now that I am leaving for the night, please restore regular traffic to the Tie-To. I'll brief the chief about what happened in Philadelphia tonight."

While walking home, I didn't notice the beautiful evening sky—I was overwhelmed thinking about the horrific murder of the warden and his deputy in Philadelphia. It could easily have been me. I thanked God that I was walking home tonight. When I got to the house, I told Joan what had happened in Philly. I caught hell for walking home alone in the dark. Why was she always right?

*

Several days later, I thought about my conversation with Rowe. So many men here with long sentences shared his concern about the youngsters in their own families. Inmates like him, serving long sentences, comprised the largest segment of Rahway's general population. This reality niggled at the back of my mind. What can we do to help them do their time, and offer some kind of guidance to their kids at home?

We called this group the "Lifers." They needed some meaningful project (enterprise) that would encourage and support them. Finding a mission with both vision and a plan would also contribute to the outside community and benefit everyone.

The vision of a new inmate group was pinballing back and forth in my mind. It was not unusual that while I toured the institution, the guys wanted to talk to me about their frustration of having nothing to focus their attention on. In addition, some had expressed an interest in doing something for the community to make restitution for their crimes.

Smiling to myself, I remembered the roaring Newark concert crowd and how fulfilling The Escorts' appearance at Symphony Hall had been for them and the Rahway inmate population.

SITTING IN MY office at home with a cup of tea, I decided the time was right to actualize the next part of my violence control plan. Our Hands-Off policy, the new Table of Organization, the Operations Unit, and the Violence Control Unit were all up and running smoothly. Finally, we were out from Ann Kline's concern about overtime costs. Circumstances were favorable to introduce my last concept. Its name is a compilation of ideas I had been considering about inmate self-help groups.

Self-Rehab is short for self-rehabilitation and signified motivated members that would develop their own career goals and help themselves prepare for release equipped with self-determined marketable skills.

Enterprise was the chosen project members would pursue. In addition, relevant community programs, in-house academic and vocational training courses, and personal and psychological counseling were therapy services now provided by the prison and available to group members, offering professional support, experienced guidance, and encouragement.

In combination, both concepts created the term Self-Rehab Enterprise Group (SREG). It offered the opportunity to help restore dignity, build confidence, and discover newfound pride in their self-acquired abilities and potential. By this time my enthusiasm was difficult to contain for the making of this program. Potentially this group could be the most important group we offered so far.

Staying true to my approach to work within the institution's inmate political structure, I approached Sam Williams, president of the Inmate Council. I developed a good rapport with Sam in the brief time I had been at Rahway. I went to Sam's cell to ask him to call the entire council together within the next day or two. Sitting on his bunk enjoying a cup of hot Maxim instant coffee with powdered creamer, I said, "Sam, I'm here to give you a 'heads-up.' We're planning to announce our readiness to implement the last leg of my violence reduction plan. It will be called the Self-Rehab Enterprise Groups.

"You're aware of the positive impact the VCU has had on unrest. Straight lines of communication between my office and the inmate population have changed the climate and environment for the better. Back in mid-November 1973, my first month on the job, you believed conditions here were still ripe for another 1971 riot. Those conditions have de-escalated, and we can make some good progress now that we all feel more secure.

"The groups we'll add will redirect and reduce the menacing control the inmate threat groups have exerted over the prison population. We hope these additional groups will be a systemic solution and put threat groups permanently out of business."

*

A few days later, at a meeting of the entire Inmate Council arranged by Sam, I explained what the term SREG meant. Council members were pleased inmates could propose the formation of different groups directly to me. I made a mental note, reaffirming that a demonstration of shared mutual respect always made a big difference. The total membership expressed their appreciation for being brought into the process.

Once we finished renovating the inmate group center, each group would have its own work area. Group membership would range in size from five members to nearly one hundred.

Now, I had an essential job to do. I needed to develop a contract that each group member would sign. We filed their signed contract in their classification folder.

The provisions included in the agreement were:

1. Group members shall not violate the prison's code of conduct.
2. Group members shall keep themselves and their living space neat, clean, and uncluttered.
3. Group members shall not use curtains or anything else to cover their cell doors.
4. Group members shall keep the volume turned down on radios and TV sets in their cells.
5. Group members shall not visit other inmates in their cells.
6. Group members shall avoid associating with other politically motivated inmate threat groups whose focus is on violent behavior.
7. Group members shall always remain respectful of each other, visitors to the facility, staff, and other inmates.
8. Group members will enroll in educational and vocational training classes and become involved with the prison's psychological and psychiatric services, life skills classes, and religious services if desired.

9. Group members shall develop a set of written goals to govern their self-rehabilitation. These contractual requirements were simple guidelines of group members' behavioral modification requirements to help them live compatibly.
10. Group members shall commit to incorporating these standards of behavior into their daily lifestyle while here and especially when rejoining their families on release.

Some qualified department heads would receive assignments to supervise the work of one group. By policy, they would oversee a group's work and directly report violations of anyone not complying with the contract to me.

If in violation of a provision of the agreement they signed, they would find themselves scheduled on my Thursday night interview lines to discuss whether they should remain in the group. I hoped my attempt to mentor them was not too apparent. I couldn't have been more pleased that it was never necessary to do what I called a "pre-emptive purge." We never had to remove anyone from a group because of poor behavior or lack of performance. It was simply all about learning how to be a gentleman and respecting others.

*

Rahway, built in the late 1800s as a reformatory, had severe physical design constraints creating limited suitable space for inmate groups to work. As usual, there was no budget to support their efforts.

We needed additional space to house these additional groups. I had been informed that there wasn't any available square footage for this enterprise. Good fortune smiled down on me when one morning after breakfast, Chief Jim Ucci and I came upon a large vacant area next to the drill hall on my tour of the prison. Jim told me the space was once a dormitory, and it would cost too much to restore it to house inmates' dormitory style. But unfortunately, it had also been the scene of a major riot staged in 1952. Since then, it was considered by the residents to be a "bad luck place," and was avoided.

Seeing the exciting possibilities, I said to Jim, "We have discovered a gold mine! This space will be Rahway's official Inmate Group Center! Once renovated, it might accommodate ten to fifteen inmate groups, each having its individual office cubicle. Jim, let's get started!"

We found several resources to help us. State Assemblyman William McGuire and my friend, State Senator Chris Jackman, offered to assist us.

Mike Israel, a native, had always been interested in Rahway Prison and would take part. The State Use Industries donated used office furniture. Some department heads, several staff members, and the Inmate Council also volunteered to join the effort.

The Chamber of Commerce, the Rahway lumber yard, and influential community resources such as judges, chiefs of police, and the community at large agreed to pitch in too.

We reached out in every direction possible. With the expert help of Frank Landers and his hard-working Vocational Training students, and the generosity of the community, we soon had a new Inmate Group Center available and waiting for us. One afternoon in October while walking behind a group of men headed for our new group center, I noticed a new vibration in the air. I thought the men had a spring in their step that I wasn't aware of before.

WITH THE COMMISSIONER'S approval and the Inmate Council on board, I set our plans in motion and created the first group myself. I called it the "Lifers Group" because it represented the most significant part of the population; it seemed natural for this to be the name.

They also wielded a significant amount of influence, and their performance as a group would set an example for other groups to follow, especially our younger guys. Finally, and not least, keeping them productively busy would help keep them out of trouble. Little did I know this group would later create an awareness movement that would capture the rapt attention of the national and international news media.

To get started, I met with several inmates serving life, including Frank Bindhammer, James Irby, and Rick Rowe.

I knew Frank from our days at the Trenton State Prison, where he served a life sentence, and I served as director of Education. My confidence in him came from an incident at the prison. He played an essential role in preventing a murder plot, orchestrated by the prison's psychiatrist, from occurring, and I too played a small part in that incident.

I shared my idea of forming a Lifers Group with them. They were receptive and enthused with the idea, saying they would discuss it with other inmates serving life sentences. I agreed they should do that, and in tandem, I would do the same.

Later, we announced all inmates serving life were invited to join me in a meeting in the auditorium. On the meeting day, I arrived at the auditorium and heard the low rumble of curious male voices, confirming what I already suspected. Assemblies such as this, held by the warden, rarely had, if ever, happened in the past. Everyone was expecting an important announcement. I could feel the anticipation in the hall.

Normally, I would have preferred to stand in front of the stage on the same level where the men were sitting. But even though the auditorium seated 450, today nobody wanted to sit in the back rows, and the overflow of men sat on the floor in the front where I would usually stand. They were waiting expectantly to learn "what was up."

Having no choice, I climbed the stairs and looked out at them. I hoped they would be receptive to my challenge of expanding their restricted world.

> "Good morning, gentlemen. Today, I have
> something important I want to discuss with you.
> I've been aware, for some time now, many of you
> would welcome a project enabling you to work

with the outside community. It has also come to my attention that there are some parents here, worrying about the future of the youngsters in their families. Those children may already be on their journey here to Rahway State Prison.

"I'm creating a Self-Rehab Enterprise Group that will act as an umbrella under which future inmate social groups will assemble.

"Those who join a group will follow clear membership and firm enforcement measures.

"Self-Rehab Enterprise groups will have two primary goals. The first goal is to improve your lives here as you serve your time, striving for personal development, and progressing toward release. The second goal is to change the course of violence here at Rahway.

"Every member of a community group will receive a copy of the SREG requirements.

"I'll create Rahway's first one myself, and I'm planning to call it the 'Lifers Group.' Membership in the group is open to inmates serving life or twenty-five-plus years. Therefore, everyone in attendance today is eligible for membership.

"If you agree to my proposal then you'll need to pick five officers to lead the group. They will decide what aspect of the project to engage in. The project may be internal to the prison, external to the community, or both.

"I devoted a lot of time thinking about that, and I want to suggest something to you. My first preference is to work with young teens, but the New Jersey State Statutes are clear that no one under sixteen can enter the prison. So, we cannot accommodate anyone under sixteen years of age.

"My next idea is to invite a small, selected group of college students to meet with the Lifers Group every Saturday morning. Each visit will include a short, escorted tour of the prison, followed by a two- to three-hour rap session with several carefully chosen members of the Lifers Group who will rotate each week.

"We need to decide what message you would like the students to take with them when they leave the prison—perhaps sharing your life experiences if you are comfortable doing that. You will meet with a different group of college students each week. It will be interesting to see how you react to one another.

"I suggest appointing our director of Education, Harold Sahm, as the liaison between participant colleges and the Lifers Group. Harold has agreed to visit with area community college presidents seeking their help. He will suggest the colleges pick from ten to fifteen undergraduates to take part in our program. I'm sure you guys will be effective talking to them about Rahway Prison and what life is like behind our twenty-five-foot walls."

The tepid response I received to what I thought was such a promising idea surprised me. So, my closing comment to the group was: "Don't forget, guys. I will review all activities and then make all final decisions. Your only job is to effectively interact with the student visitors."

The first word I got back was the group had elected Frank Bindhammer president. Next, they planned to create several committees to develop goals and decide on their mission.

Frank reported to me and said the Lifers agreed to act on my suggestion to work with college students. So now the ball was in my court. I had several important things to plan and organize.

I met again with Harold Sahm to discuss the program. He enthusiastically agreed to be involved.

When Harold got back to me, he reported talking to several area school administrators and had at least two groups of students ready to visit.

WHILE SERVING AS director of Education at the Trenton State Prison (TSP) from 1967 to 1973, we developed the Prison Education Network with MCCC. It broadcast classes from the college to three remote prisons via an amplified Bell Laboratories System. The Victor Electrowriter, modern technology (then), produced written images on an electronic blackboard and completed a total system called Telelecture. The Electrowriter was an early version of a fax machine, but we didn't know that in 1967.

Oregon State University, under a federal grant, was researching an identical system; however, we implemented ours while they were still studying theirs. Thus, we were the first to use the joint technologies, fully implementing them for the first time.

Once we completed our research, we applied for and received a Pell Grant for $276,000 to carry out our innovative "invention."

The college students in these online classes received invitations to Saturday morning sessions with the Lifers Group at the prison. Some students and Lifers were already aware of each other from their courses on the automated system. It was clear in the first session that it pleased them to meet in person.

The program began slowly, but after a brief time, there were waiting lists of students.

I WAS PLEASED with the Lifers' rap sessions with the students and how they received each other's messages. The tone was low-key and excluded profanity. The guys were on their best behavior, as I knew they would be. They did themselves proud.

Most of the Lifers were reformatory graduates before they landed in prison. So, there was no shortage of questions asked by the students and no lack of answers from the inmates. These animated young people, whose lives had been so different from those of the inmates, inspired the Lifers, and the students learned about a different view of the world from our guys.

I sat in on several of these sessions and believed we had found a suitable project (Enterprise) for the Lifers Group. I was comfortable with the possibility that Lifers could continue this work into the future, and the program would produce positive benefits for them all.

But not long after the program began, Frank Bindhammer's name appeared on my upcoming Thursday night interview line. I was expecting a glowing report about the sessions.

At the interview, I told him how happy I was with their work. "Frank, this is such an excellent service you guys are performing. So far, everyone is pleased."

Frank took a deep breath and said, "I'm happy you're pleased, sir, but the Lifers Group officers wanted to request that you consider an idea they were kicking around at group meetings. But please, he said, the troops hope you do not become unhappy with what I am about to say." He shifted in his chair and continued…

"Warden, the Lifers Group wants to pull the plug on the college program. We want you to consider shifting the focus from college students to juvenile delinquents. We all remember the day we met with you in the auditorium. From the stage, you said: 'My first choice would have been working with troubled kids.'"

"'That is what we would like to do, too!"

"We believe we have more to offer kids in trouble than we do to college students."

It took me a minute to realize what he had said. Then, not wishing to appear disappointed, I answered, "Frank, please put your request in writing, providing me with as many details as possible. It may not be possible to do this. I'll have someone look at the law about youngsters entering the prison, and I'll get back to you as soon as I review the details you supply me."

I wasn't expecting the Lifers' suggestion, but I knew Frank remembered correctly; working with juveniles was what I had initially wanted to do. It was easy to understand the guys also felt strongly, considering their own experiences and personal histories with the juvenile justice system. They were right! They had more to offer to the teens. It was a logical and potentially more promising solution to their search for a project.

*

If state law allows youngsters inside "to visit the Lifers Group," we will have a lot of adjustments to make switching from college students to juvenile delinquents. I told myself not to get too excited—realistically, it might not happen.

The press and the local politicians might take a dim view of kids entering the prison. Would anyone take up our cause and champion our effort?

We could step on land mines of disapproval. Support from a prominent local figure could help lend credibility to our venture. We'd need a judge, a police chief, or some influential public figure involved in juvenile justice with enough gravitas to lend integrity to the project. Also, other than our staff members, someone representing the teens must always be present during each session.

I asked myself the following questions:

1. Will our director of Corrections agree to undertake a program involving juveniles, especially a program capable of generating a significant amount of public controversy?
2. How will the juvenile justice community react to a group of inmates, especially Lifers, interacting with teenage delinquents in need of help?
3. What do the Lifers offer?
4. How do we find youngsters to take part?
5. How will they get transported to and from the prison?
6. What will occur during the visits?

7. Who will assume the telephone costs for a phone line the Lifers will need to conduct business?
8. How many days per week and times per day will the program run?
9. Should the Prison Classification Committee get involved in selecting which Lifers Group members may come into personal contact and interact with visiting juveniles? Again, the answer was an imperative yes.
10. Where will the group perform their work?
11. Who will lead the tours inside the prison?
12. How many, and which correction officers, at no overtime cost, will oversee the rap sessions?
13. What legal concerns and liabilities come into play?
14. How do you make sure that only the central office or I handle contact with the media?

These were the questions—among many others that would arise along the way—that needed answers. Depending on those answers, I would make a final decision on the Lifers' request. A prudent man would vote no, stating it simply couldn't happen. But…what a possibility this really was! We could help kids, seriously, right here in our community. What a terrific enterprise for the Lifers Group. Would it be as beneficial to the young people?

I suffered from anxiety over the safety of the teens. Is it too risky to bring kids into a maximum-security prison? They have already had enough trauma in their young lives. Also, if anything goes wrong, it would be the end of launching future inmate community groups.

Were the risks more significant than the benefits? Was it worth the effort it would take? After much thoughtful consideration, I asked for advice from two staff members I had confidence in, Rich Curran and Jim Ucci. We held many brainstorming sessions, and each of the three of us arrived at the same conclusion. A risk versus benefits analysis could help me make a go/no-go decision.

We did that, and guess what? The risks side of the chart was much longer than the benefits side. Now what? We still felt enthusiastic about helping young people, and we were not ready to give up.

If I were to move ahead with the project, we all agreed we would move slowly and with extreme caution out of necessity. We must interpret the law as written.

Once again, I recruited the help Rich and Jim could provide. Our next step was to prioritize the actions required to launch the program. The plan included several options requiring a go/no-go decision. The more we learned and talked, the more promising and exciting the project became to us.

And so, I searched for someone prominent in the juvenile justice community to sponsor us.

RICK ROWE'S WIFE suggested to him that I speak with New Jersey Superior Court Judge George Nicola. Before calling him, I did a little research. I learned the judge dealt firmly, but in a friendly way, with the youngsters appearing before him. In a newspaper article, I read his approach was a simple one. He asked the juveniles appearing in his courtroom: "Select what you wish, the carrot or the stick."

Eagerly, I placed a call to him. He was away from his office, so I left a message requesting a return call. Several days later, he called back.

"Judge, I am looking for a sponsor for a potential inmate Self-Help Group at Rahway Prison. We call them the Lifers Group.

"They are a large group of inmates, some seventy-five strong, wishing to help juvenile delinquents avoid a life of crime."

We had a brief discussion about the work the Lifers were doing with college students. He seemed impressed, and he later mentioned it in a book he wrote.

I told him they planned to take carefully chosen juveniles on a short inmate escorted tour of the prison, followed by a presentation made by a small group of inmates. The purpose of these lectures would be for the kids to have a firsthand glimpse of a prediction of what they could expect from their life in a maximum-security prison. They would see, hear, smell, feel the institution's oppression, and experience its residents' intensity. This alert would hopefully bring about an awareness that would ring alarm bells and suggest an alternate life choice.

"Judge, I have some concern about the Lifers' plan to lace their presentations with decidedly salty language."

Judge Nicola requested to meet with the group to hear firsthand from the Lifers about their plans. We arranged a date and time to meet with the group's officers and listen to a draft presentation.

SEVERAL DAYS AFTER their meeting, I heard from the judge. He told me, "I decided to sponsor the group. Their willingness to reach back to help kids in trouble is commendable. However, you will have a significant obstacle to overcome. Currently, state law prohibits juveniles' entry into a state prison. If you agree, I will pursue a special waiver from the state. I'll ask the former mayor of New Brunswick, John Flynn, a state legislature leader, to help me get a waiver."

Next, he suggested recruiting local Police Chief Anthony O'Brien from Woodbridge Township.

"The chief can help by speaking with his counterparts in the area. They could help refer youths to the program."

What shocked me most was when the judge said, "Bob, if you approve the project and decide to move ahead, I will offer my support. I will sentence some kids who appear in court before me to one-half day at Rahway Prison working with the Lifers. I think if we handle this correctly, we can make it work."

Following our conversation, I felt cautiously optimistic. Could this idea work out?

During our next conversation, I shared with the judge the extensive list of questions I had that needed answers. The judge stepped up to help. First, he agreed to follow up with Chief O'Brien. Further, he suggested he would take responsibility for contacting juvenile agencies to inform them of our plans and seek their active support. As a result, he found several willing agencies to come forward and agree to refer teenagers in trouble to the program. Most helpful in his recruiting efforts was informing juvenile agencies he would sentence youths appearing before him to spend one-half a day at the prison with the Lifers.

*

Back at Rahway, our group of three—Rich, Jim, and me—were still unraveling the remaining snags in our plans. The first reservation we resolved was the safety and security of the kids. We decided security was our primary concern and one we could address with confidence. Our standard institutional procedures would far exceed the requirements for their safety.

I had a conversation with Frank Bindhammer about the presentations the Lifers planned to give the judge. First, Frank said he would put together a group of five inmates he thought could do the best job talking to the teens. Then, when they were ready, he would ask me to schedule a demo presentation.

I invited several critical assessors, who were experts at working with juveniles, to sit in on the demo with me and evaluate what we would hear. Included were Judge Nicola, Chief O'Brien, juvenile justice agency leaders, and acting Commissioner of Corrections, my friend, Bill Fauver. All but Fauver agreed to join me.

After listening with the group to the demo presentations, I disappointedly concluded that "this dog won't hunt!" We heard profanity never heard in Notre Dame High School halls in Trenton, New Jersey, where I had taught and coached teenagers.

It was a good thing someone already braced us for a two-hour-long presentation peppered with explicit and foul language. We understood this was an exaggeration for the sake of making a dramatic impression. I knew this foul language was typical in most prisons around the country. Until recently, this form of communication was the norm at Rahway, too. However, staff and residents now acknowledged Rahway's behavioral shift, and as the control of violence had brought about an improved demeanor, civility was displayed—at least sometimes.

Unexpectantly, the judge and the juvenile justice representatives were not as appalled as I was. Their thoughts were that the inmates' language was correct, with some modifications for the group to hear. Further, the information conveyed was right on the money. Parts of the presentation dealt with rape, stabbings, and other forms of everyday prison violence.

Once again, it was decision time. Should I move ahead or find some other project less controversial than the Lifers Enterprise?

The Lifers agreed to tone down the language they initially used; however, they would still present the reality of prison life as they knew it to be.

In discussions with the judge, I stressed the importance that this would be an entirely voluntary project. Children should not take part against their will. Further, parents or guardians must sign a waiver on behalf of their child. I told the judge the release must include a clause to the effect that the parent or guardian knew fully that their child would hear explicit language.

Parents and guardians would receive invitations to attend a Parental Awareness Program session at the prison on the Saturday following their teen's participation to offer follow-up support with our Lifers.

*

In mid-summer of 1976, the judge, the Lifers Group, Chief O'Brien, a few juvenile justice administrators, and I ironed out the program's essential elements.

We included an around-the-clock telephone hotline to the Lifers for the teens to call. After every session, one Lifer distributed business cards to the kids, including the group's name and the hotline's phone number.

Preparing a document describing how the Classification Committee would work with inmate groups and their members took us considerable time to write. Since this material covered all new ground for the committee and me, we needed to ensure we had overlooked no aspect of our newly proposed endeavor.

*

Sitting on the sun porch of the Superintendent's Residence one evening, I recognized another potential problem the program presented. I worried it could become extensive and would demand all my time. We needed a full-time liaison between the group and me. Envisioning this would be an inundating job, and Chief Ucci suggested I consider only a sergeant for the post, because a sergeant would bring more authority to the job than a correction officer would.

When I talked to the sergeant whom the chief had suggested, he was eager to accept the assignment. I cautioned him: "You are not to consider yourself a decision-maker. I will make all final decisions, especially judgments concerning security, publicity, or program decisions. Please refer all media contacts directly to me. I will then send the media requests to Jim Stabile, the department's public information officer, or refer them to the Lifers office." This procedure was standard.

ONCE SATISFIED THAT we had considered every aspect of our project, I still viewed this as a high-risk venture. But I was convinced we had carefully planned and would supply and support a safe environment for the visiting teens.

*

I once more called for a meeting in the auditorium, with only the Lifers Group members. Early in their development as a group, their membership totaled seventy-five men. To their credit, again they all attended the meeting.

My message to them was simple: "Men, I have decided you are correct. We need to accept the opportunity to help vulnerable teenagers already in trouble, as the focus of this project. They need to be convinced that the last place they want to end up is in prison. You have successfully worked with college students, even though this was not the first choice your group or I would have preferred. You undertook the challenge without the enthusiasm we all feel now for the opportunity to work with teens. Without that enthusiasm, you have performed admirably.

"We have encountered some legal blocks concerning the project involving juveniles—this is something we are vigorously addressing and are close to resolving."

"There is the possibility that the public may not be ready to accept our venture. We must be willing to not succeed. We have learned that success is achieved if we have the courage to try. But we will not be discouraged if we fail. Your success with the college kids proves that extraordinary things often happen with the willingness to fail. You can make these encounters more than an 'aha' moment; the reality of your message will not fade away quickly. Hopefully, the youngsters meeting with you will cause a significant shift in their outlook. Remind them of the hope and promise of their future, if they listen up and reimagine the possibilities that lie ahead."

With that, to my complete surprise, seventy-five men stood up and clapped, and I could not help myself… I clapped with them. Everyone was eager to start.

I wondered to myself, since when do inmates applaud wardens? *That may be one for the books!* Their enthusiasm immensely encouraged me.

On his way out of the auditorium, I pulled Lifers Group President Frank Bindhammer, aside to say, "Frank, the last point I want to make is, I expect only you to select every member who will interact with the visiting youths, or I will choose the members of your group to address the visiting juveniles."

Frank responded, "Don't worry, Mr. Hatrak, Rahway's Lifers Group members, as men, recognize your confidence in us. Many of us knew you were for real when you placed The Escorts out on a chaperoned leave to appear live at Symphony Hall. They were all maximum-security inmates, just like us. Not one inmate here believed you could, or would, make something so rare happen. We've been waiting and hoping you would think of a project for the rest of us."

WOW.

Over the next few days, when word leaked out to the general population about the formation of the Lifers Group, the excitement generated was contagious. Requests asking for, and suggesting other additional groups, flooded my in-basket. But, again, I never expected such enthusiasm. I felt grateful.

*

On September 6, 1976, the first group of arrogant delinquent young offenders visited Rahway to experience the Lifers' version of life in prison.

I was present in the auditorium on that historic day. I needed to see, for myself, the newly formed Lifers Group bravely take its maiden step.

They proceeded, unscripted and uncensored, to deliver their emotional messages.

I will forever remember the first Lifer, in the tense silence, to open the program unexpectantly, shouting into one youngster's face in his raspy smoker's voice: "When you wake up in the morning, do you think that maybe I might have to kill somebody today? When I wake up in the morning, I believe I must kill somebody today! Is That Paranoia? Yeah, for you, it might be paranoia. For me, it's a reality! THIS IS PRISON!"

Everyone jumped when he suddenly and angrily shouted, "This is Prison!"

Suddenly, there was fixed attention. I watched as tears ran down the face of one young girl, while the others sat captivated, motionless, their eyes wide in disbelief. As I sat silently through the two-hour session, I watched the spellbound reaction of the juveniles. Gone were the smug "tough guy" attitudes. And now, inside the prison, listening to the "real tough guys," some cried while others sat stone-faced, not knowing what to expect next. One youngster lost his breakfast.

I wondered how the young girls in the group were handling the information shared by the Lifers. No one made a sound.

The most effective star of the event was inmate James Irby. He quickly got the teens' riveted attention when he pointed to the empty socket where his right eye had once been and loudly admonished: "Do you see this? I had two eyes when I got here, and I consider myself one of the lucky ones!"

Those who had slumped in their chairs now sat bolt-upright at the edge of their seats. At the conclusion, after two hours, everyone, including the Lifers and me, were emotionally drained.

The Lifers had hit a grand slam for the Juvenile Awareness Program.

At its end, I left the session satisfied and hopeful that at least one kid would change their deviant behavior because of this dramatic advice. (It was a lot more than just one.)

Many random thoughts crossed my mind. How will the juvenile justice experts react to a group of Lifers inserting themselves into the Juvenile Justice System? What will these kids tell their parents and friends about the experience? How will the press, citizens, and police react to what we are doing?

*

Concerning the juvenile justice expert's reaction, I could not help but think this group of Lifers was personally far more involved in the Juvenile Justice System than any critic might be. The Lifers had firsthand experience with the probation system, juvenile justice detention facilities, city and county jails, courtrooms, and finally a maximum-security prison. Indeed, their firsthand experience should count for something and deserve to be respectfully acknowledged and assessed.

The proof of our program's effectiveness was in the changes seen when looking back after twenty years at the group of seventeen kids who went through the program initially. Those same kids (then adults in their mid-thirties) were much more forthcoming in discussing their illegal and dangerous behaviors than they were when interviewed as teens. They gave total credit to our Juvenile Awareness Program for their behavioral change. Some said their change occurred quickly; others said it took longer. But the majority did change, and they gave glory to the program for their new outlook.

Of the seventeen kids interviewed, one died of a drug overdose, one was (then) in jail for armed robbery, and one had been in prison for heading a bookmaking operation but was now law-abiding. There was one other kid who was a suspect in a rape/murder a few years after visiting the Lifers, when he was about eighteen or nineteen—the case, tragically, went unsolved for many years, until modern-day DNA evidence finally surfaced and proved him to be undeniably guilty of the crime.

That left thirteen juveniles who turned their lives around for the past twenty years after a half-day at Rahway Prison. Not bad.

THE PROGRAM BECAME so popular that sometimes teachers or counselors sent entire classrooms to us, whether they were prone to crime or not.

It didn't take long for our work to reach the local and national newspapers and appear on local and national television. It amazed us to learn that our idea had "crossed the pond" and adapted into a Juvenile Awareness Program, in full swing, in England on the BBC! Even Prince Harry sat through a complete session.

Naturally, we were concerned that excessive publicity could diminish the Lifers Group's purpose, designed to create awareness and redirect the future of youngsters in trouble. But the kids kept arriving at Rahway from all over the country. We and the Lifers Group never expected the reaction the Juvenile Awareness Program received.

There simply is no way to know the total number of juveniles who have gone through a Lifer's session (in its various adopted versions throughout the world) of the Juvenile Awareness Program since the program's start in 1976. What we know is in the first five months—the program ran from September 6 until February 1—over five thousand kids experienced the best my guys had to offer, and I was proud of all of them and their unwavering focus on their message to the kids.

Since our application is still in operation in many states and foreign countries, I would guess that by now, hundreds of thousands of young people have received help from their experiences with our and other models of Juvenile Awareness Programs.

New Jersey Senate Minority Leader Chris Jackman paid us a personal visit when he learned of the program's existence. He became a staunch supporter and my friend.

State Assemblyman William J. Maguire accepted an invitation made by the Lifers Group to become their advisor. Everyone valued and appreciated his able guidance.

*

Deeply proud of what we created and relishing in the program's overall potential, my primary focus was on my job – running an entire prison – so I was cautious about avoiding personal publicity.

I always had a staff member escort a reporter to the Lifers Group office to speak with a Lifer and never to a staff member. I believed the Lifers Group should have center stage. They deserved it.

We now had a second model group, following The Escorts, to pattern future groups after, and it was successful. But, again, the credit belonged to the Lifers. The Lifers did all the work; the staff only helped make it happen.

Our contract with the Lifers Group members not only had an extremely positive effect on the group's future behavior, but we also saw the violence curve spiral downward, changing the environment in the institution.

Dr. Sid Langer, when researching his doctoral dissertation, reviewed the classification folders of twenty of the more prominent members of the Lifers Group. He searched their classification records for how many disciplinary charges these men had received since the program began. He found a significant reduction in the number of disciplinary events attributed to those twenty inmates actively involved in their Self-Rehab Enterprise Group.

I, too, did a similar research project, except I included every Lifers Group member, and my research confirmed his findings. As a result, violations of the prison's disciplinary rules had dramatically decreased, and violent incidents were now a rarity.

At last, I was ready to act on the mountain of requests I received for future groups yet to be created. Our success inspired confidence and offered support and encouragement to future endeavors.

As it sometimes occurs,
a moment of satisfaction comes along,
floats, and stays suspended for only a heartbeat.
And then the phone rang…!

CHAPTER 16

Scared Straight!

James Irby addressing the youngsters featured in the *Scared Straight* Film

"Whatever you can do, or dream you can, begin it.
Boldness has genius, power, and magic in it."

– Goethe

On a cloudless morning in March, I answered the intercom, and my Executive Assistant Mary Mularz said, "Mr. Hatrak, I have an Arnold Shapiro on the phone. He claims he is a film producer and wants to speak with you. Would you like to talk to him?"

My first thought was, Oh yeah, sure, sure, he's a producer. He's looking for a story to write about the Juvenile Awareness Program. The last thing we need is additional public attention. I was pleased with the press received to date. My idea about publicity was to stay below the media's radar. To put it more succinctly, I preferred quieter success.

Mary, waiting for me to answer, walked from her office to mine, asking, "Shall I tell him you'll call him back?"

"No, Mary, I'll talk to him now. Please put him through."

After brief introductions, I understood that Mr. Shapiro was indeed a film producer from KTLA-TV in Los Angeles. He wanted to discuss a story he'd read in the January 1978 Reader's Digest concerning our Juvenile Awareness Program.

Asking Arnold to hold the line, I buzzed Mary and asked her to go and get a copy of that month's publication from the Woodbridge Public Library.

According to Mr. Shapiro, there was a positive story about our Lifers Program in that edition called "Don't Let Them Take Me Back."

I wondered if our public information officer, Jim Stabile, knew about this publicity because this was the first I heard of it.

As Arnold and I talked, it became apparent that he was exploring the possibility of filming a Lifers Group Juvenile Awareness Program session. But, Arnold said, "I have some concern about the amount of public interest the film could generate."

I remember thinking how different our perspectives were as he spoke. He was weighing whether or not this project would generate enough interest to make it worthwhile, and I was worried that too much attention to the inmates and the drama of the prison would detract from the brilliant message the Lifers delivered. They took this program seriously—having conducted sessions with countless numbers of juveniles over the last couple of years.

I SAID TO Arnold, "I have two major concerns: Will the film project exploit the stereotypical image of a penitentiary inmate, and will viewers come away with a negative opinion about Rahway Prison? There are many people here who have worked diligently to improve our image. Today, the prison's climate and environment are nothing like the one portrayed in the press back in the '60s and early '70s.

"Another initial worry that comes to mind is how the media and juvenile justice community will react to what could become a controversial film. Juvenile justice agencies might have opposing opinions and disagree with the Lifers' methods of creating awareness.'

"What the Lifers don't need is negative publicity. If left alone to do their work, they can, and have been for almost two years, help large numbers of troubled youngsters."

*

Once we hung up, I began thinking about how the Lifers responded to past requests for publicity. They were always levelheaded and considered their work was far more rewarding than any personal gains. Interestingly, they had little concern about what people would think of them on an individual level. Instead, their commitment was solely to help youngsters avoid prison. They were truly dedicated to preventing teens from following in their footsteps.

Most of them shared the same life story. They started by first going to a reformatory, then life in some horrible county jail, and finally, landing in the big house. They knew the system from the inside out. I believed the Lifers had a lot to offer kids walking on the wrong side of the tracks.

A WHILE LATER, Mary returned from the library and handed me the Reader's Digest January edition, saying that she'd read it and liked the way the author portrayed the program. She asked me if she "could sit in the audience during a presentation sometime."

I was pleased to hear all of this and said, "Of course, Mary, you got it! I'm eager to hear what you think of the Lifers program. Pick either the morning or afternoon session tomorrow. I'll ask Howie Beyer to escort you to and from the auditorium." Howie was a young student doing an internship at the prison. I turned to Raul Tunley's story in the Reader's Digest and began reading.

The story repeated what the Lifers said to the kids verbatim. It showed them talking about what crimes they had committed to end up incarcerated and gave them brutal details about what their life was like in prison… how they were scared all the time.

Placing the Reader's Digest in my in-basket to finish reading later, I told Mary, "Based on what he read in the Reader's Digest, Mr. Shapiro is exploring the possibility of producing a film documentary, but we have a long way to go before that happens."

*

One morning early, the red hotline telephone in our home rang. It was the Center Keeper lieutenant. "Good morning, Lieutenant. Now, what could happen at 5 a.m. that warrants your waking me up this early?"

"Sorry, boss, you have a surprise visitor! She told me she drove nonstop from Florida with her son handcuffed in the car's back seat. Even though his feet were tied together during the trip, he kicked out the glass in the back windows! She's parked in your reserved parking spot and says she won't leave until you see her. I think she means business! She's very determined."

"Oh boy! Okay. Put on a pot of coffee for her and tell her I'll be over as soon as I can. Please have the kitchen send out breakfast for the two of them to the conference room. Assign a correction officer to stay with them until we're sure the boy has calmed down."

By the time I arrived at 7 a.m., the boy, now fed and relaxed, had changed his mind, and wanted to attend the morning session. He walked voluntarily to join the visiting kids in line. Satisfied now, after our conversation, his mother waited in the conference room.

Making it a point to be in the auditorium when the group of youngsters entered, I was already seated on the stage and motioned to Irby to come over to me. "Hey, 'Irb,' I need your help. Do you see the young dark-haired boy sitting at the end of the line?"

"Yup!"

After telling him the story about the mother driving straight through from Florida to get him here, I asked, "Will you give him some 'special counseling' to make certain he wants to be here today?

"You got it, Warden. Consider it done!"

Several weeks later, the mother called me. She was overjoyed. The boy had returned to school, met with his counselors regularly, and stopped hanging out on the street corners at night. Seeing Irby later that day, I made sure to share with him the feedback from that boy's mother.

*

The next time Arnold and I talked, I told him I planned to meet with the Lifers Group officers to discuss the prospects of doing a film documentary.

When I met with the group's officers to discover how they felt about being filmed, I told them I had some concerns. "Primarily, I'm thinking about each one of you. Someday, no matter how far into the future, you'll meet the Parole Board, and hopefully, your work won't reflect poorly on you. You must see the negative picture you will paint of yourself and other inmates in the documentary as a distortion. If you don't care about yourselves appearing as prisoners in this film, then consider your family's feelings."

The group's officers decided they welcomed the opportunity to have their work seen on the West Coast…if I was okay with the idea.

The next move was mine. I needed to give Arnold's request more thought and gather additional information before making a final decision.

Closing myself up in my office to think, I had the overwhelming feeling that this film would be an important one if I approved of its making.

My decision would affect the lives and the futures of many young people who were not alerted to the result of a criminal lifestyle.

After several hours of deliberation, I decided that the message of the Juvenile Awareness Program was potentially powerful enough to help thousands of kids. Therefore, we should allow the men and their project to become all that it could be, not limit its potential or silence its messengers. They deserved a chance to deliver their alert to the destructive consequences of a life of crime. Their voices should be heard by as many teens as they could reach. This documentary could be their best opportunity to introduce "awareness" of having a different life path and a fulfilling future.

BEFORE TELLING ARNOLD of my decision, I called Jim Stabile, the department's public information officer, to inform him of my plan. As per standard departmental procedure, Stabile said he'd get back to me if the boss had a problem. He never got back to me.

I called Arnold, informing him everyone agreed to have him sit in on one Lifers Group session. Apparently, he was not about to let any grass grow under his feet! In early March he called, informing me he had booked a flight to Rahway. He said that should his viewing of a Lifers Groups session be successful, he would make four more trips during March and April.

*

On the first of these trips, he would bring a film crew and film an actual session.

His work plan included doing more research and filming a series of pre-filming interviews before shooting a session. His goal was to return in August to film Peter Falk as narrator both inside and outside the prison. I heard the enthusiasm in his voice, and without him saying so, it told me he had already decided he would produce a film documentary. I think he recognized from the very beginning the powerful impact the Lifers' message would have.

I had to take care of some preliminary details before Arnold's return visit. I scheduled a meeting with the sergeant Chief Ucci had recommended to be my liaison with the Lifers Group. The most important task I gave him was to remind every member of the Lifers Group scheduled to be presenters that on filming day, or any day, they were never to touch any kid, in attendance, no matter what!!!

*

The big day in April 1978 finally arrived. Arnold and his crew sat wide-eyed and silent throughout the filming of an entire Juvenile Awareness Program session. I'm sure they hadn't expected the stark reality of the Lifers' performance.

As he was leaving for the day, Arnold stopped by my office to tell me, "After the presentation ended, and the kids were on their way out of the auditorium, I realized I had a raging stress headache."

I said, "Arnold, just think about how the kids felt as they were leaving."

The following day, Arnold came to my office to tell me he had telephoned Jim Stabile to inform him about his crew's filming the previous day and his next steps. Jim's job was to get approval for all publicity in the department. I was relieved by this development, because Director Fauver had not responded to my invitation to attend our Lifers' demo with Judge Nicola, nor had he ever attended any of the early sessions of the Lifers' program in two years. I was happy that Commissioner Mulcahy came unannounced to see a session, and enthusiastically approved it to continue.

ARNOLD WAS EAGER to return to Los Angeles. He had a scheduled meeting with the top executives at KTLA-TV to discuss his observations at Rahway. In addition, he planned to brief them on his vision for the film documentary he now wanted to produce.

We spoke on the telephone before his meeting. Arnold said he had a significant concern about the profanity in the film already in the can. He assumed film clips would litter the floor.

He said he thought about station owner Gene Autry's clean image on the plane ride back to Los Angeles, and wondered if it was possible for the excess profanity to survive Autry's careful examination?

Explaining further, he said, "Bob, for a viewer to get your program's full impact, the street language must remain in the film. Besides, with what I heard, there is just too much profanity to bleep."

Arnold had his meeting with the station's executives, and following the meeting, he called me to say, "In a show of courage rarely seen by television executives, I got permission to make the film just as I initially outlined it to them!"

The executives told Arnold to let them worry about the language, meaning, Mr. Autry and the Federal Communications Commission.

Even if I owned a crystal ball, I could not have foreseen film history would occur at Rahway Prison in 1978, presented by a group of surly inmates serving life sentences.

*

Once Arnold checked all his bases, he shot interviews with all the seventeen juveniles scheduled to attend the Lifers session.

He also filmed interviews with their counselors, Sergeant Chuck Martini, a Ridgefield Park Police Department Juvenile officer, and Sandy Shevack, a youth counselor in Passaic, New Jersey.

THE FILM AIRED for the first time in November 1978 in Los Angeles. A premiere screening occurred at the prison in early 1979. National syndication occurred in March 1979. It became a national sensation and every parent across the country concerned about their child clamored for them to attend a Lifers Group session.

The KTLA executives renamed our Lifers' Juvenile Awareness Program Scared Straight! for their film. The new name obviously attracted interest and added drama. The Lifers had been creative and dedicated to their mission, and their message rang out clearly in the film.

In July 1978, Arnold did a press tour to a half-dozen big cities with Lifer President Frank Bindhammer, who left prison just before making the journey.

When the film premiered (on KTLA-TV) to a national audience on a Thursday at 10 p.m. in November 1978, it received a higher rating and audience share than the CBS, NBC, and ABC network stations combined! KTLA was an independent station not affiliated with a broadcast network.

Premiering nationally, in all top ten markets, the same ratings happened. In addition, Scared Straight! airing on independent stations got a higher rating than the three network-affiliated stations combined.

Arnold taped a follow-up program hosted by Dick Cavett that aired in most major cities following the national premiere of the film.

In March 1979, Scared Straight! received an Academy Award for the outstanding Feature Documentary of the Year. In addition, the film received eight Emmys (national and regional).

ARNOLD FILMED OTHER Scared Straight follow-ups: Scared Straight! Another Story, Scared Straight! '99, Scared Straight!

Ten Years Later, Scared Straight! Twenty Years Later, and Beyond Scared Straight.

If you are interested in knowing how the Lifers and the seventeen kids turned out over the long term, watch the YouTube video Scared Straight 20 Years Later.

Sitting back now in September 2021, some forty-plus years later, I am pleased and proud about the time and energy a dedicated Rahway staff, a group of unselfish and committed Lifers, and me, devoted to the creation of the Juvenile Awareness Program. The result is that, up until today, in 2023, the program continues internationally.

We all continue to be grateful to Arnold Shapiro, Scared Straight! producer, for shining a spotlight on our Juvenile Awareness Program and advancing our efforts to highlight the consequences of continued criminal behavior to youngsters everywhere.

Thank you, Arnold, for your achievements, and your continued friendship.

Governor Brendan Byrne made the following statement: "I am proud to add my congratulations on the Academy Award for Scared Straight, the documentary on New Jersey's prison inmates' effort to depict life behind prison bars.

"We have tried to be innovative in New Jersey to foster new ideas and new programs. We have won some and lost some, but it's nice to have so spectacular a winner.

"Thanks belong to the prison's Warden, Bob Hatrak, the inmates, and Arnold Shapiro of Golden West Television in Los Angeles. Mr. Shapiro produced and directed the film.

"And thanks to the Lifers Group to bring their story to a broad national audience. I hope your efforts are successful in deterring young people throughout the country from crime."

DR. SIDNEY LANGER titled his doctoral dissertation Scared Straight: Fear in the Deterrence of Delinquency (University Press of America).

In his study, Sidney Langer, an assistant professor of sociology at Kean College in Union, New Jersey, tracked sixty-six "graduates" of the program. Although delinquent behavior increased for both groups, he found that forty-seven percent of the graduates improved their behavior while only twenty-five percent stayed the same.

The answer to the question raised earlier in this book— "Why worry about preparing someone with a life or life equivalent sentence for release?"

Who said they never go home!!!!

CHAPTER 17

Boxing Association

Bob Hatrak & James Scott jogging together

"Let me tell you something, my friend.
Hope is a dangerous thing. Hope can drive a man insane."

– Andy Dufresne, in a letter uncovered by Red after
Andy's jailbreak, Shawshank Redemption

It was August 1947, and in three weeks I would return to school as a third-grade student. I remember being very uncomfortable because the temperature was in the low nineties, and the humidity was nearly the same. Pop and I were sitting, after dinner, on the couch in the living room of our small row house. We were eating pretzels and listening to our new Zenith radio as Trenton native Ike Williams defeated Bob Montgomery to win the world lightweight championship. Williams knocked out Montgomery, New York State Athletic Association lightweight champion, at Municipal Stadium in Philadelphia. The fight lasted six exciting rounds, and at its conclusion, Williams was the undisputed world champ in his weight class, and I became a dedicated boxing fan at a very young age.

*

Years later, boxing was still in my blood. As director of Education at the Trenton Prison, I often thought about introducing boxing into our program activities. But there were too many obstacles to overcome to make it happen. I didn't have the resources I needed (staff, indoor space, money, and the approval of high-level security supervisors) to introduce a boxing vocational school at the Trenton Prison. So, only in the back of my mind, I continued to conceptualize my unique idea, a "Boxing Vocational Training Program," which had to remain a fantasy (for now!).

I understood that there were several professional trades associated with prizefighting. Training to be a referee, trainer, cornerman, judge, timekeeper, promoter, manager, and boxer offered genuine employment opportunities for inmates when released from prison. And so, I imagined men learning the trades associated with a viable vocational training program leading to a career opportunity.

As hard as I tried, I could not get the program off the ground at Trenton Prison because Chief Deputy Arthur Edmonds had banned boxing at the institution. Edmonds was concerned that inmates would use newly gained boxing skills as an advantage over staff. He never accepted the concept that inmates boxing each other would help equalize antagonisms at the inmate level and offer them the opportunity to vent their frustrations in a controlled environment by participating in the boxing program.

*

I met James Scott when I worked at the Trenton Prison. It appalled me to learn he had been transferred there from a New Jersey Reformatory when he was just thirteen years old!

He was serving hard time in a maximum-security prison for truancy! James was a child incarcerated with much older and more sophisticated inmates, many of whom attempted to prey on him.

Today, I remember him as a young, restless, defensive youngster who had to carry a steel pipe around to protect himself. I found him to be both intelligent and determined to survive in his new environment.

While at Trenton, James met inmate Albert Dickens, a former pro boxer who would play a significant role in his future.

With Dickens' help and tutelage, James became one of the prison's best pugilists. He spent many hours sparring with other inmates in the recreation yard. While still at a very young age, he was the only inmate ever to last three complete rounds against the inmate Rubin "Hurricane" Carter. Carter was acknowledged as the best fighter in the prison. That particular fight occurred secretly in the recreation yard without the knowledge of Chief Edmonds. I had nothing to do with this event.

During his time at Trenton Prison, James attended the school program and worked hard at preparing to earn his High School Equivalency Certificate.

In 1974, while sitting in my office enjoying a cup of coffee, I looked up and there in the doorway stood James Scott!

"Scotty, am I seeing things? What are you doing here? For you to be standing there, you must have a minimum custody status."

"Mr. Hatrak, I'm only days away from parole release, and I wanted to begin my parole leaving from Rahway.

"I asked for a transfer to Rahway because I believed you were the only warden in the state who would grant me an escorted leave to take part in a local fight card. The same leave you introduced at Trenton."

"Oh, Scotty! Warden Bill Fauver implemented that furlough program. He designed it to allow inmates with maximum security status to get what he called an 'escorted furlough.' Since you're standing in the doorway to my office, you don't need that kind of release."

A few weeks later, Scott left Rahway on a work-parole program. Before his release, he had contacted many boxing managers and promoters across the country to find representation as a professional boxer. Finally, Miami architect Gaby Murray offered him a managerial contract on behalf of a group of Miami Beach businesspeople.

The morning James was leaving Rahway to start his parole, we stood at the front door of the Front House. He was a free man on his way to Miami Beach, Florida, to pursue a career as a light-heavyweight boxer.

As we shook hands on the concrete landing just outside the front door, I remember saying, "James, make the most out of this opportunity you have earned. You're an excellent brawler, and if you can stay out of future trouble, I'm hoping you'll get to fight for the light-heavyweight championship! Send me a note or call me if you ever need to talk to someone to help you get over a problem. I'll always accept a call from you even if you need to call collect."

ONCE IN MIAMI, James walked to the gym owned by the Dundee brothers. It was a world-famous gym frequented by many champions, including Muhammad Ali.

Dr. Ferdie Pacheco often visited the gym and is best known as Muhammed Ali's fight doctor. The first time I met Ferdie, he told me about the day he met James in Miami.

"On a typical hot and rainy Miami Beach morning, James Scott crossed over the threshold and entered Angelo Dundee's (of Muhammed Ali fame) 5th Avenue gym with the anticipation of finding someone to represent him.

"When he walked through the gym's front door, every head in the gym swiveled to get a look at him. He didn't look like a tourist or typical Floridian.

"Why? Well, to me, James looked like a vagrant looking for a handout. In Miami's steamy climate, James had dressed appropriately, although certainly not elegantly. Later, I learned everything he was wearing was part of the release clothing issued to him as he left Rahway. His footwear was a well-worn pair of high-cut, dirty white sneakers. His pants were prison-issued Bermuda shorts in need of a good washing—or better yet, destroyed. His once white T-shirt was a dull, dark gray.

"I approached him, hoping to get him to leave. But he introduced himself and told me of the time, in prison, he lasted three complete rounds in a three-round fight with Rubin "Hurricane" Carter. He said he was the only Trenton State Prison boxer able to make that claim."

Ferdie continued, "James was very glib, talking a mile a minute about himself and his dreams. He was able to convince me to give him a shot at sparring with the gym's best heavyweight.

"Maybe granting his request would get him to leave the facility. But first, he would need to pull himself together once he got himself off the canvas!

"Since James arrived empty-handed, I helped him borrow headgear, boxing shorts, someone's used boxing shoes, and other miscellaneous equipment.

"Once he entered the ring and began throwing punches, everyone stopped talking and watched him in awe. Then, he knocked out his much heavier opponent in the second round."

*

Scott's professional Miami debut took place on January 22, 1974. He weighed in at 178 pounds. He climbed off the canvas in the first round's opening seconds to score a sixth-round knockout of undefeated John L. Johnson, who weighed 217 pounds.

After eight consecutive wins, Scott fought a ten-round draw against Dave Lee Royster. Two fights later, on February 25, 1975, Scott outpointed undefeated Jesse Burnett over ten rounds, advancing his record to 10-0-1 with five knockouts.

After every bout he had in Miami, Scott invited his opponent to dinner, and only one declined.

*

James called me to tell me how well he was doing. He told me about his Miami fights, his car, his apartment, and his girlfriend.

"Mr. Hatrak, I hope to fight for the light-heavyweight championship soon. I'll send two ringside tickets for you and Mrs. Hatrak. You'll have to spring for your airfare. Please don't let me down—I expect you to be there!"

He told me he was on the verge of a title shot against World Boxing Council light-heavyweight champion John Conteh. But before that happened, he violated his parole's conditions and drove to Newark, New Jersey, and got in trouble. Whomever or whatever may have influenced that decision changed the course of Scotty's life forever.

*

In May 1975, the police arrested Scott in Newark and charged him with armed robbery and the murder of Everett Russ.

The jury found Scott guilty of robbery, but the jury hung on the murder charge. Even though he beat the murder rap, he received thirty to forty years in prison.

Scott returned to the New Jersey penal system on March 22, 1976, as a parole violator. He first went to Trenton State Prison. Not long after, the administration transferred him to the Vroom Building Readjustment Unit. His transfer occurred because other members of the New World of Islam sect were there.

It was reported in a couple articles in The New York Times that the New World of Islam (NWOI), a militant Muslim sect, based in Newark, New Jersey in a place known as Temple 25, had a cell in Trenton State Prison. It was noted as "a force to be reckoned with". The religious group was suspected of having staged over 100 armed robberies to finance the organization and black separatist community. Scott was the alleged captain.

Albert Dickens, the leader (general) of the New World of Islam, occupied a cell at Rahway when I arrived there.

Police authorities believe Dickens ordered the Shabazz murder in Newark, New Jersey from his Rahway Prison cell.

The Trenton State Prison's Nation of Islam retaliated for the murder of Minister Shabazz. A bloodbath in the new school building resulted in the group's administrative separation.

Some inmates remained at the Trenton Prison while others went to the Vroom Building. Those staying at Trenton waited patiently for two years for the Shabazz killers to be convicted and sent to the Trenton Prison, thus giving the Nation of Islam access to those convicted of the Shabazz murder.

On October 17, 1975, The New York Times reported on a fight between two inmate Muslim groups at Trenton where one prisoner was killed and six were stabbed. The weapons used were sharpened chisels and screwdrivers. It was suggested that the clash might have been in revenge for the 1973 murder of James Shabazz (the spiritual leader of the Black Muslim mosques in neighboring cities) who was shot in his driveway. Four of the injured inmates were members of the NWOI.

Things took on a more stable environment at the Rahway Prison following the separation of the sects. The wars had the potential to destabilize Rahway. The atmosphere at Rahway had made significant improvements, and now we had to be on the lookout for a possible retaliation by Dickins and his followers. The anxiety had already begun, and the general population was keenly aware of the dangerous possibilities. So were we.

By March 17, 1977, the department head meeting fell on Saint Patrick's Day. I was about to adjourn for lunch when Ken Hamner, regional laundry manager, raised his hand.

"Yes, Ken."

"Warden, members of your management team need a timeout. We need a chance to catch our breath and to solidify all which we have put in place."

"Go on, please, Ken."

"Everyone, including yourself, has been 'frenetically busy.' The simile 'as busy as a one-armed paperhanger' seems to apply to our current situation." There was a soft murmur of agreement in the room.

"Ken, I agree with you, one hundred percent. Folks, let's do it! Barring a dire necessity, let's commit to a two-month moratorium on implementing anything new!" Starting now!

We were all thrilled with this idea, and the meeting was happily adjourned.

*

As everyone predicted, the timeout didn't last long. Two weeks later, Captain Curran and Chief Ucci purposefully came to my office and solemnly closed the door behind them. Obviously, something was up, and from the distressed look on their faces, it would not be pleasant.

I cautiously asked, "Gentlemen, what's going on?" Curran spoke first.

"Boss, something's come up which requires your immediate attention."

Curran, a member of the Inter-Institutional Classification Committee, then told me, "A federal judge has ordered the release of the two Muslim groups being held in 'keep separate' status at two separate facilities. He's demanding their immediate release to the general prison populations at Trenton, Rahway, and Leesburg. I don't know if we can select those headed our way. But if I were a betting man, I'd say we'll get those the committee sends us!"

That brief statement touched off a five-alarm fire in my head.

"Warden, let's prepare for the inevitable. We can be sure that we're going to get our share of inmates from each sect. As a committee member, I hope I can influence the selection of suitable candidates you'll agree to accept." I asked Curran and the chief to spend the next several days exploring our options.

"It will take several weeks for the committee to decide who will go where. We have very little time. Let's find a solution before their next meeting."

I asked Curran and the chief, "Let's reconvene in a few days to explore the possibilities for safely absorbing these once-warring factions into the general population."

Here we go again.

Knowing that these guys were all troublemakers and adversaries, it would be harder to maintain the peace and safety we'd achieved here over the past four years.

I spent several stressful evenings calculating and considering what would work best for everyone. The first thing that struck me was that we had the New World of Islam's general, Al Dickens, right here at Rahway. My second thought was, if we could work quickly enough to establish a challenging focus, we might derail any incoming storm, maintain our stability, and keep everyone safe. We owed it to our staff and inmate population. We had invested so much effort to build the safe Rahway we all now expected. Which meant we had a lot more to lose.

*

The leadership of the Nation of Islam was weak at Rahway and powerful at Trenton. I recall Trenton inmate Imam Lester 2X Gilbert rising in power there. Upon Fauver's arrival as warden, he determined he would parley peace between the two opposing Muslim factions by building a bridge with Lester Gilbert, encouraging a working relationship to prevent more unrest. The result was that Gilbert became the most potent inmate leader in the state's prison system. This caused a distinct power imbalance between the two Muslim factions. Al Dickens, leader of the New World of Islam at Rahway, deeply resented the power of Lester Gilbert, the leader of the Nation of Islam at Trenton Prison.

The leadership of the Trenton Prison's correction officers' labor union (PBA) was blaming Trenton Warden Bill Fauver for creating a monster in Lester Gilbert. People were upset, and there was a lot of turmoil surrounding this accusation at Trenton.

One morning while in the shower, I was still deliberating on a plan of action. I thought about James Scott and that he would surely be one of those scheduled for release from the Vroom Building. I knew James for many years at Trenton. I would gamble on his good behavior at Rahway, especially if he had something important he could get involved with and concentrate on. Since his sentence was a life equivalent, he might decide to join the Lifers Group with his brother Malcolm. I hoped not. His boxing ability and leadership were his greatest assets and applying them to his future progress would be to his best benefit. His skills would be invaluable to a third Enterprise Group if we had one ready for him to join.

With the general (Al Dickens) and the captain (Scott) in the same prison (RSP), they would overpower the Nation of Islam's weak leadership. That could mean that Dickens might launch a counterattack on the Nation of Islam. This would not be good for anybody.

The next day while driving back to the prison, I thought about how badly I'd always wanted to develop a boxing school. Both Dickens and Scott had experience as boxers and leaders. They were also good friends. I could use their help to set up a third inmate Self-Rehab Enterprise Group and center it around the boxing trades. That would keep people productively busy and most everyone happily involved when the new men arrived.

However, placing them in a critical role in the vocational school could also be dangerous. The Nation of Islam would feel slighted if they had only a student participatory role in the new program. This endeavor clearly still required more thought. We needed to identify a civilian from the Nation of Islam living in New Jersey to volunteer to assume a critical school management role. Where would we find a qualified volunteer? The whole undertaking seemed overwhelmingly impossible. There must be a way to put this together, accommodating everyone responsibly.

Another important variable was how my boss would react to the timing of setting up a school for inmate boxers now, given that, so far, there was only one filmed session of the Lifers' Juvenile Awareness program (which later became the Academy Award-winning film documentary Scared Straight!). The project was still in full swing, and currently, our staff and residents were already functioning at maximum capacity.

Adding a boxing program would put both projects on parallel tracks, operating simultaneously. I would never have purposely scheduled the projects so close together. But I had no choice. The Juvenile Awareness Program had been well underway for two years. A boxing program had been strategically planned for implementation but not for several months from now.

WE SERIOUSLY HAD to get things going much sooner than expected because I learned there would be at least two busloads of Muslim inmates heading north on Route 1 coming to us! Getting the boxing school operational was the only idea I could come up with that hopefully averted disaster and potentially encouraged both groups to sing together from the same sheet of music. (Or at least not try to kill each other straight away.)

Once at the office, I settled into my chair and called the Control Center lieutenant to ask him to have the kitchen send a large pot of coffee and some coffee cups to my office, and to please ask Curran and Ucci to come to see me post-haste.

I greeted Rich and Jim with two empty coffee cups and a tentative plan that apparently didn't surprise either of them.

"Well, guys, to contend with this transfer of Muslims to Rahway and avoid a holy war like the one at Trenton, I have a proposal I hope will refocus everyone's energies. Unfortunately, that means our much-needed 'timeout from new projects' is officially over!"

I shared my idea, suggesting that now was the right time to create our third inmate Self-Rehab Group. I explained that none of our current groups met the needs of either Black Muslim sect and that it would require more than a little "insightful creativity" to keep everyone alive!

An additional Enterprise Group offered qualified men, from both sects, something of value that they wouldn't want to risk losing by starting a battle with each other again here at Rahway.

I told the chief and the captain I would have James Scott transferred from the Vroom Building before the arrival of those men scheduled for release from the segregation unit to us.

With James Scott and Al Dickens here, their combined talents offered us a chance to staff and begin forming the new group. We could call the group the Boxing Association. Should we do that, I proposed opening a Boxing Vocational Training Program and putting Scott in charge. He was in Florida and not here when the incident in Trenton went down. So, that could work in his favor with both groups, and it could help him get beyond the turn his life had taken.

Scott's career and expertise as a professional boxer, and the contacts he made while in Florida, could help us get equipment donations and maybe even some volunteer tutors from the public. It could be a win/win situation for everyone.

*

I had decided earlier that if my boss didn't respond to my request to begin a new project, I would call him again to try to interest him once more.

As I anticipated, again he failed to say no, but I sensed he was less than enthused with my striking out to do something else new.

Since he didn't offer a solution to the likelihood of "our impending peril headed up Route 1," I decided we needed to keep moving forward developing our boxing school while at the same time keeping him fully informed. Hopefully he would become interested and decide to champion our efforts.

The next time I met with Jim and Richie, I reiterated my sentiments. "Suppose we can put together a coalition of boxing people from both Muslim sects. In that case, my hope is each denomination would have parole and career investments to risk, important things to lose should they decide to go to war. I can't see them taking that chance."

"Well, men, what do you think? Can it work?"

Curran spoke first. "Boss, you know the security people at Trenton didn't allow you to put boxing equipment in the big yard.

"Well, Rich, then I was the director of Education. But here I'm the warden and the decision is mine. Also, the security staff here at Rahway has become more open and receptive to new things than the administrators at Trenton. This could be a project everyone can wrap their arms around. And it could turn out to be a lot of fun."

I was pleased that we agreed to give my proposal a try since we were without a better idea at the end of our meeting. Fortunate, in that their agreement was more than I had expected. I now nervously realized that up to this point, I had only my own enthusiasm to bring this desperate last-minute idea to life.

I had the distinct feeling that Ucci and Curran believed Scott was beyond reclamation. If they were right, we could be placing ourselves in a high-risk position. But I was more than willing to attempt to pull it off. I sensed it was doable, and success would keep the peace—and blood off the walls.

It would have been easy for me to take the position that Scott should not get a second chance, given his lifelong antisocial behavior. However, the same could have been said of The Escorts and the other inmates in our Lifers Group. The opportunity given to them worked out fine. So, why not give another chance to Scotty too?

I always offered inmates a fair shot at resocialization, self-actualization, and self-rehabilitation. If they wanted to try, I was there to support their effort.

Several days later, I asked Curran to go to the Vroom Building to interview Scott.

"Tell him I'm willing to have him sprung from there. I'll ask the Inter-Institutional Classification Committee to consider his immediate transfer to Rahway on one condition. Tell him I have an idea for a program he could work in. He must understand I'm only willing to risk his transfer to Rahway, provided he has something to keep him busy when he gets here! If we work it out, I want him here before the other Muslim transferees arrive. That means yesterday!"

It felt good to be proactive at last, instead of taking a "wait and see position" and then picking up the pieces (or body parts) of a passive strategy.

When Curran returned from the Vroom Building, he said, "Scott wants me to tell you you've always been willing to help him. So, he is excited to transfer to Rahway to help you set up a boxing school. He said he had never heard of anything like that, and he'll do whatever Mr. Hatrak needs me to do to get out of this hellhole!"

*

Scott arrived at Rahway on Friday, May 27, 1977. I hadn't seen him since he left Rahway on parole in 1974 to pursue a professional boxing career in Miami Beach. Please God, may this plan have a better outcome.

When we finally met a few days later, James reached out and gave me a very firm handshake when Sarge let him into the office I was using in the Tie-To.

"Hey, James, it's been a long time since we last talked! You don't look too bad considering what you've survived. I was sure you would become the world light-heavyweight champion, but you had to figure out some way to screw things up."

"I know. I know. Mr. Hatrak, I didn't come here to see you tonight for you to harass me!"

"You know better than that, James. I was your biggest fan when you were fighting out of Miami. Officer Charley Butler, an ex-light-heavyweight, kept me informed about your progress. Charley told me your record fighting out of Miami Beach was ten wins, five knockouts, no losses, and one draw. He said you won your first professional fight right out of Rahway, and you won by points in a ten-round fight against someone named 'Sugar' Ray Anderson. At one time, Anderson defeated Bob Foster to win the light-heavyweight championship of the world. Was Anderson past his prime?"

"Maybe a little. Sounds like you really were following my progress."

"And so, James, are you ready to stay out of trouble and help me build a boxing school?"

"You're something else. You haven't changed a bit. If anyone other than you told me what you just said, I would have said that person was full of shit. Nobody but you could ever think of such a school."

"I remember Chief Edmonds at Trenton banning boxing there."

"It's impossible to continue my boxing career while I'm in prison, but you never know." You've always preached to the men that 'inmates must assume the responsibility for their own rehabilitation,' and that's what I plan to do."

James had not been at Rahway long when I introduced him to the concept of Self-Rehabilitation.

For James to make the statement three years later that "the boxing school... promotes rehabilitation because an inmate can do what he wants [sic; chooses] to... reassured me that we were going about things the right way at Rahway.

James and other members of the various SREGs at Rahway took my focus on Self-Rehabilitation seriously. Inmates pursuing career paths of their choosing is the hallmark of self-rehabilitation. And James Scott said as much.

"Mr. Hatrak, I'm ready to get to work. When do I start, and can Al Dickens be assigned to assist me?"

Despite his lengthy sentence, James told me he planned to launch a demanding training regimen that would include 1,200 push-ups and 1,200 sit-ups each day. Multiplying that by seven days in the week results in 16,800 per week. He said he would run in the yard every morning in the rain, sleet, or snow, and at lights-out (10 p.m.), he would shadowbox, going toe-to-toe with his shadow.

"Why would you want to train as if you were training for a fight I asked for?"

"Well, since you want me to train young boxers in your boxing school, I never want to ask them to do anything I wouldn't do. You never know when one of these youngsters will get a title shot of their own someday."

"I agree to your request. I'm going to ask your friend Al Dickens to help you with this endeavor. Since you and Al are in leadership positions in the New World of Islam, I'm looking for someone with a name in boxing and in the Nation of Islam to balance you and Al. I believe many prospective students will come from each group and will build an enthusiastic enrollment."

"In short, James, you will manage an inmate Self-Rehab Enterprise Group called the Rahway Boxing Association. In addition, the association will run a Boxing Vocational School Program that will prepare our students for licensure and probable employment upon release.

"There is still a lot of preliminary work to do, James. You'll have to reach out to your contacts to find sources for donations. We'll also need boxing equipment donated. We don't have a budget to help us, and so you'll fully depend on donations and volunteers. We'll need volunteer instructors for each trade area—boxing, refereeing, managing, judging, timekeeping, cornermen, cut men, etc. I have an office ready for you to use. It's above the Tie-To."

"You and Al should report for work Monday morning. I'll see to it your housing unit officer is aware of this.

"Tomorrow morning, I'll meet with the assistant superintendent and the senior classification officer to set up two new jobs: Boxing Association president and Boxing Association vice president. Both positions will be full-time, and their work locations are the Big Yard and the Drill Hall."

"Mr. Hatrak, what in the heck is the Inmate Group Center everyone is talking about?"

"You'll soon find out. We've been swamped with ideas and developing opportunities for our group members. You'll be surprised at how much progress we've made.

"Both of you will receive the same pay as other inmates working in the recreation department. You will also earn work credits. You'll need a sponsor to pay your telephone bills."

ONCE SCOTT ASSUMED his job in the Boxing Association, he began, as the saying goes, "moving heaven and earth" to carry out what I had assigned him to do.

As soon as word got out about the Boxing Association, the naysayers crawled out of the woodwork. They included my boss, the director (later commissioner), and his deputy.

I arranged a meeting with several representatives from the State Department of Education. I was looking for advice and support for our Boxing School. I was also seeking funding for the program. Unfortunately, I learned the department could not help us with funding.

Next, I met with my boyhood idol, "Jersey Joe" Walcott, the former world former heavyweight champion! I was thrilled to meet the champ.

I found Joe to be softspoken and extremely polite. The first thing he said to me was, "Bob, in 1968, I worked for the Camden County Corrections Department and I was also elected Camden County sheriff."

When I told Joe about Scott, he surprised me when he said he was aware of him and his record fighting out of Miami Beach for Murray Gaby's management group.

I asked Joe for his help.

"Commissioner Walcott, please consider licensing our school's students once they become qualified for licensure. We will use civilian volunteer instructors in the program. They will certify an inmate when he is ready for his New Jersey license."

Joe responded very positively even though inmates or ex-inmates could not receive state licenses at that time. He kept his word; the first license he issued was to Scott.

I asked his agreement to be the school's sponsor, the same way Judge George Nicola agreed to sponsor our Lifers' Juvenile Awareness Program. Joe agreed.

I made sure he always had a reserved ringside seat at our boxing matches, and he attended every one of them!

*

On my way to the officers' dining room for lunch, I stopped off as usual at the Boxing Association office.

"Mr. Hatrak, I have some good news. My friend Ferdie Pacheco, once Muhammed Ali's fight doctor, has agreed to help me get boxing equipment donations and volunteer tutors needed to get the school started! He's talked to many boxing celebrities and feels confident we should begin receiving contributions soon."

One afternoon, I received a phone call from Ferdie Pacheco. He confirmed he was communicating with James and would help as much as he could to get the school off the ground. After several months, we became friends, and by then, he was not only a frequent visitor at the institution, but he also volunteered to be Scott's "fight doctor." The exact role he performed for Muhammad Ali!

One of my fondest memories of Ferdie was when one day he said to me, "Warden, the world-famous Dundee 5th Avenue Gym in Miami Beach, Florida, has been referred to as the World's Boxing University. When talking to my friends about what you're doing at Rahway, I refer to your boxing school as the 'Rahway Prison Boxing College.'"

Somehow James connected with a boxing gym in the city of Rahway, and he convinced owner Deke Taylor to volunteer as a part-time volunteer trainer for the school and to help train our men.

We got lucky and found someone to give us high-level exposure to the Nation of Islam. The most important goal for the plan to develop a boxing school was to keep the Muslims from attacking each other. A boxing school student told me about Murad Muhammad. We needed a prominent Nation of Islam figure to balance the leadership control of the program. Murad had once been a member of Muhammed Ali's security team. He also carried the afro pick that Ali used after each fight while awaiting the judge's decision…. Cool.

Murad Muhammad agreed to accept my offer to take on the role of boxing school promoter. We now had the right balance needed in the boxing program. Each Muslim sect had a leading role—Scott, the president of the Boxing Association, and Murad promoting the association fights.

Before the school could begin operation, I needed a boxing ring and several heavy bag standards. The prison's Vocational Training director, Frank Landers, working under a federal grant, came through as he always did. It took little time for his students to construct a professional-quality and official-size ring and two heavy bag standards.

Slowly but surely, things were coming together without a budget. Everyone involved in the boxing program was a volunteer. It was gratifying to see how much spirit they all generated for the project.

Scott was doing his job making contacts and securing the donations of much-needed equipment. The inmate population talked nonstop about the boxing school. The basket on my desk was full of notes from men requesting placement in the program. I was not surprised to learn that many Muslim inmates from both sects applied for admission to the program. I was both grateful and relieved that the men intended to work together. During a conversation, I said, "James, we need to get the school open for business before the end of the week. I need a day or two of rest, and then I'll be ready to go again."

"Mr. Hatrak, I have an idea. I run laps in the recreation yard every morning. How about tomorrow morning you run laps with me?"

I did it.

Rahway's Boxing Association was born in 1978, and yet, many years later, it continues to appear in current media.

**The boxing school's bell has
rung again more than forty years later!**

CHAPTER 18

Boxing Vocational Training Program

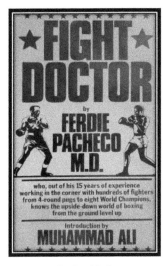

The 'big' fight

*"Only those who will risk going too far can't
find how far it is possible to go."*

– T. S. Eliot

Being creative and having a reputation for thinking outside the box to solve problems was part of what was expected of me by the Rahway State Prison, employees, inmates, and the media. My propensity to get things done quickly was only possible with the efforts of the talented teams I was blessed with during my years as warden at the Rahway State Prison.

The boxing school's survival and success would influence and enable the prison's staff and population to move forward in harmony, by capitalizing on the newly found peace between the two Muslim factions.

*

One evening I took some time to contemplate the extensive, inventive work our skillful implementation teams carried out over the past five years. We began by refurbishing and nearly reinventing the prison and how it functioned. We eliminated almost all violence and reduced overtime spending by $1.9 million. Now, most residents were in school, vocational training, or a member of the various Self-Rehab Enterprise Groups we developed.

*

Our most recent group, the Boxing Association, was now in place and the participants were eager to get going. The boxing program could well turn out to be our most important project to date. Its success would set aside the potential threat of two warring Muslim groups and enable the prison's staff and population to move forward in harmony.

*

I remember standing on the front porch of our house one morning, looking toward the entrance of the prison just across the road, and when my gaze settled on the copper dome crowning the institution, asking myself, half-jokingly, *What will we do if the dome suddenly begins vibrating from our many activities? Will steam seep up from around its base?* But, of course, if it had been doing both, it wouldn't surprise me, given the energy already exerted under the dome daily. We were all carrying a workload that would have staggered an entire army.

*

Finally, the dreaded transfer of Muslim inmates from the administrative segregation units at both Trenton and the Vroom Building occurred. One late morning we absorbed a busload of silent men into our peaceful population. As I watched them disembark from the big green transit bus, I wondered, *What next?* I could have sworn I heard Pop's voice exclaim, in exasperation, from the dome above us, *"Ježiš, Maria, a Josef."*

I almost responded to him, *"Please stick around, Pop. We're going to need help."*

*

We distributed an introductory memorandum announcing the new boxing program to everyone by placing a copy in every cell in English and Spanish. It explained how the new program would provide training opportunities for anyone interested in learning to box or the trades related to boxing.

Soon, the number of applications, including various attachments for enrollment in the new and exciting boxing school, filled an extra in-basket on my desk. Mary, my secretary, neatly arranged corresponding classification folders on my desktop, requiring me to peek over the top of the piles to see beyond my desk and into the rest of the room. It took me the better part of one morning to review it all.

My primary concern at that moment was about the number of enrollees from each Muslim sect. We didn't want one sect to far outnumber the other. Thankfully, that didn't happen. Forty New World of Islam men applied, and there were thirty-five Nation of Islam men also seeking enrollment. James Scott, "Scotty," a captain in the New World of Islam, was already at Rahway and placed in the role of Boxing Association president, establishing the presence and leadership position of the New World of Islam sect.

We hoped fervently that all boxing school members would make an emotional investment in the future release opportunities offered to them in the boxing program.

When at last, the school had a volunteer promoter, Murad Muhammad, with ties to the Nation of Islam through Muhammed Ali, we achieved a vital power balance. This balance would ensure, to the greatest extent possible, something meaningful and promising for each side to lose should they create problems or withdraw from the program.

THE CLASSIFICATION COMMITTEE acted quickly and approved seventy-five qualified candidates to include in the boxing school—*we were officially on our way!*

*

On opening day for the boxing program, I arrived early and went directly to the recreation yard. I wanted to show my commitment to the new program. Standing and waiting under an officer sentry box (tower) on this early spring day, I enjoyed the soft breeze. To me, it seemed like an omen that opening our boxing school, earlier than planned and for precise reasons, was the correct answer.

"Scotty" (James Scott) and seventy-five energized young men soon bounded into the yard, prepared to do morning calisthenics and run laps around the large area. I thought about joining them in their jog but decided against it when I realized how young and energetic they all looked.

Suddenly I heard someone yell, "Okay! Line up!"

James commanded the boisterous students entering the yard to prepare to begin. He was a calisthenic fanatic and wanted each of the young men in the program to pursue his rigorous regimen.

I watched for a while and then left the yard, making my way up to the Drill Hall to await the students' arrival. As they filed into the gym, Scotty told the men to form a group at the center of the room.

"Okay, guys, the hard work begins today! We'll train until lunch, go to lunch, and return here to finish the day.

"Now let's break down into groups: boxers, referees, managers, trainers, and cornermen. I'll circulate between groups to provide instruction. Deke Taylor, our volunteer pro trainer, will do the same."

James and Deke worked the men very hard. I knew from my basketball coaching days at Fairleigh Dickinson University that a diversion from the daily routine of calisthenics and other school activities would help to prevent the students from burning out. We might think about a fight for Scotty, as he was the only boxer ready to compete against a fighter from the outside.

If the spring weather continued, such a match could occur right here in the recreation yard. Then, the inmate population could watch the new program happening live. That would provide an exciting diversion and incentive for the students to train. If we were able to somehow work that out, then we'd also need a new procedure for visitors to arrive and leave safely outside through our receiving gate.

The first day of classes had a good beginning, and Scott's enthusiasm motivated everyone. Unexpectedly, the group worked well together. It relieved me when we got through the first day peacefully and no one was bleeding!

THE BOXING ASSOCIATION scheduled a late afternoon fight in the recreation yard on Friday, May 5, 1978. Boxing Association President James Scott carefully coordinated the event with Murad, who contracted for a four-round fight with Diego Roberson. Until we prepared additional students to fight on an undercard, we held off scheduling undercard exhibitions.

Once Friday finally arrived, many interested, but laid-back, fellow inmates attended the fight. Scott quickly knocked out Roberson in the initial fight of the school's program.

The Roberson fight unexpectedly legitimized the boxing program. As a result, many more men began seeking admission to the program. Some from Trenton and Leesburg prisons requested transfers to Rahway. Once again, my in-basket runneth over! Our enrollment now topped one hundred students.

*

Now, it was back to the grindstone. We were actively pursuing donations of equipment and volunteer tutors from the community, while Scotty was diligent in encouraging the students to keep pace.

My agreement with Scott and Murad was that I planned, by observation, to manage the program from a short distance, leaving them to work together and maintain the mission as designed.

I told Murad that the next fight card, and every fight after that, must include several undercards. Each undercard must comprise students from the various boxing trades so that everyone took part.

The relationship between Scotty and Murad was not good. I had suspected as much. There was only one incident between the two that required me to intervene. When I sat down with each of them separately, we resolved the problem quickly and easily. Our essential strategy worked—each sect had something of value to lose and they weren't about to walk away over a simple disagreement.

It was great to have both Muslim sects take part on equal footing in a program designed to keep the peace between them. To everyone's relief, that arrangement worked out, and there were never any violent incidents between the two sects at Rahway.

The second boxing program card occurred on Saturday afternoon, September 9, 1978, when James Scott fought Cleveland Brown. I remember that afternoon fight well because we held it outdoors again. It felt cold because of a breeze wafting through the yard.

It surprised me when I saw my boss, Bill Fauver, walk in (*finally*)! He didn't tell me he'd be there. Happy to see him, I hoped he had come to give our up-and-coming boxing program his blessing at last. He was cordial but distant. He seemed to be nonplussed by what he was seeing. I was so pleased with how the program and the students had progressed that the buttons on my shirt were about to pop off.

THE STUDENTS WORKED hard all summer, getting themselves and the program ready for prime time. James Scott deserved a tremendous amount of recognition for his work as president of the Boxing Association. We had just enough donated equipment to open the school. His exercise regimen for himself and the students was outstanding. However, we needed more volunteer tutors' help.

Gratefully, "Jersey Joe" Walcott was looking out for us. He provided us with the names of people who could help us locate tutors. James, always and without hesitation, offered his help to all the students. One of them was Dwight Braxton's brother Tony. With Scotty's help, Tony became a far better boxer than he was when he first enrolled in the school.

Because of my insistence, Murad scheduled four bouts to take place before the main event on September 9, 1978. Students enrolled in all the trades had progressed so well that they were ready to display their talents on that memorable afternoon.

At the last minute, the "Godfather of Soul," James Brown, made a surprise appearance at the fight. It was a rousing success!

At the start of the fourth round of the main event, I walked back toward the door that would take me to the Tie-To. I stopped in the officers' dining room for a cup of coffee to take with me on my way out to the receiving gate. I wanted to check on our readiness to process the sizable crowd of people on their way out of the prison using this new departure procedure. This would have been a good time to talk with Bill, but I couldn't find him.

It wasn't possible to relax until I saw one more time that there were only visitors leaving, and no "adventurous residents slipping out with the crowd." It was times like this that validated my daily walking and talking trips throughout the institution. I was not only familiar with nearly everyone's face, but I knew almost everyone's name. No one was going to slip out past me, or the five correction officers assigned to that post. The fans' arrival had taken place so smoothly, we didn't need any problems going in reverse, as people left through the receiving gate.

I lost track of my boss in the crowd. I tried briefly to find him because I wanted to thank him for coming. He had said he was leaving a little early and would miss the end of the fight, but I would have liked to see his reaction and hear his thoughts on our fledgling new school program.

Over an officer's radio in the receiving gate sallyport, I heard that the fight was over. Scott won by a knockout in round five! The crowd had exploded, and I stayed on watch until most of the chaos subsided. Once we processed everyone out through the receiving gate, I walked home thinking how proud I was of everyone and what a good job they had all done.

*

As I usually did on Sunday mornings, the following day I went to Rudy's hole-in-the-wall storefront diner on Avenel Avenue. I picked up the Sunday newspapers, two cups of coffee, and two toasted and buttered Kaiser rolls for Joan and me.

Rudy greeted me. "Good morning, Bob! The *Home News* has a story about yesterday's fight. Bob Knobelman did a good job writing it. Have you seen it yet?"

"No, I haven't, Rudy. I will, though, just as soon as I get home."

When I arrived home, I quickly read Knobelman's story in *The Central New Jersey Home News* (September 10, 1978) titled "Rahway Inmates Show'em Some Fancy Footwork." It talked about how the prison yard came alive during the boxing event that featured five inmates who all had victories! They also said that the 950 spectators watched James Scott take a giant step toward a light heavyweight title bout when he stopped Freddy Brown after the fourth round.

What? Where did a title fight come from?

That expectation wasn't factual and was not in my crystal ball *(yet)*. New Jersey's boxing Commissioner, Jersey Joe Walcott was reported to have told the audience, "We hope to see more boxing behind these walls... these fellows are in tremendous condition." The article went on to talk about all the bouts. But I will never forget what I read next. It set off a fire alarm in my head!

They actually said that the Scott bout was *billed* as a title shot for an October 12th fight against the number-one ranked contender Eddie Gregory. The Home News article continued by describing what happened after the fight, when Scott said, "I'm going to knock that punk out" and then Gregory entered the ring, took off his shirt and rushed Scott in an impromptu event that turned out to be a great promotion for what was to come... and the crowd loved it!

Holy crap! Did what I just read occur while I was at the receiving gate? My mind was racing! Had Murad made the arrangements for a Scott vs. Gregory fight without talking to me first to get my permission? I wondered if he went to the commissioner instead and got his approval. Did the "comish" leave before this obviously planned spectacle in the ring took place? He must have!

The story ruined our Sunday. It left me really pissed. *How could all of this have happened with no one here knowing about it?* I suspected from the beginning that Murad was very self-serving and was freelancing to build his new career as a fight promoter. He used Scotty as his steppingstone into a career as a boxing promoter.

I stopped reading to call the Center keeper.

"Lieutenant, please contact Murad Muhammad and tell him I expect him to be in my office, without fail, no later than 9 a.m. tomorrow morning. His phone number is on the Rolodex on top of my desk. Please get back to me to confirm that Murad got the message. Thank you."

I picked up the newspaper again and continued reading Knobelman's article. It said that Murad had approached David Meister, the person running the sports department for Home Box Office (HBO), which at that time was a new subscription channel looking to establish an audience, to discuss a fight. This was a surprise. Murad went on to state that the event must be held at Rahway, because the fighter would be James Scott, the inmate. David agreed.

How could Knobelman have known this when I didn't, and how could David Meister have assumed Murad had the authority to make such a deal? Meister never called me.

I spent all of Sunday night seething. Had my boss witnessed the goings-on in the center of the ring, he would have called me, so I suppose he missed the action in the ring too. Bill would have had a reason to be angry with me if he heard first about an HBO fight some other way than from me. I called Bill at his home and learned that he too was shocked. He hadn't seen the paper and was unaware of Knobelman's story. Bill had a lot of questions, but I was grateful he wasn't angry with me. I was mad enough for both of us.

ON MONDAY MORNING, September 11, Mary buzzed me to say Murad Muhammad was there to see me.

"Send him in, Mary!"

Before Murad entered my office, he threw his hat in first, and then loudly said, "Warden, I'm gonna tell you something that's gonna knock your socks off."

I answered, "Murad, I already know! You've sandbagged me! I learned what you have done from page sixteen of the Sunday edition of the *Home News*. You've gone around me and have scheduled a fight for October 12 without my knowledge or approval. And, on national television! You've certainly got a lot of nerve, sir! Call HBO and tell them there is no October 12 fight, straight away!"

Murad said, "But Bob, I want to bring HBO into your prison to televise a fight live right from Rahway State Prison nationally. And, to top that off, Eddie Gregory has agreed to come to Rahway to fight Scott! He has a title fight scheduled and wants to use the Scott fight as a tune-up. Do you even know who Gregory is?"

"Oh, okay! So, now is when you tell me? After the fact, and after you have already made the arrangements. You sound like you expect me to be impressed by your arrogant presumption! You had to have that planned before the Brown fight. Why did you keep me and the Department of Corrections in the dark?

I continued, "You should have told me you were going to HBO and what you would propose to them before going there! How could you think I would entertain such an outlandish proposal? You stabbed me right in the back. Call HBO to tell them I won't allow the fight. You can be sure I'll check to determine that you called! Murad, we'll talk when I calm down."

I asked Jim Ucci and Rich Curran to come over to my office. I said, "Murad has gone rogue! On his own, he scheduled a nationally televised fight on HBO, live from Rahway! This puts us all in a critical position. If we cancel the fight, we will become the bad guys, and Murad becomes a martyr!"

"Guys, after all the effort and stress exerted to create a delicate balance between the two Muslim groups, Murad has put us in a position to piss off one or both groups. This could result in a Muslim blowout like the one we tried so hard to prevent. How in the hell do we get out from under this rock? Murad has put us back where we started."

Jim was very reassuring. "Bob, we've been in tougher positions than this in the past, and we'll figure out how to handle this to keep too many people from getting mad at us."

As usual, Jim was an excellent strategist.

Richie didn't seem concerned either. "We've both been through a lot of tougher spots together at Trenton. We'll figure it out."

I said, "Thanks, guys. It's nice to know that you're always there to help me get our fat out of the fire. I've thought about his freelancing, and I have an idea. Murad doesn't seem to want to understand that he's not working for himself. He had no business scheduling a fight on television.

I have clearly defined his role as a volunteer to him. He knew my expectation was that he promote the school and all the students prepared to fight opponents from the community. Not just Scotty, whose success was helpful to Murad. People like Eddie Johnson. Eddie is prepared right now to referee a boxing match. Others, like Mike Baldwin and Tony Braxton, are ready to fight opponents he finds for them. What I don't want him doing is using Scott to promote himself."

Rich said, "We should begin looking for someone with the same connections he has with the Nation of Islam should we decide to replace him! Are we expected to believe it never crossed his mind that he had no authority to speak for us?"

Jim said, "This venture introduces new and challenging security situations for us to manage if we allow his arrangement. He knew, of course, he had absolutely no authority to commit to any kind of business deal for Rahway Prison."

I replied, "Jim, it seems to me he counted on us not being able to reverse a 'done deal' once he had already shared it with Bob Knobelman! Behind my back, he scheduled a Gregory fight with HBO and brazenly announced his unauthorized arrangement to the press!"

Immediately, I added, "*You know what?* He may have assumed correctly. There may not be a way to stop this runaway train! When you think about it, Murad made one hell of a deal with HBO and Gregory. If we cancel his arrangements, it will cause a great deal of disappointment, and mistrust with the boxing students and Scotty. Beyond that, and because of Knobelman's article, the public expects, and is now waiting with wild anticipation, to see a nationally televised fight live from Rahway! I believe Murad has deliberately put us in this vulnerable position and we're screwed. If we attempt to cancel the fight, we'd be severely criticized and taken apart in the press. More importantly, we would lose the trust and support of staff and residents. We've painstakingly established a delicate balance of power between the two Muslim groups. Withholding support for an 'ardently expected event' could tip our entire community over and quickly undo the fragile working relationship that most everyone now expects and maybe even trusts. Murad played his cards just right. We may not have a choice. He purposely put us in an awkward position. I believe to maintain the peaceful coexistence we've established here, we need to allow the HBO spectacle to take place!"

Weighing which choice was worst, we decided to go forward with the fight. But forward with our complete and total control.

*

The more I thought about it, the more I could see this unwelcomed development might not be a bad thing after all. It could get the word out about our boxing school and acknowledge the progress that one hundred of our men were making. That progress was clear when each of our four students won their undercard bouts when they were part of the Cleveland Brown vs. James Scott fight.

God knows it was not easy to establish the program without budgeted funds. We desperately needed equipment and volunteer tutors in each of the boxing trades. A nationally televised event might make it easier to enlist organizations willing to donate to the program and attract volunteer tutors.

Students fighting and refereeing undercard bouts on the night of a nationally televised fight would be motivated to continue their efforts while receiving the same recognition as the headlined boxers. Not to overlook the pride they and their families would enjoy. Their families and friends needed to see the positive progress the men had made. Their reaction would help boost the students' self-esteem, vital for their personal success.

Wow, I suddenly thought, *what a positive 'release preparation possibility' for the men!* I designed the program based on my philosophy of Self-Rehabilitation, and the enthusiastic participation acknowledged that self-directed efforts produced success!

Richie Curran said, "I think we all agree! Let's do it!"

*

When doing my risks/benefits analysis, I soon confirmed that a nationally televised fight would be fraught with security nightmares. This is where I would depend on Chief Deputy Jim Ucci. If anyone could structure a protected and secure environment for such an event, it was Jim.

Before taking another step, I asked Jim to educate Murad about the security requirements for an extravaganza like the one he was proposing.

In one of our several *mind-bending* discussions about providing security for a nationally televised fight, Jim stated, "Bob, besides our regular staffing that night, we'll need to hire many more correction officers and supervisors at overtime, simply to process the people and their equipment and supplies in and out safely. I know how you feel about overtime spending, but that's what it'll take."

"No sweat, Jim. You tell me what you need, and you'll get it. But, before asking staff to add a significant burden to their workload, we need to make sure they are on board to make this happen. There will be many people and equipment to frisk, more doors to open and close, and a bunch of civilians requiring escorts. But I don't need to tell you that!"

Jim answered, "I know the media will have pre-fight night visits here to shoot some footage they will use during the telecast. This activity, too, will need correction officer coverage. At least five doors on fight day will be extremely busy, much busier than otherwise would be the case. Officers will have sore arms, hands, and backs at the end of the night and will, out of necessity, be on duty again the next day. That could be a problem."

I added, "We'll need to assign an officer to each HBO production staff visitor. All equipment will have to get inventoried on the way in and checked against the inventory on the way out. They will bring with them millions of dollars' worth of equipment. I'm sure they will bring in ladders and wires and ropes and cords and things that inmates could potentially steal and use to escape. This will require careful attention. I hope they bring some security of their own too! We'll need prior interaction with their security to make certain they understand our requirements."

ONCE I WAS sure Murad had been advised of our strict policies, and that he clearly understood his role, I decided to get in touch with him.

In my conversation with him, I said, "I've decided, Murad. We'll do the fight, but it won't be easy on our security staff. You need to climb into the chief's back pocket to recognize potential security problems—so you don't create any! I expect you to run everything you're doing past him. If you don't do that, or if Jim is not satisfied with your preparation, there will not be a next fight until I get another promoter."

Soon after, Murad came back to see me. Again, he had another angle!

"Warden, Gregory's purse is $15,000, and I need to raise some money to meet this requirement. How many seats are there in your auditorium?"

What? "About 400 to 450. Why?"

Murad, always the promoter, complained to me "...about not having enough money available to pay Gregory's purse, all expenses, and then to pay himself too!"

I asked him "Why is this my problem?" And told him, "Surely, you were aware of Gregory's expectations all along!"

My suspicions were once again aroused, and I was on high alert for a follow-up scheme.

Murad visited me a few days later with a proposal that made my head spin. He proposed:

"If you allow me to sell tickets to the public, I'll be able to get close to the money I need to pay Gregory."

His modus operandi was becoming familiar. To execute his ideas, he identified those in a position to enable his plan. He drew in their interest a little at a time, and when it was to his advantage, he revealed his next step.

"Murad, you're crazy. There's a limit to the amount of risk I'm willing to assume, and this is more risk than I would ever consider.

"This is a prison! You're asking me to allow 450 civilians into Rahway Prison to watch a fight. Now you want me to allow you to sell tickets! Why didn't you plan better? Or did you?"

Unabashedly, Murad grinned and said, "Of course I did. I will take care of the ticket sales, and you'll never have to touch a nickel. The tickets will get sold before fight night and away from the institution.

"Murad, if we positively agree there will be no exchange of money anywhere near state property, nor will there be any state employees involved, then there will not be any problem. Remember, it's imperative we don't exceed our capacity of 450."

*

Later, at lunch, I updated the chief. Jim was unconcerned.

"Bob, that's no big deal! We handle hundreds of inmate visitors twice a week already! It will be like inmate visiting on Saturday and Sunday. We routinely process large numbers of inmates to and from their cells to join their visitors in either the indoor or outdoor visit areas, depending upon the weather. Each visit day, scores of visitors, with the food packages they brought with them, are processed through the receiving gate to the outdoor visit area."

Jim offered, "Once assembled in the visiting area, corrections staff supervise them until it's time for them to leave. Then, we do it all over again, in reverse! It's the same process as visiting days, only with different people!"

So Jim, "You're saying, moving 400 to 500 civilian spectators (instead of inmate visitors) to and from the auditorium, without food packages to contend with, is a piece of cake?!"

"Yes, but processing the media will be a lot of extra work, Bob. They'll be lugging notebooks, typewriters, cameras, tape recorders, and other miscellaneous things with them that require careful processing. All that stuff will have to be opened and searched, both going in and again coming out."

*

It did not surprise me when, before I expected, Jim and our security supervisors figured out how to make it all happen safely. The secret was to have more than enough officers and supervisors to process the civilians in and out and provide super-abundant security coverage once everyone was together in the auditorium. To keep the place safe and secure, we'd need to overkill normal security.

A crucial element was the unique roster plan developed by Lieutenant Bill Miller. Lieutenant Miller did a masterful job scheduling the second shift, a split shift, and finally, the third shift to provide the coverage for fight night. Adding to the complexity of it all, at 10:20 p.m., our shift change would take place while the fight was still in progress. Also, we needed enough fresh and able officers to cover the third shift later that night.

Procedures for processing the guests, fans, and media in and out of the facility were carefully thought through and then committed to paper. We repeatedly practiced the entire plan until its execution became second nature. Even I was impressed with our painstakingly thorough preparation.

Fans entering the prison had to sign in and produce a picture ID with a signature that was checked on the way out. Then, we required them to allow an officer to stamp the back of one hand for easy viewing under ultraviolet light on their way out.

Getting to the auditorium required that visitors pass through a metal detector and then get processed through three locked metal grill gates, each staffed by a correction officer and a few carefully chosen additional security checkpoints, each also staffed by an officer.

Most maximum-security prison wardens would not want to establish a boxing school, let alone allow fans to enter the prison to watch a nationally televised fight. But we were not most prisons!

We did it with ease, thanks to the knowledgeable and precise security planning by our innovative, bright, and hardworking chief of security, Jim Ucci. Aided by my friend and go-to guy, Captain Richie Curran, Richie did an excellent job implementing our Control Unit, which reduced our prison violence to never-seen-before low levels!

Our correction officer "scheduling wizard," Lieutenant Bill Miller, who ran the Operations Unit, produced amazing and complicated daily schedules for all three shifts, providing total coverage and ensuring everyone's safety.

To name all the supervisors and correction officers who contributed to the effort, now some forty years later, is impossible for me to do. But I want to memorialize their contributions in this book. I wish I could thank each of them again face-to-face.

Today, gratefully, Jim Ucci is still alive. I have told him recently how I feel about his contribution to helping make a model for other maximum-security prisons to follow.

And so, we faced our risky event head-on, eyes opened wide, while holding our collective breaths!

And then it was time to rumble!!!!

CHAPTER 19

Live From Rahway

A poster announcing James Scott Vs. Eddie Gregory
in *'The Battle For Survival.'*
(The gloves shown in the picture are those Scott
wore when he fought Gregory.)

*"When you try to stand up and look the world in the face like
you had a right to be here, you have attacked the entire power
structure of the Western world."*

– James Baldwin

My "Walkin' and Talkin'" management style helped me consistently take the prison's "temperature."

Staff and residents were fired up about the first-ever nationally televised prize fight between the world's number one ranked light heavyweight, Eddie "The Flame" Gregory, and Rahway's own James Scott. The fight was scheduled to be aired on HBO on October 12, 1978.

I'm proud to say that during each of our seven publicly attended and nationally televised fights, we never had a single incident. Not even a minor one.

I knew nothing untoward was going to happen inside the prison on a fight night because I had enormous confidence in our chief deputy, the correctional supervisors, and the correction officers.

*

Correction Officer Tommy "Rocky" Laurienti asked me, "Boss, will the inmates be allowed to watch the fight?"

"Tommy, I'd like to do that, but first we would need to develop procedures that will assure us all that we can do it safely."

After I thought about it, I had an idea. I asked Murad to get the producer to erect two giant screens (closed-circuit TV) in the Drill Hall. If they did that, then the entire population could watch the fight.

Again, more risk-taking.

However, I had confidence in both our excellent security staff and our inmates. They didn't disappoint me and came through one hundred percent.

We set up the auditorium with a professional quality boxing ring constructed by our training students, led by Vocational Training Director Frank Landers. We used the same ring for every one of the boxing cards sponsored by the Boxing Association.

*

On my daily tours of the prison in late September, inmates in high spirits stopped me to talk about the upcoming fight. They looked forward to the battle, and a festive atmosphere inside the prison was apparent. It seemed like nearly everybody was talking about the contest—correction officers, civilian staff, and inmates alike.

Excitement was in the air. Anticipation was absolutely a palpable new "vibe" here. Inmates being excited about anything positive happening inside a maximum-security prison is beyond compare. It isn't often that something positive is going on.

Inmates were betting on the outcome of the fight. The betting odds in the prison were three cartons of cigarettes (any brand) to one against Scott.

Even our correction officers, people like Officers Paulison and Harold Turk, liked the idea that a nationally televised contest was happening in the same prison where they worked.

New York Knicks' "voice" Marv Albert made a trip to the prison to do a pre-fight interview with Scotty. Instead, Rahway's inmates swamped him, asking basketball questions. Marv told Andrew Mambo, producer of ESPN's The Fighter Inside 30 for 30 podcasts (2017) with Bob Hatrak, that the inmates "are all well informed, James and his friends. So, you would forget that you were in prison. It's like you were sitting around with a bunch of guys just talking sports. And I think we all felt like this: It was like visiting a kid at camp. After packing up and getting ready to go, Scott would stall; he wanted to show us everything in his cell. Anything to have us stay there."

It was a compliment that Albert noticed the positive attitudes and calm background inside Rahway Prison. We had come a very long way, transforming the violent prison I inherited following the 1971 riot into the prison Marv Albert observed.

It took a lot of hard work by an army of staff, the correction officers' union, the Inmate Council, and the inmate population to develop the prison into the safe, productive, and organized facility it became.

Before I knew it, the date was Wednesday, October 11, 1978, the day before our groundbreaking event was to take place under the, now percolating, dome. I got to work at 6 a.m. because I couldn't stay in bed. There was a lot to do. By 7 a.m., everyone involved in planning the event assembled in the conference room. I was there to greet them.

"Okay, folks, give me the good news."

Chief Ucci, the chair of the planning task force, reported, "Well, Bob, we're as ready as anyone can be."

Following the meeting, I contacted my boss to brief him. I learned he would attend the fight and listened to his concerns regarding the movement of the paying customers. He also expressed apprehension about how we would move 1,000+ inmates from the Drill Hall to their cells after the fight to lock in for the night.

His comment to me was, "Bob, I've been losing sleep over the complexities surrounding this event. You could lose the prison."

"Bill, a lot of strategic planning went into staging this event. We're beyond prepared. Rahway's staff is up to the job, and at the end of the night you'll be proud of our success."

I'd have bet a dollar to a donut that nothing unexpected or untoward would occur on fight night. He should have been aware of how well the sub-currents had improved inside Rahway Prison. I never knew if he did, because he never gave me any feedback about the positive and progressive things we were accomplishing.

I couldn't sleep that night. I kept going over and over our procedures. Finally, after I'd concluded that Rahway's security staff were the best in the state and everything was in order, there was a little respite for rest. I was confident that everyone involved could be counted on to do whatever it would take to have that night go down in the history books as a glowing success.

On fight day, Thursday, October 12, 1978, I got to work again at 6 a.m. I wanted to do a two-hour tour of the prison to psych myself and everyone else up. I found nearly everyone was sky high. Most inmates I spoke with fully understood they were to be part of a very memorable night. Memorable in the annals of boxing history, and unique in the history of Rahway State Prison and for the state of New Jersey.

I left for home at noon to nap, satisfied with the state of our readiness. It felt good knowing this would be a stressful but exciting night. Before I left, I made sure my guest list was up to date at the front door. I didn't want anyone I invited to be turned away.

I returned to the prison at about 4 p.m. I wanted to be there when the boxing celebrities arrived. I greeted "Jersey Joe" Walcott, Len Berman, Don Dumphy, Larry Merchant, Sugar Ray Leonard, Larry Hazard, and my newly made friend, Dr. Ferdie Pacheco. Ferdie was a very active boxing school volunteer. Part of his role as a volunteer included being in Scotty's corner during the fight (just as he was for Muhammad Ali).

Processing prepaid guests went smoothly, and we moved the inmates to the Drill Hall without incident. Everything happened as planned. So far, so good.

During a pre-fight interview, HBO's Tim Braine paid our staff a compliment when he said, "The warden was a pretty progressive guy, and they're meticulous in maximum security."

*

I met my boss in the rotunda under the dome, and we walked to the auditorium where we had reserved seats on the stage just above the ring. To say I had butterflies would be a trivialization of what was going on inside me.

A thought crossed my mind: It would take an awful lot of positive future happenings under the Dome to top the Escorts, the Lifers' Group (Scared Straight!), the Boxing Association, and the Boxing Trades Vocational Training Program. Hats off to the tremendous security and civilian staff working during that time at Rahway. Also not to be forgotten, are Rahway's inmates, most of whom turned their attention to the positive opportunities we offered and supported our efforts for them to have a better chance at a more successful future. It's important for me personally to mention that I knew I could depend on the inmates' behavior. I trusted many of them, just as many of them came to trust me.

The reality of this event proved that our boxing program put two explosive Muslim groups of men together and showed them how to work and live peacefully with each other. Both staff and inmates were overwhelmingly proud of this accomplishment.

*

As I walked through the crowd, several inmate leaders whispered to me, "There was a summit meeting with both Muslim groups involved, and it had been decided that 'Rahway was holy ground,' and that I had nothing to worry about tonight."

Former inmate Belton Williams, a ranking member of the New World of Islam living in New Brunswick, New Jersey, also assured me both sides had agreed Rahway was neutral territory tonight and there wouldn't be any trouble from either side. I trusted Belton and felt extra reassured. Whew!

WHEN I ARRIVED at the auditorium, I took my seat next to my boss, Bill Fauver, and had just enough time to breathe in the energy of the crowd and feel the thrill of the lights dimming. It was showtime!

Next, loud music announced that James Scott was making his way from his locker room (an office) to the ring.

The discernable anticipation and rolling roar of excitement running through the crowd of spectators was deafening.

James Scott, his trainer Deke Taylor, Murad Muhammad, and boxing students Keith Hill and Walter Barry assembled and began the short walk to the boxing ring. As they walked, many animated attendees started to pound their feet on the floor and shouted words of encouragement to Scotty. Everyone was psyched, and within moments the whole place was bustling and up on their feet!

James Scott was calm and composed. When the entourage got to the ring, Eddie Gregory was already there. Five hundred paying customers exploded in applause. One thousand inmates in the Drill Hall did the same. They were chanting, "Rajan! Rajan! Rajan!" Rajan, meaning "King," was Scott's Muslim name.

Sitting in my seat on the stage, I thought how surreal this was. It felt like we were in the heart of Madison Square Garden, not inside a prison! It dawned on me that instead of frustrated rioters, the auditorium was joyfully full of excited fans. "Switch-er-Rooney!"

Scott, standing in the ring in the same spot where the inmates had rioted seven years earlier, taking the warden and six correction officers hostages, was my proof that I had met one of my objectives: "To transform the auditorium into a space where positive inmate activities would predominate."

I took time to say a short, silent prayer: "Lord, please keep all fighters from being hurt, and let the night end without incident. Please help my boss relax and enjoy the evening."

Announcer Don Dunphy told the HBO audience, "We're about to witness an event that's never happened before in the history of television sports! A top boxing contender is coming inside the walls of a prison to fight an inmate, the comparable James Scott!"

If you were to ask me, did Scott have much of a chance? I'd have to say, I don't think so. I just couldn't conceive of an inmate in prison defeating the number one light-heavyweight contender.

Well, he was about to be amazed, as were some 1,500 fans (inmates and paying customers combined) inside the prison on that memorable night. We were all witnessing a truly extraordinary moment.

At the sound of the opening bell, James sprang from his stool and stealthily stalked Gregory. To my mind's eye, right from the start, James was dominating the fight.

Sportswriter Larry Merchant declared, "If you asked me, I would tell you this is a testimony to what willpower can do for a man."

Walter Barry, an inmate boxing student, reported, "The prison was on fire. Everyone in the auditorium was chanting, 'Rajan! Rajan! Rajan!' I mean, the whole prison was reverberating. To me, I sensed everyone could feel the energy in there. The vibration rocked the Dome standing atop the jail as if it were a crown."

James won the fight unanimously and decisively on points. The Drill Hall, packed with jubilant inmates, was the scene of a celebration like none ever witnessed at Rahway.

A small crowd gathered at the center of the ring from where Len Berman asked James, "What can you do for a celebration here? What kind of celebration will you have?"

James responded, "Mr. Hatrak's got a steak dinner for me downstairs. That's my celebration. One other thing, maybe Mr. Hatrak will let me go home."

I required that James pay for room and board as if he were renting an apartment. And so, a steak dinner he paid for himself, following a grueling fight, was not out of the question.

Standing on the stage next to my boss and James DePiano, the father of Michael Rossmann, the current light-heavyweight champion of the world, I wondered, how in the world will James be able to sleep tonight in his small three-wing cell after all this excitement?

*

I spent the rest of the night filled with pride about what our Boxing Association, in coordination with Murad Muhammad, had just accomplished.

Having a glass of wine and unwinding at home with Joan later, I realized that the evening's event would most likely be a "big deal" for the boxing program and the students, now and in their futures.

The four school students fighting on the undercard each won their fight, too. Eddie Johnson, the only student enrolled as a boxer and referee, refereed each of the four undercard fights. I believed Commissioner Walcott should license him as a referee. We made it happen.

*

The morning after the fight there was definitely a little extra 'pep in my step' in my routine walk up the two flights of old cement stairs leading from the Tie-To and into the Drill Hall. All the school's students were already there and hard at work. When I entered the hall, they stopped what they were doing. They all grinned in silence as they waited to hear what I had to say. Cool.

I talked to the men and told them how proud I was of all of them, and that I couldn't wait to see what we would accomplish next. All the handshakes and congratulations had happened the night before. But we were still overwhelmed and needed a chance to let it all sink in. Before I left, I remarked that the camaraderie they had built was proof that their unified effort was unbeatable. I told them, "I believed all along you could do it! We all appreciate your loyalty to Scotty!"

I knew I had to keep my eye on the ball. My job was foremost running the prison safely for staff and inmates. I dared not lose sight of that fact. "I was not there to punish. That was the job of a judge." So, for the time being, along with my usual workday running the prison, I added evening and weekend work time to ensure all bases were covered.

It was the work done previously by Captain Curran and his Control Unit that helped provide the controlled setting, which made it possible for every one of our groups to function.

Our established groups were now operating on their own steam. They generated a lot of activity that needed to be directed appropriately. Since the boxing school was our newest group, my focus was now on their continued progress. Also, future activities for the students in the boxing trades program had to be in place to showcase the students' talent, and to help them maintain their current enthusiasm and continued progress.

Scott did a terrific job organizing and running the boxing school. The precise aim of all the Self-Rehab Enterprise Groups was to fully support each member to the fullest of his capabilities. Scott's victories positioned him to take the next step. Unbelievably, the next step could be to fight for the light-heavyweight world championship.

And... the media was picking up on the possibility. The Oregon Statesman Journal, on March 15, 1979, in an article titled "Promoter Wants Convict To Fight On The Outside As a Favor To Rossman", reported that promoter Bob Arum had appealed to the state officials to give Scott the "freedom" to fight for the title outside of the prison walls. Arum, promoter of the light heavyweight champion Mike Rossman, was asking the Governor to allow Scott, who was known to be a model prisoner, to be awarded minimum custody status so he could participate in a fight that took place outside of Rahway... in the community. He stated that "it would be a tremendous boost for prisoners all over the country."

The governor himself praised the prison's boxing school during an interview with NBC. He said that "Rahway Prison's boxing school was one of his 'pet projects.'"

In the story, I told the reporter that James had to be in minimum custody status before he could be released for a fight, which was true. What I wasn't ready to tell him was that I was working on a plan to release him for one day on an escorted furlough. Until I had the details worked out, an announcement would be premature.

I knew I had a way to release James for a fight in the community. I had the authority to grant James an escorted furlough, like the one I had granted to the Escorts singing group to do a live performance at Newark's Symphony Hall.

Bill Fauver himself granted a three-day escorted furlough for a maximum-security inmate when he was the warden at the Trenton State Prison. My furlough would be for only one-half day, and we would proceed with our additional constraints. And so, the past practice could become precedent.

Given that set of facts, I would ask Senator Jackman to approach my boss with me, asking him to go with us to meet with the governor. At that meeting, we could assure the governor there was a safe way to get James Scott out in the community for a title fight.

With the support of the governor and my boss, I could approach Murad Muhammad, the boxing school's volunteer promoter, to ask him if he had an interest in co-promoting a Scott title fight with Bob Arum. If I could interest Arum and Murad to co-promote a title fight, they might help me secure the Meadowlands as the site of the fight.

Worked out in theory, these were complicated arrangements to actualize. Planning with Deputy Chief Ucci and Captain Richie Curran was time-consuming because there was no room for mistakes.

We met regularly to think through and document the procedures we would follow. Our agreed-upon plan would start by meeting with Senator Jackman and getting him on board, then selecting the escorting officers, touring the fight arena with the group of escorting officers to detect any security concerns we would confront, and finally implementing the furlough.

Before we could pull all these things together, certain "events" took a sharp turn in a very strange direction!

CHAPTER 20

"Footsteps"

Warden Robert 'Bob' Hatraks' Rahway State Prison badge.

"Everything must come to an end."
"There is an end to everything, to good things as well."

– Chaucer proverb (1374)

Over the following months, Rahway, as an institution, was operating smoother than ever. While the Boxing Association was still basking in Scotty's win, what was most noticeable was that the collective positive energy generated from that spectacular event had clearly contributed to a more peaceful prison environment.

*

On April 17, 1979, after six-plus years as the warden of Rahway State Prison, I was getting fired! But incredulously, my previously encouraging buddy, my boss, the correction commissioner, Bill Fauver, simply and directly said, "You're being transferred to a position here at the Central Office and I'm not allowed to tell you why!" WHAT?

"Bill, we've been friends for a long time. Given this and our history together, I deserve a proper explanation from you. I am confident that in my role as warden, I have been successful, and I am personally proud of all the improvements we've made in-house (for Rahway). Our achievements are unequivocally recognized institutionally and by the media.

"Haven't you at least taken the time to consider how, under my watch, the violence at the prison has all but disappeared? You yourself, not too long ago, told a reporter, 'Rahway is in better condition than it ever was!' So, unless I hear an actual reason for this action, I have no choice but to be pissed off and take it personally."

"I'm sorry, Bob but the deputy attorney general, my attorney, advised me not to give you a reason because it could be used against me should you decide to file a 'wrongful transfer' action with the courts! And besides, you serve at my pleasure, so I don't owe you any reason."

We didn't shake hands as I got out of my chair and left his office. I rejoined Joan and we drove home to Rahway in utter disbelief.

*

Coping with adversity was not a new concept to me. I did that as a nineteen-year-old youth, and now twenty-two years later, I had to summon up the courage to do it again. I was overcome by the familiar feeling of total loss once more!

I never saw that coming! The shock was like a lightning bolt trauma similar to the one I felt when my left pitching hand was torn apart in an industrial accident so many years ago. Not the physical pain, but the life-changing blow to my gut, realizing my life had changed once more, losing forever something I loved doing most. And, apparently, until now, doing well.

*

The innovative solutions I brought to the trainwreck of the administration of Rahway Prison after the 1971 riot brought positive national attention to what had been a disgraceful blot on the New Jersey prison system. Now those changes, all of which I had implemented successfully, and with the approval of the then Warden Bill Fauver at the Trenton State Prison, were now being eliminated by him.

It was impossible for us not to empathize with those inmates who had made personal investments for their futures and in the trust for their success they had placed in me. I understood that the distress of my leaving the prison was as real to them as it was to me!

The years of work by our carefully organized teams of dedicated and committed professionals were now considered valueless by the commissioner. Many of Rahway's inmate population embraced my approach to the "Do It Yourself Rehabilitation," and now they too had the rug pulled out from under them. Gone was the opportunity for students to work hard at becoming all they could successfully realize. For example, seventy-five young and aspiring boxers, referees, timekeepers, managers, cut men, and corner men (under the leadership of James Scott) were "being floored" after an entire year of strenuous training and studying by a commissioner who chose to protect his own future over caring about theirs.

It took some time to sort out my injured feelings from the real-time need to make rational decisions regarding this dramatic disruption to my life.

But *why* was this happening?

JOAN'S MEMORY OF the advice given to us by our friend, State Senate Majority Leader Chris Jackman, who worked in the New Jersey statehouse, and who was attuned to that building's grapevine, should have given us a heads-up about what was coming.

My good friend Chris came to our home one Sunday to watch the New York Giants play the Philadelphia Eagles, and during the visit, said to me, "You need to be careful, Bob. The talk around the statehouse is that your boss is hearing footsteps creeping up behind him. YOURS."

My transfer out of Rahway proved the warning from Chris was to be prescient. Still, this was hard to believe. Bill and I had enjoyed a close relationship while working together at Trenton. He gave me free rein there as his assistant superintendent and again at Rahway as warden. We positively trusted each other, and there had been no competition between us. Bill had my respect and complete loyalty. I believed the sun rose and set on his hat brim for the longest time. His consistent encouragement of my reformative projects at Trenton enabled me to continue the path Warden Yeager had put me on. These "innovative changes" dramatically reduced Trenton's violence. They satisfied Commissioner Clifford's marching orders to Bill: "Get rid of the violence at Trenton."

Our accomplishments, noted by Commissioner Bob Clifford, got Bill promoted to division director, and I was appointed Rahway Prison warden. Our hard work at Trenton produced dividends for us both!

What was behind Fauver's refusal to tell me the reason for my purge?

*

W hen Bill moved to the Central Office the decline in our communication was noticeable, becoming steadily strained and infrequent. However, we did continue to have pleasant social get-togethers for dinner and cordial conversations on many occasions. So, for a long while, I attributed much of this to us both having our hands utterly and completely full in our new jobs with the added difficulties of now working in separate and distant locations. It turned out that I had also, wrongfully, assumed Bill's silence about Rahway's accomplishments and his recent lack of opinions or critique was his way of showing agreement and acquiescence.

Instead, it was anything but. *Why hadn't we talked about this?*

NOT LONG AFTER I was transferred from Rahway to the Central Office, the boxing program was disbanded and closed. James Scott was transferred from Rahway to Trenton, where there was no boxing program.

Swiftly, in one fell swoop, Fauver (with his reputation as being a reformer) eliminated what was perhaps the best program ever designed for New Jersey's inmates. The overarching reason, in my opinion, was that "Bob Hatrak" was getting much too much national and international publicity for *Scared Straight!* (something I purposely avoided and followed procedure properly by directing all media to Jim Stabile). I gave only one interview, to Dick Cavett after the Academy Award was awarded to the producer. My sole purpose was to use that platform to give well-deserved credit to the Lifers Group for their role in the creation and success of the Juvenile Awareness Program. It was the first and last interview I agreed to sit for about *Scared Straight!* to anyone. Still, all Bill heard was "footsteps."

Fauver's self-preserving cancelation of the inmate boxing program no longer reflected the actions of a reformer, but the compliance of someone intimidated by the challenge of criticism and departmental politics. Moving me to the Central Office all but eliminated the sounds of footsteps he was hearing in stereo.

I accepted the transfer, *temporarily.*

*

If Scared Straight! publicity (which I vigorously attempted to avoid) had distressed the commissioner (he stated in the press that we had become a "Hollywood film set"), then the public attention Rahway's Boxing Vocational Training Program generated in its infancy must have been intolerable for him. Added to that, the excitement of a probable title fight, hyped by the press, and an enthusiastic prison population, was more "innovation and publicity" than he wanted to deal with.

I believe it was the confluence of Scared Straight having just earned an Academy Award, followed closely by the very real possibility of a highly televised world championship fight for James Scott, that finally tipped him over the edge.

The overwhelming success of Rahway's projects was a shock to both inmates and staff. It was never planned or anticipated by any of us. Our ideas seemed to take on a life of their own. But Bill avoided talking about it with me and I never knew why.

We at Rahway extended several invitations to the director to view or in some way participate in our new projects. We were always disappointed when he didn't respond to our requests for his involvement.

*

There was one instance in the press when Bill mentioned "an investigation" into me to a few reporters. His reference to the word "investigation" was a simple allegation, involving two disgruntled employees and should have taken less than a full day to sort out, which lasted for more than a year.

THE BUSINESS ACTIVITIES in question concerned a company we invested in while at Rahway, led by another state superintendent at Woodbridge State School. The company's holdings consisted of owning several small stores in Rahway and one restaurant at the NJ beach. The accusation against us was that we had been inappropriately mixing business between the ice cream shop and the prison. No legal documents or official communication was ever presented to us.

We learned, through internal chatter and harassment, that the claim against us involved "someone" who had bought twelve popsicles on a hot summer day, brought them inside the prison, and distributed them to inmates. This was followed by another false accusation from the employee, who was then polygraphed, which he failed, and everything was immediately dropped.

*

The lack of any substantiated or official rationalization for my transfer also forced me to contemplate the situation on my own. At that time, another factor I suspected might be pertinent was the old "overtime problem" we had tackled and resolved at Rahway.

Within the first year, the $2 million overtime problem we'd inherited was reduced by $1.6 million, and the following year that balance was cut in half.

Our new approach was effective because we had devised a unique system for the scheduling of correction officers and developed a formula for calculating a precise shift relief factor with the assistance of a friend at the Federal Bureau of Prisons. We developed all this manually without the use of computers.

We were all excited to share these results with Bill Fauver, so it was a complete shock to hear from him that he had *"no interest"* in learning about how we had accomplished our solutions to solving overtime.

A FEW DECADES later, as we wrote this chapter (June 6, 2023), we were using the Newspapers.com app when we stumbled on news stories as far back as 1979. Back in those days, we only knew what was reported in local newspapers because there was no internet at the time. According to Hackensack, New Jersey's *The Record*, Bill Fauver "had a very cozy relationship with the correction officer's union."

But for the first time, another reason for my dismissal jumped out from the page. In 1997, *The New York Times* stated that Bill had resigned (retired) because he was placed under investigation by the attorney general because of a scandalous overtime problem at the Leesburg State Prison. Two correction officers who reported directly to him were themselves abusing overtime. They had been sent there by him to investigate the prisons' superintendent. (Imagine assigning a correction officer with no experience as an investigator to investigate a superintendent, and to look into overtime abuse at the facility.) Another reason for his resignation was that the department had a $73 million correction officer overtime problem. Several state legislators were calling for his resignation.

The New York Times, who had chronicled many events that happened at Rahway and in my career, reported on November 7, 1997, in an article titled "Prison Chief Is Resigning Amid Inquiry", that Fauver's resignation came as his department was currently under investigation for possible abuse of overtime. They stated that in the prior year, overtime was $73 million, which was close to 10% of the department's $750 million budget. The *Times* said that officials attributed the overtime to severe overcrowding in the prison.

Days after reading several news stories, out of the blue, Joan recalled the details of that day when Jim Ucci, Bill Miller, and I had excitedly telephoned the boss and triumphantly informed him that we three had developed a brand-new Relief Factor formula that could dramatically reduce the department's staggering current overtime problems of over $70 million! *It was a big deal.*

HE COULD HAVE HAD OUR SOLUTION, WHICH WE USED AT RAHWAY WHILE SAVING $1.6 MILLION IN ONE YEAR.

Could there have been some correlation between the rejection of our solution to overtime and his strange reaction to our accomplishment? Was it possible he didn't want to decrease the department's overtime problem because that would jeopardize the relationship with the union? If so, was it in *someone's* best interest to move Bob and his solutions out of the way so that the overtime could continue?

*

The day following my "ousting," I wasn't sure what to do next. I reached out to Tony Travisiono, the American Correctional Association executive director. When I called him to introduce myself, it surprised me when he responded positively, saying he "was aware of who I was, and of the 'transformation and the accomplishments' that had taken place at Rahway." He told me, "I'm astonished by what has happened to you. I'll do all I can to help you relocate." And he did!

If anyone had any joy in my transfer from the warden's job at Rahway Prison, they would have been disappointed to learn that my corrections career opportunities suddenly blossomed at the beginning of the following week. *Karma?*

Several days following my exit from Rahway, I was contacted by a headhunter representing the state of Arkansas. The search committee chair for Arkansas's newly elected governor, Bill Clinton, contacted me to interview for the position of corrections commissioner.

I declined the interview and returned the airline tickets they had sent to me. *Why did I decline the interview?* Well, I just had the rug pulled out from under me, not only on a professional level but in a personal betrayal as well. I needed time for Joan and I to make sound course corrections before embarking on a new challenge.

Then, within a week of my transfer, Tony Travisiono arranged for me to fly to an interview for the warden's position at the Brushy Mountain State Prison in Tennessee, the same facility from which James Earl Ray (Martin Luther King's assassin) had escaped.

They were clearly pleased to have me there, and they believed I could help resolve their problems. An interview and tour took up the morning. We met with inmate representatives who had requested a meeting with me. I was with them for the entire afternoon, and it amazed me that all they wanted to talk about was *Scared Straight!* and the boxing program at Rahway. They asked, "Can we do those things here, and how quickly can we get started?"

Unfortunately, the prison's location was too remote for my young family, and I declined the job offer.

But what a tonic that visit was for my deflated morale!

*

Meantime, I stuck it out and went to work at the Central Office in Trenton every day, from April until September, while still living in the warden's residence at Rahway. I traveled by state vehicle between Rahway and Trenton.

The new management of the Rahway Prison became bleak with the return of regular violent events. I learned from retired Captain Richard Gilgallon that shortly after I left Rahway, the new administration built two cages suspended from the ceiling in the inmate dining room: one at the entrance and one halfway down the left side. From there, the officers observed the activity in the dining room safely from the cages. The officers performing direct supervision in the dining room were removed.

According to Captain Gilgallon, "Many of the veteran officers did not favor removing officers from the dining room posts."

New dining hall procedures required posting an officer in each cage who would hit the riot bell when the need arose, and the second officer began videotaping the incident.

Responding to a riot bell, riot squad officers suited up in riot gear and rushed to the mess hall to deal with the bedlam until order was restored.

Thankfully, they did not arm the officers in their lofty perches above the room, but riot-squad response teams wielded batons when they appeared on the scene. I can't recall ever using batons or removing them from their place in the armory at any time during my tenure.

That move was the response by the new administration to help protect the officers from being injured or killed in the returning mess hall violence.

Still, there was a particularly scary instance when, at the entrance to the mess hall, an inmate cut Officer Colello's throat with a piece of TV antenna. Luckily, he survived. The assault was in response to the officer confiscating a cigarette lighter, and the lack of close and direct supervision.

Among other stories recounted by Richard Gilgallon, an inmate hit another inmate from behind and knocked him out. The assaulted inmate was then dragged to the large, hot coffee urn, where the aggressor turned the scalding coffee onto him, burning his skin and breaking his back in the process. These few examples tell only a part of the story regarding the return of violence in the '80s. With the absence of direct supervision in the dining room by correction officers, the inmates were totally in charge. As a result, the movement of contraband, circulation of drugs, many fights, and sex acts were possibly looked past. Certainly, riot squad officers' violent response to violent events would have been new to my established and effective former dining room policies.

*

Again, by invitation, in early September, I interviewed for the manager of Institutional Services position at the Multnomah County, Portland, Oregon Department of Corrections. Several days following my interview, Bill Fauver, to my astonishment, gave the county a glowing recommendation concerning my work at Rahway, and they hired me.

After only several months, Multnomah County promoted me. I was now the county's director of Corrections.

In a telephone conversation to me, Bill Fauver expressed, "I'm surprised at the salary they will pay you on a county level." I still wonder what that meant. I was now earning a larger salary in Portland as county director of corrections than I had when I left New Jersey.

*

Working in Portland was thankfully calmer than working in New Jersey. But I was only there for six months when a hair-raising event occurred. An individual we called "The Portland Bomber" had already successfully caused several explosions in the Portland area. There was much anxiety in the community as officials awaited the bomber's next threat.

The Portland police received calls at 10:25 a.m. on April 23, 1980, from the bomber to announce his next target. He chose the public restroom in the park directly across the street from the Multnomah County Courthouse. *Jeez.*

The Multnomah County Department of Corrections maintained a booking facility on the top floor of the courthouse. The booking facility housed approximately thirty pre-trial detainees.

Several weeks before the current bomb threat, in anticipation of an emergency, I met with my facility managers to develop an emergency plan to evacuate the Courthouse Jail should the courthouse or immediate area be threatened. The goal was to move the inmates from the top floor of the courthouse to the Fourth Avenue mall. Correctional supervisors would commandeer the free public busses that traveled on the mall to transport the detainees from the downtown facility to the Rocky Butte Jail, a short distance away.

In preparation for the threatened explosion, we commandeered two city buses on the Fourth Avenue Mall, and with the passengers' full cooperation, (though they were in total shock) we emptied both. We used the busses to transfer all the jail's detainees to the Rocky Butte Jail, where they were detained in the jail's recreation yard.

Unfortunately, the bomber followed through with his threat, and the public restroom was indeed blown up. Thankfully, there were no injuries, and the bomber was apprehended, tried, and convicted. Eventually, the demolished restroom was slowly rebuilt.

*

Funny, many of our family's most memorable moments occurred on cold rainy nights. But one especially thrilling and wondrous memory took place on a brilliant and sunshiny Sunday afternoon in February 1980, when we were blessed by the arrival of our little youngest daughter, Caydi. She arrived wearing a big frown and a dear tiny shock of golden, fluffy hair! Naturally, we all fell in love with this little bundle, whose first declaration of independence much later was, "I can't want to!"

*

After working for three years as Multnomah County's Corrections director, Alaska's popular governor, Jay Hammond, contacted me and invited Joan and me to visit him and tour Anchorage. He appointed me to lead the Alaska Department of Corrections as state commissioner and a member of his cabinet. Alaska was magnificent.

But...surprise, surprise, following the next gubernatorial election, the new governor-elect, Bill Sheffield, "requested" and accepted the written resignations from retiring Governor Hammond's entire cabinet! *No one had seen that coming.* None of us were invited to join the new administration. In hindsight, this turned out to be for the best because the new governor was soon to be indicted!

EARLIER THAT YEAR, in a national election, the membership of the American Correctional Association elected me to sit on the association's Board of Governors. Also, the association's director, Tony Travisiono, appointed me to the association's powerful Standards Committee, which oversaw audits and granted, or withheld, accreditation to all of America's prisons and jails.

Upon leaving the great State of Alaska, Alan Breed, National Institute of Corrections executive director, arranged a one-year grant for me to move to Nevada and help Director Vernon Housewright. My assignment included implementing a new correction officer scheduling system to help control their runaway overtime expenditures statewide, just as I had done at Rahway with the Operations Unit for Commissioner Ann Klein.

Three months before the expiration of the grant, Director Housewright asked me to take over at a prison in Indian Springs, Nevada (in the outskirts of Las Vegas) that had significant problems. That kept me busy for three years before being promoted to deputy director of the State of Nevada Department of Prisons.

After a short time in that position, I retired.

*

Joan and I spent the next twenty years owning and operating a successful corrections consulting corporation.

With our children all grown up, our contracts took us all over the country, and kept us busy and happy, making many new friends along the way. Joan's desire to travel was now somewhat realized, and our adventures almost took the place of the vacations we never had the time to take!

Now, forty-three years have passed since that dark April day in Fauver's office, and a different perspective illuminates what was then a devastating event. Reviewing those subsequent years, I can now see my departure from the New Jersey Corrections System was a lucky gift for my personal career and family life.

We retired for the second time in 2010 and are busier now than ever, living in and exploring the great Pacific Northwest.

*

I've never thought about being remembered personally. But I began thinking about the work of the wonderful civilians, correction supervisors, and correction officers that I worked with and who performed skillfully.

I owe a debt of gratitude to those men and women who lived and worked at Rahway during the Warden Bob Hatrak era (1973-1979).

Working together, we all reformed what the media once referred to as "a violent and riot-torn turn of the century maximum-security prison" into one that the American Justice Institute listed as being among "the top five most stable maximum-security prisons in America."

Many of you are gone by now, but none of you are forgotten. Thank you all for the hard work and one-of-a-kind memories.

Bob Hatrak was inducted into the New Jersey Boxing Hall of Fame on November 10, 2022.

Bob & Joan
Wedding Day